Dictionary of
Jewish Usage

Dictionary of Jewish Usage

A Guide to the Use of Jewish Terms

Sol Steinmetz

ROWMAN & LITTLEFIELD PUBLISHERS, INC.
Lanham • Boulder • New York • Toronto • Oxford

ROWMAN & LITTLEFIELD PUBLISHERS, INC.

Published in the United States of America
by Rowman & Littlefield Publishers, Inc.
A wholly owned subsidiary of The Rowman & Littlefield Publishing Group, Inc.
4501 Forbes Boulevard, Suite 200, Lanham, Maryland 20706
www.rowmanlittlefield.com

PO Box 317
Oxford
OX2 9RU, UK

British Library Cataloguing in Publication Information Available

Library of Congress Cataloging-in-Publication Data

Steinmetz, Sol.
   Dictionary of Jewish usage : a guide to the use of Jewish terms /
by Sol Steinmetz.
     p.   ; cm.
   Includes index.
   ISBN 0-7425-4387-0
   1. Judaism-Dicionaries. 2. Jews-Dictionaries. 3. English
language—Foreign words and phrases-Hebrew Dictionaries. 4. English
language-Foreign words and phrases-Yiddish-Dictionaries. I. Title.
BM50 .S75   2005
296′ .03—dc21   2002018144

Printed in the United States of America

To my wife
Tzipora Mandel Steinmetz
and to
our children and grandchildren
with love and thanks

*   *   *   *

*IN MEMORY OF
OUR PARENTS*

Philip and Leah Steinmetz ע״ה

Abraham and Chana Mandel ע״ה

The words of the wise
are like goads,
and like nails well driven
are those that are composed
in collections.

—Koheles (Ecclesiastes 12:11)

Words are like bodies,
and meanings like souls,
and the body is like a vessel for the soul.

*—Abraham Ibn Ezra, Commentary
on the Decalogue (Exodus 20:1)*

Contents

Preface

The idea for this book came to me some thirty years ago, when, in the course of my work as a lexicographer, I was struck by the fact that English dictionaries were noticeably inconsistent in their treatment of Yiddish- and Hebrew-origin terms. The two greatest English dictionaries, the British *Oxford English Dictionary* (OED) and the American *Webster's Third New International Dictionary* (W3), presented two diametrically opposite approaches to Jewish terms. While the OED treated them as foreign, marking them with a tramline symbol (‖) to indicate their unnaturalized status in English and labeling them variously as *Judaism, Jewish Ritual, Jewish Cookery,* and the like, W3 treated such terms as *bentsh* (spelled *bensh*), *daven, shul, nudnik, meshuge, meshulach,* and *meshummad* as completely naturalized, without any usage label or other indication of how and by whom they were used.

Even more conspicuous was the failure of English dictionaries to standardize the spellings of Jewish terms. Instead of providing one or two spellings that users could adopt, a dictionary as influential as W3 often listed as many as eight different spellings for a particular word. Thus, for the word *shammes* or *shammash*, 'synagogue beadle', W3 listed *shammash, shamash, shammas, shamas, shammes, shames, shammos,* and *shamus*, plus the plurals *shammashim, shamashim, shammasim, shamasim, shammosim,* and *shamosim*. I understood, of course, that the dictionary editors were merely recording the variety of spellings they encountered in their research, which consists of reading a variety of books and periodicals and highlighting unusual words. Still, I believed that sensible editorial practice would recommend picking *one* or at most *two* spellings, preferably the ones reflecting most closely the original Hebrew and/or Yiddish forms of the words.

These discoveries prompted me to start a file of Jewish terms that could serve as the basis of a standardized dictionary or guide. The specialized dictionaries of Jewish-interest terms that were available to me were not of great help, being rather limited in their coverage. Generally speaking, Jewish-interest terms fall into three categories: religious, cultural, and popular. The religious category includes the names of Jewish holidays, Jewish months, sacred objects, and rituals such as *bris milah, bar mitzvah, kiddush,* and *havdalah*.

The cultural category covers the names of Jewish leaders and scholars, classical works, historical events, languages, movements, and sects. The popular category encompasses the stuff of everyday ethnic speech, including numerous food terms and many Yiddishisms like *naches, nudnik, maven, schlemiel,* and *heymish.*

In the 1970s there were two English-language dictionaries and one encyclopedia devoted to Jewish terms—the *Concise Dictionary of Judaism* (by Dagobert D. Runes), *A Popular Dictionary of Judaism* (by Hugh Schonfield), and *The Encyclopedia of Jewish Religion* (ed. by R.J.Z. Werblowsky and Geoffrey Wigoder). These books covered only the religious and cultural categories of Jewish terms. The popular category was represented by Leo Rosten's informal compilation, *The Joys of Yiddish,* which established a genre regularly imitated in subsequent decades. However, none of these works aimed for inclusiveness, or attempted to standardize the Jewish terms, or tried to serve as a guide for what is proper or improper usage.

As the file which I began in the 1970s had grown over the years into thousands of terms marked on slips, I was able to divide the terms into various types: those with established English spellings, such as the names of the Jewish holidays (*Yom Kippur, Rosh Hashanah,* etc.); those with variant spellings reflecting Ashkenazi/Sephardi doublets, such as *Shabbos/Shabbat, tallis/tallit, golus/galut*; those that followed a standard system of romanization for Yiddish or for Hebrew; and—by far the largest category—those that were entirely haphazard improvisations or ad-hoc attempts to represent pronunciation, such as *mishpawchah* and *mishbawchah* for the Hebrew word for 'family.' After a few false starts, I managed to reduce the list of variant spellings to either a single form or to two variant forms, where one reflected the Ashkenazi and the other the Sephardi pronunciation.

My file also revealed other deficiencies in the treatment of Jewish terms in both the standard and specialized English dictionaries: discrepancies in the definitions of parallel terms, confusion in the pronunciations, and mistaken etymologies.

All of these findings led me to the decision to compile a dictionary of those Jewish-interest terms that needed explanation or correction based not on preconception but on actual usage. In so doing, I took the position of *Webster's Third* that English loanwords of Hebrew, Aramaic, Judezmo, or Yiddish origin are not foreign but, by definition, English. For, as long as these words are used by English-speaking Jews and are fully integrated into English sentences, they are perforce English words. At the same time, I had to admit that these words belong in a special category, since they are all of Jewish origin and are used primarily if not exclusively by Jews. The OED, in its "General Explanations," calls such words *denizens,* and describes them as "fully naturalized as to use, but not as to form, inflexion, or pronunciation, as *aide-de-camp, carte-de-visite,* and *table d'hôte.*" This, then, is a dictionary of English denizens, which, like the examples cited by the OED, need to be clarified and elucidated far more than native words do.

In writing this book, I drew upon my experience as a longtime dictionary editor and as a lifelong student of the history, traditions, customs, and practices of the Jewish people. I also benefited greatly from the help and knowledge of various scholars and teachers who generously gave me valuable insights over the years and thus steered me in the right direction: the late Professor Uriel Weinreich and Professor Mordkhe Schaechter, of Columbia University; Professor Robert A. Fowkes, of New York University; Professors Joseph C. Landis and Samuel C. Heilman, of Queens College; Professor Ivan G. Marcus, of Yale University, and Professor Harvey I. Sober, of Yeshiva University. Special thanks are due to the scholars who read and commented on parts of the manuscript: my great teacher and friend Rabbi Reuven Fink, of Yeshiva University, spiritual leader of Young Israel of New Rochelle, my esteemed friend Rabbi Dr. Alter B.Z. Metzger, Professor of Judaic Studies at Yeshiva University's Stern College, and my respected colleagues David L. Gold, editor of *Jewish Language Review* and *Jewish Linguistic Studies,* and Professor Bella Hass Weinberg, of St. John's University, editor of *Judaica Librarianship.* I am deeply indebted to all of them.

I also wish to thank my distinguished editor, Brian Romer, and his dedicated staff, especially Marian Haggard and Sonya Kolba, for helping me bring this work to light. Their interest and cooperation is greatly appreciated.

S. S.

Introduction

The *Dictionary of Jewish Usage* is neither a conventional dictionary of Jewish terms nor an expanded glossary of Yiddish or Hebrew words. As its title indicates, it is a guide to words and meanings used mainly or exclusively by Jews, arranged in a dictionary format. The term *usage* refers to the way in which a group of people customarily speak or write a language or a variety of a language. *Jewish usage* is therefore the usage particular to Jews, especially the many words and meanings of Hebrew, Aramaic, or Yiddish origin that are part of the speech and writings of Jews.

This dictionary covers specifically the usage of English-speaking Jews. Although Jews speaking other languages have their own particular Jewish usages, all Jews share a core of Jewishness derived from their common heritage, be it Ashkenazi, Sephardi, or any other kind. In this respect, many of the entries in this dictionary are relevant to all Jews, regardless of their nationality or language.

The need for guidance in the use of Jewish words and meanings in English is self-evident. The spelling of many such words tends to be haphazard, their meanings often unclear. For example: Which is the proper spelling: *mikveh* or *mikvah*? Which designation is preferable: *marrano* or *converso*? What is the difference between *Judezmo, Ladino,* and *Judeo-Spanish*? What is the Jewish equivalent of the Christian abbreviation *A. D.*? Is an *Israelite* the same as a *Hebrew*? Is "chained wife" a proper translation of the term *agunah*? Is the term *Old Testament* acceptable to Jews?

A thorny issue in Jewish usage is that of spelling. Even a cursory survey of the Yiddish- and Hebrew-origin words found in English-language publications reveals a morass of haphazard spellings. The problem is not that there are no standards for transcribing Yiddish and Hebrew loanwords into English. Since the 1940s there has existed a transcription system for Yiddish (the Standardized Yiddish Romanization) and there has been since 1975 several transcription systems for Hebrew, both popular and scholarly (the American National Standard Romanization of Hebrew). The problem is that most writers and editors have chosen not to adopt these standards. One reason for their choice may be that the systems are designed for two different languages and hence differ in their transcription of the Jewish alphabet. For example, in the Yiddish system, the letters *khes* (ח) and *khof* (כ, ך) are both transcribed (i.e., romanized) as *kh* (as in *khutspe*, 'impudence', *brokhe,* 'blessing'), whereas in the popular Hebrew system the same letters (*chet* and *chaf*) are transcribed as *ch* (as in *chutspa, beracha*).

A further complication is that general English has absorbed hundreds of Jewish terms and naturalized them with spellings of its own: *Yom Kippur* (not *yon-kiper, yom-kiper,* or *yom kipur*), *Yiddish* (not *yidish*), *bar mitzvah* (not *bar-mitsve* or *bar-mitsva), chutzpah* (not *khutspe* or *chutspa*), *maven* (not *meyvn*), *yahrzeit* (not *yortsayt*), and many others. Since these spellings are thoroughly established in English, it would be impractical if not foolhardy for writers and editors to ignore them.

Still another factor to be considered is that among Ashkenazim, a host of Hebrew terms from the Scriptures, from the traditional prayerbook, and from other sacred texts are romanized, however roughly, to reflect either an Ashkenazi pronunciation or a Sephardi one. For example: *bris* or *brit, Shabbos* or *Shabbat, Shavuos* or *Shavuot, tallis* or *tallit, zemiros* or *zemirot*. In cases of such variant spellings, the Ashkenazi form comes closest to the word's pronunciation in the Diaspora, where Ashkenazim and their institutions are dominant. Yet quite commonly many writers use the more prestigious Sephardi Hebrew form even where the word is Ashkenazi in pronunciation (a phenomenon known in linguistics as schizographia).

In sum, though ideally Yiddish loanwords should be spelled in English according to the Yiddish Romanization system and Hebrew loanwords according to a standard Hebrew Romanization system, we cannot reject out of hand those English spellings that do not conform to either system yet have become rooted in common usage. It is hard to quarrel with a spelling as long as it is consistently spelled the same way. Both the Yiddish *ganef,* 'thief', and the Hebrew *ganav* are acceptable doublets; what is unacceptable is an inconsistent shifting from one to the other, or worse, impromptu made-up spellings like *gonnof, gonoph, gunif,* and *ganof*.

In this dictionary, therefore, naturalized (i.e., generally accepted and recognized) English spellings of Hebrew and Yiddish loanwords are listed as main entries: **Hasid, kabbalah, yahrzeit.** However, common variant spellings (**Chasid, cabala, yortsayt**) are both cited at the main entries and separately listed and cross-referred to the main entries.

Where two variants spellings are shown, usually in such pairs as **aliyah** or **aliya, Tanach** or **Tanakh,** the first represents the more common usage. Occasionally the spellings do not clearly reflect the pronunciation. In such cases, the pronunciation is shown in parenthesis with the accent indicated with a stress mark immediately following the stressed syllable, for example, **derasha** or **derashah** (*Ashkenazi* dro'she; *Sephardi* derasha').

Where no pronunciations are given, the Hebrew and Yiddish loanwords should be pronounced in syllables; for example, *a-gu-nah, a-li-yah, da-ti, da-ven*. Generally, Yiddish loanwords of more than one syllable are accented on the next-to-the-last syllable, as in *hash-ko'-fe, a-li'-ye*, while Hebrew loanwords are accented on the last syllable, as in *hash-ka-fah', a-li-yah'*. The consonants are pronounced the same as in English except for the following:

ch	as in Scottish *loch* and German *ach*	e.g., *acharon*
tsh	as in *chair, watch*	e.g., *bentsh*
tz	as in *hats, Ritz*	e.g., *am-haaretz*
zh	as in *azure, treasure*	e.g., *zhlub*

The vowels and diphthongs are pronounced as follows:

a	as in *ah, car*	e.g., *agunah*
e	as in *red, set*	e.g., *ger, mezumen, choge*
i	as in *fit, tin*	e.g., *dati, Ivrit*
o	as in *ford, tall*	e.g., *vort, bobkes*
u	as in *put, foot*	e.g., *luach, mezuzah*
ay	as in *lie, guy*	e.g., *halevay*
ey	as in *day, ape*	e.g., *sheytl*
oy	as in *oil, toy*	e.g., *goy*

Other matters of usage dealt with in the dictionary are synonyms (*Holocaust, Shoah, Churban*), related terms *(kasher, kashrus, kosher)*, terms often confused or misused *(aufruf, bashert, opsherenish)*, unacceptable (non-Jewish) usages of various kinds, and clusters of terminology (clothing terms, food terms, mourning terms, synagogue terms, wedding terms). Finally, a number of entries are included for the sole purpose of elucidating some aspect of a word, such as its spelling, etymology, or pronunciation, that may be helpful to readers.

The purpose of a dictionary of usage is to describe how words are used and to offer guidance on disputed, erroneous, or divided usages. Jewish usage is essentially an uncharted territory. This dictionary is thus offered as a general guide to Jewish usage and will hopefully be received as spadework rather than as the last word on this subject.

The Dictionary

– A –

abba. The Hebrew-origin word for father, dad, or daddy. The corresponding word for one's mother is *imma*. After the establishment of the State of Israel, many Zionist Jews in the Diaspora adopted *abba* and *imma* (or *ema*) as terms of address for their parents. This usage is in contrast to that of traditional Ashkenazim of East European descent who retained the Yiddish words *tate* and *mame* (taken from Slavic), often pronouncing them in English *tati* and *mami*. Those who use *abba* and *imma* may also use the Hebrew *sava* and *savta* for grandfather and grandmother, whereas the others may refer to grandparents by the Yiddish *zeyde* and *bobe* (also from Slavic), pronouncing them *zeydi* and *bobi*.

abbreviations and acronyms. Jewish abbreviations and acronyms occur mainly in the religious realm. Clipped forms are usually romanized transfers from Hebrew, Aramaic, and Yiddish and include such formulas as *B″H* (for *Beezras Hashem*, 'with the help of God'), *BS″D* (for *Bisyato Dishmayo*, 'with the help of heaven'), *IY″H* (for *im yirtse Hashem*, 'God will-

---

The word *abba* comes from the Aramaic for 'father.' It is found in the Talmud as a familiar title for a teacher or rabbi, such as the tanna Abba Saul and the amora Abba bar Akha. It was later adopted by the Christian Coptic, Ethiopian, and Syriac churches as a reverential title for bishops and patriarchs. The Christian use is reflected in modern times in such words as English *abbot* and French *abbé*, both of which came from the Aramaic through Latin and Greek *abbat-*, *abbas*. Ultimately the Aramaic word, which is closely related to the Hebrew word for father, *av*, influenced the use of such words as *father*, *padre*, and *pope* (from Latin *papa*, 'father') as eccesiastical titles.

1

ing'), *z"l* (or as an acronym *zal,* for *zichrono livrochoh,* 'may his memory be for a blessing'), *A"H* (for *alav [aleha] hashalom,* 'may he [she] rest in peace'). Some English abbreviations are also used, such as *R.* (for *Rabbi*) and *OBM* (for *of blessed memory*). Common acronyms include *shelita* (for *sheyichye leorech yomim tovim omeyn,* 'may he live long and well, Amen'), *shatz* (for *sheliach tzibbur,* 'cantor,' literally, 'deputy for the congregation'), *shub* (for *shochet ubodek,* 'ritual slaughterer and examiner'), and *ram* (for *rosh mesivta,* 'head of yeshiva'). Another convention is the abbreviating of the name of the Deity as *G-d* and also sometimes *A-mighty,* and *L-rd,* as a sign of reverence deriving from the practice of not writing out fully any of the Divine names in Hebrew except in the sacred texts. In the secular realm, abbreviations tend to be informal and somewhat facetious, as *M.O.T.* (for 'Member of the Tribe,' i.e., a fellow Jew), *B.T.* (for *Baal-Teshuvah,* 'a returnee to Judaism'), *J.A.P.,* usually pronounced *jap* (for 'Jewish American Princess'), and *Ph.G.* (for Yiddish *papa hot gelt,* 'Papa has money'). See also **notarikon.**

academy. A formal English term used by Jewish scholars and historians for a *yeshiva,* especially the great yeshivas of Babylonia (Sura, Pumbedita, Nehardea) and Eretz Israel (Yavneh, Tzipori, Tiberias) during the Talmudic period. The term should be used only in highly formal and historical contexts. In general, the preferred term today is *yeshiva* (plural *yeshivas* or *yeshivot*).

acharon, plural **acharonim.** An *acharon* (Hebrew, literally, 'last one, latter one') refers to any of the later rabbinical expounders or codifiers of Jewish

Academy is one of a group of English terms used formally to replace words or phrases borrowed from Hebrew or Yiddish. Some other terms in this group are: *services* (for *davening*), *synagogue* (for *shul*), *ritual bath* or *ritualarium* (for *mikveh*), *prayer shawl* (for *tallis*), *Sabbath observer* (for *shomer shabbos*), *ritual slaughterer* (for *shochet*), *holy ark* (for *aron kodesh*), *skullcap* (for *yarmulke* or *kippah*), *chapel* (for *beis midrash,* often in contrast to *sanctuary* for *shul*), *sidecurls* (for *peyes*), *Day of Atonement* (for *Yom Kippur*), *High Holy Days* (for *yomim neroim*), etc. *Academy* is among the subset of scholarly formal terms that include *responsa* (for *shayles (un)tshuves*), *novellae* (for *chiddushim*), *decisor* (for *posek*), *approbation* (for *haskamah*),* etc.

law (*the acharonim*), as distinguished from the *rishonim* or earlier rabbinical authorities. (See **rishon**.) The start of the period of the acharonim is usually set after the 16th century, when Rabbi Yosef Caro's *Shulchan Aruch* was completed. The term *acharon* is also used in synagogue ritual to refer to an extra aliyah given before the last (the maftir), or to the person accorded this honor. The acharon may be a kohen, a Levite, or an Israelite. Used in this sense, the plural is usually Anglicized as *acharons*. The regular plural **acharonim** normally refers to the rabbinical authorities.

adafina. The Judezmo name of a Sabbath dish of slowly baking meat and vegetables, similar to the Ashkenazi *cholent* (from Yiddish *tsholnt*) and the Sephardi *chamin* (from Hebrew, literally, 'hot water'). The Judezmo term was adopted from Arabic *ad-dafīna*, '(the) hidden, (the) covered,' because the dish is covered on Friday and left in the oven to simmer until the next day. See also **food terms.**

Adar. The 6th month in the Jewish calendar, consisting of 29 days in ordinary years and 30 days in leap years. Adar occurs usually in March. In the Bible, where the year begins with the month of Nisan, Adar is the twelfth month. The leap year is called *Adar Sheni* ('Second Adar') or *Adar Bet* ('Adar Two'). Another name, now obsolescent, is *Veadar* ('Additional Adar'), adapted from the Yiddish (*oder*) *veoder*, '(Adar) and Adar.' The 14th of Adar marks the holiday of Purim, which gives a joyous character to the entire month, expressed in the Talmudic saying (*Taanis 29a*), "With the beginning of Adar, rejoicings are increased." (Compare **Av.**)

adloyada. A modern Hebrew-origin term for a Purim carnival, originally the name of the Tel Aviv Purim carnival. The term was coined from the Talmudic phrase *ad delo yada* ('till he does not know') in the amora Raba's saying (*Megila 7:*), "It is a man's duty to carouse on Purim *till he does not know* the difference between 'baruch mordecai' (blessed be Mordecai) and 'arur haman' (cursed be Haman)."

admor. A title of a Hasidic spiritual leader (a rebbe or tzaddik), usually placed after his name. The word is an acronym formed from the Hebrew phrase *ad(onenu) mo(renu) (ve)r(abenu),* 'our master, teacher, and rabbi.' It is sometimes used as a common noun, especially in the plural form **admorim.** See also under **Hasidic terms.**

Adonai or **Adonay.** A sacred Hebrew name of God, derived from *adon*, 'master, lord,' used in prayers, blessings, Torah-reading, and other rituals as a substitute for the Tetragrammaton or unpronounceable four-letter name of God, as set forth in the tractate *Kiddushin, 71a*. The sanctity of *Adonai* itself is protected by substituting for it *Adoshem* (a blend of *Adonai* and *Shem*, 'Name') or *Hashem*, 'the Name,' in nonsacred contexts. In English translations, *Adonai* is translated as '(the) Lord.' See also **Hashem.**

afikoman. Also spelled **afikomen.** This Hebrew-origin word, cited in the Passover haggada and found originally in the Mishna (*Pesachim 10:8*), has been given various derivations. The Gemara derives it from an Aramaic phrase *afiku mon*, 'bring in (sweet) food.' A more common belief is that the word came into Hebrew from Greek *epikomion*, 'festal merrymaking.' Both are questionable etymologies. The word means an aftermeal delicacy or 'dessert.' According to the Mishna, no *afikoman* may be eaten after consuming the paschal lamb at the end of the seder meal. In practice, the afikoman has come to refer to the last piece of matzo (broken off the middle of three matzos on the seder plate) eaten at the end of the meal, after which nothing may be eaten.

aggadah or **aggada.** The part of the Talmud and Midrash that does not deal with halachah or legal matters. It consists of stories, sayings, folklore, sermons, and other forms of religious and ethical instruction. The word should not be confused with **haggadah**, which is the narrative of the Exodus recited at the Passover seder and means literally 'narrative, communication.' Though etymologically the two words are related, *haggadah* derives from the Hebrew verb *higgid*, 'to tell, say,' whereas *aggada* is a variant of the Aramaic *aggadeta*, meaning literally 'story, tale.' The derivative adjective **aggadic** means 'pertaining to the aggadah; nonlegal, homiletic.'

agunah, plural **agunahs.** A married woman who is separated (but not divorced) from her husband and is unable to remarry for various reasons, usually because (1) the husband has deserted her and cannot be found, (2) the husband has disappeared (as in wartime) and there is no evidence that he has died, (3) the husband is mentally ill and legally unable to grant her a *get* (bill of divorce), or (4) the husband willfully refuses to grant the wife a *get*. In the latter case, a *bet din* may issue a summons (*hazmana*) to the husband, or a *shtar seruv* (a document noting the husband's refusal to appear before the *bet din*). While rabbinical authorities have enacted numerous statutes to relieve the plight of the agunah, permission to remarry has always been withheld when the remarriage might be considered adulterous, resulting in *mamzerim* (see **mamzer**).

The Hebrew plural of *agunah* is (Ashkenazi) *agunos* or (Sephardi) *agunot*. (The Anglicized plural is given above.) The masculine form, referring to a man who for various reasons is unable to divorce his wife, is *agun*. The condition of being an agunah or an agun is called *igun* or *aginus*. The Hebrew-origin word *agunah* can mean either a deserted or abandoned wife (from the root *igen,* 'forsake, desert,' *agen,* 'be forsaken') or one who is tied down or bound to an absent husband (from the root *agan,* 'to tie down, anchor, moor'). The popular English rendering of *agunah* as 'chained wife' or 'chained woman' is based on the second meaning, and though not entirely accurate, it has served to dramatize the plight of such women.

akkum. In talmudic and rabbinic literature, an idolater or heathen. The word is a Hebrew acronym of the phrase *oved(e) kochavim umazzalot,* 'worshiper(s) of stars and constellations,' and is used both as a singular and plural noun. It should not be confused with **goy** (plural *goyim*), which refers to a non-Jew or gentile, or with **min** (plural *minim*), which refers to a Jewish heretic.

aliyah or **aliya.** A Hebrew-origin word meaning literally 'a going up, ascent,' originally referring to any of the three festival pilgrimages made to Jerusalem. The two common meanings of the word are: (1) the honor of being called upon to recite the blessings on the Torah scroll, or any section of the Torah over which the blessings are recited (as in *There are four aliyahs on Rosh Chodesh*). Used in this sense, the word is pronounced among Ashkenazim as it is in Yiddish, with the stress on the second syllable: (ali'ye). (2) immigration to to Israel, usually in the phrase 'to make aliyah.' In this sense, the word is pronounced with the stress on the last syllable (aliya') and the plural is usually spelled *aliyahs, aliyas,* or (Sephardi) *aliyot.* One who makes aliyah is called an *oleh,* feminine *olah* (plural *olim*). Another, less common, use of *aliyah* is in the mystical sense of 'ascent of the soul to heaven,' which is the basis of the Hasidic custom of wishing a person observing a yahrzeit, *Di neshome zol hobn an aliye* 'May the soul have an ascent.'

almemar. A chiefly Anglo-Jewish term for the raised platform on which the Torah-reading desk stands in a synagogue. Among Ashkenazim it is called a **bimah**, and among Sephardim, a **tevah**. The term is thought to derive ultimately from Yahudic ("Judeo-Arabic") *al-minbar,* 'the platform.' The Yiddish equivalent, **balemer,** was probably a variant of *balmemer,* an alteration (influenced by the Yiddish prefix *bal-,* as in *bal-koyre,* 'Torah-reader') of *almemer,* an Ashkenazi German form of *almemar.*

The honor of being called up to the Torah-reading is called an *aliyah* or 'ascent' because traditionally the Torah scroll is read on a **bimah** or raised platform, which a person ascends, as distinguished among Ashkenazim from an **amud** (Yiddish, *omed*), the cantor's stand, which is traditionally on or below ground level.

Altneuland: A tale of two names

Altneuland, a German coinage meaning "Old-new-land," was the title of a utopian novel by Theodor Herzl describing the creation of a new Jewish state and society in Eretz Yisrael. It was published in 1902. In his diaries, Herzl describes in a note dated August 30, 1899, how he coined this word:

> While riding out today . . . on the jolting omnibus, the title for my novel about Zion suddenly occurred to me: *Alt-Neuland*—reminiscent of the name of the Prague synagogue, Altneuschul. It will become a famous word. (translation by Marvin Lowenthal)

In the novel, the title is the name of the ideal future Jewish state envisioned by Herzl. The year is 1923 and Altneuland is a vibrant country, with a flourishing agriculture, great cities, and many industries. Education is free, the economy is based on cooperation, tolerance is widespread, and racial hatred has disappeared.

Though criticized by various Jewish intellectuals of the day, notably the Hebrew writer Ahad Ha-am, for ignoring historical development and the Jewish national character, the book was translated into many languages. Nahum Sokolow translated it into Hebrew, but retitled it *Tel Aviv*, after a Babylonian city mentioned in the Bible (Ezekiel 3:15) which suggested the 'old' and 'new' of the original title (*Tel* = hill of ruins; *Aviv* = spring).

Not long after, on May 21, 1910, a rapidly growing Jewish suburb of the ancient city of Jaffa (Yaffo) was given the name *Tel Aviv*, after the title of Sokolow's translation of *Altneuland*. Thus the title of Herzl's visionary novel became transmuted in the short span of eight years into the name of the first Jewish city in modern times.

Amalek. The Biblical name of a nomadic people of the Sinai desert who descended from Esau and became the archenemies of Israel. Haman is described in the Book of Esther as a descendant of Agag, the king of the Amalekites. The Bible (*Deut. 25:19*) calls for the obliteration of the memory of Amalek. In popular Ashkenazi usage, derived from Yiddish, the phrase *an amolek* is synonymous with any enemy of the Jews, and, by extension, with a wicked Jew. **Amalekite** and **Amalekian** are used as adjectives to describe irrational or unjustifiable hatred of Jews: *Amalekian anti-Semitism.*

amen. An interjection used to express assent or affirmation upon hearing a blessing. It is the prescribed response to all benedictions and to parts of the kaddish. The word occurs thirty times in the Tanach and though its etymology is unclear, it is used in the general sense of 'It is true, So be it.' The Talmud (*Sanhedrin 111a*) explains the word homiletically as an acronym of the phrase *El Melech Neeman* ('God, King, Trustworthy'), which precedes the Shema prayer ('Hear O Israel') when recited in private. The Christian scriptures employ the word over a hundred times and the early church adopted it into its liturgy. Its use in English dates back to 1000 C.E. The English spelling does not reflect the Ashkenazi pronunciation, which is *omeyn.*

am-haaretz, plural **amei-haaretz.** This Hebrew-origin term, literally meaning 'people of the land,' has been used mostly pejoratively, whether referring to the lower classes or commoners in Biblical times, or to the peasant population which neglected Jewish laws in the Talmudic period, or, in later popular usage, to any Jew who is ignorant or uneducated in the Torah. The Yiddish word *amorets* (plural *ameratsim)* was borrowed from Hebrew in the latter sense. Yiddish coined the word *ameratses,* meaning ignorance or illiteracy in things Jewish, which colloquial Hebrew adopted as *am-haara-tzut.*

amidah. The Sephardi term for the **shemone-esrei**, the principal prayer in the Jewish liturgy. It literally means 'standing,' because it is recited in a standing position. The term is found in the minor tractate *Soferim (16:12).* *Amidah* has been adopted by many Ashkenazim as a more formal synonym of the traditional name *shemone-esrei.* Its advantage as a term is that it covers every variety of this prayer, including those of the Sabbath and holidays, which have fewer blessings than the daily eighteen implied in the term *shemone-esrei* (literally, 'eighteen'). In the Talmud, the amidah is called *tefillah* (literally, 'prayer').

amora, plural **amoraim.** Often capitalized: **Amora, Amoraim.** Any of the Talmudic sages of Babylonia and Eretz Israel whose teachings form the Gemara. The period of the amoraim extended from the death of Judah the Prince (219 C.E.) until the completion of the Talmud (c.500). From Aramaic, literally, 'speaker, lecturer.' The adjective is **amoraic,** as in *amoraic teachings.* Compare **tanna.**

amud (*Ashkenazi* o'med). 1. The page, side, or column of a book. See **daf.** 2. The stand or lectern in a synagogue at which the cantor or leader in prayer stands.

Anglo-Israelite. An Anglo-Israelite is not an English Jew. The Anglo-Israelites are supporters or advocates of a theory proposed in the 18th century that the Anglo-Saxon people are descendants of the Ten Lost Tribes. The theory, known as **Anglo-Israelism**, became popular in the 19th century and still has adherents today. It was based chiefly on various ingenious interpretations of certain Biblical passages as well as some spurious derivations of English words, such as the word *berry* being derived from Hebrew *peri,* 'fruit.' Anglo-Israelites hold that the Stone of Scone, which is the coronation stone of English sovereigns, is the stone upon which the patriarch Jacob laid his head on his way to Haran (Genesis 28:11). Anglo-Israelism is one of a number of theories attempting to trace a particular ethnic group to the Ten Lost Tribes.

Anglo-Jewish. The primary meaning of this adjective is 'pertaining to English Jews or Jewry,' as in the phrase *the Anglo-Jewish population* or *the Anglo-Jewish rabbinate.* A second meaning of the term is 'English-Jewish,' referring to Jewish publications written in English, as in *the Anglo-Jewish press in Canada.* This is the sense in which the term is generally used in the United States.

Ani Maamin. The thirteen articles of Jewish faith formulated by Maimonides, each beginning with the Hebrew phrase *ani maamin* ('I believe'). After the articles appeared in 1168, they became the subject of controversy between the Maimunists and their opponents, who criticized the manner of the credo's formulation. But eventually the articles became enshrined in Judaism and incorporated in most prayerbooks both in their original form and in the versified form known as *Yigdal* (from the first word of the poem), which appears at the beginning of the morning prayers. During the Holocaust, the twelfth article, which expresses perfect faith in the coming of Messiah, became a defiant song from which the victims of Nazism drew the courage to face martyrdom.

annos. A Judezmo word, meaning literally 'year' and derived from Latin *annus*, used among Sephardim for the anniversary of the death of a relative to whom the laws of mourning apply. It corresponds to the Ashkenazi **yahrzeit.**

anti-Semitism. This notorious term for hostility toward or hatred of Jews is a misnomer. It first appeared in 1879 in the writings of a Jew-hating German journalist, Wilhelm Marr (1818–1904), who used it to emphasize the Semitic origin of Jews in order to identify them as a race, in accordance with the then-popular pseudoscientific theory that distinguished between the "superior races," especially the so-called Aryan race, and various "inferior races," which included the Semites. (This theory became subsequently the ideological basis of Nazism.) Marr justified the existence of *Antisemitismus* by blaming Jews for attempting to dominate German culture and society. The term quickly became a politically acceptable euphemism or code word for Jew-hatred. It was adopted into English as early as 1881. But the term fooled no one. Though it was coined to cover up traditional hostility toward Jews with a veneer of scientific respectability, it came to be used within a short time as the standard term for anti-Jewish prejudice and discrimination.

Judeophobia, which literally means 'irrational fear or hatred of Jews,' is a far more accurate term to designate what came to be known as anti-Semitism. Yet it was not coined until the early 20th century as French *judéophobie,* and its use became almost exclusively the province of historians, who applied it to the hostility toward Jews manifested throughout history, as in pagan antiquity, medieval Christendom, and Czarist Russia. "On the whole, . . . the peculiarity of the Roman attitude toward the Jews seems better expressed by the term 'Judeophobia' in its ambivalent combination of fear and hatred." (Peter Schafer, *Judeophobia*, Harvard University Press, 1997).

For those who would like to discard the term *anti-Semitism* and its derivatives both for their racist connotation and nefarious origin, *Judeophobia* and its derivatives, *Judeophobe* and *Judeophobic*, are good alternatives.

anusim. See **marranos.**

apikores, plural **apikorsim.** Also spelled **apikoros.** A Jew who does not believe in or who rejects the divinity of the Torah or of Biblical prophecy; an unbeliever, heretic, or freethinker; (loosely) a nonobservant Jew. The source of the word is Mishnaic Hebrew (*Avos 2:14*; *Sanhedrin 10:1*). According to Maimonides, the word is Aramaic and derived from the root *pakar,* 'declaring free, renouncing.' Most scholars, however, regard the word as a direct borrowing from Greek *Epikouros* (Epicurus, died 270 B.C.E.), the Greek philosopher, whose followers rejected Judaism. Compare **meshummad, min, mumar.**

Aramaic. A northern Semitic language closely related to Hebrew. It derives its name from Greek *Aramaios,* 'of Aram,' Aram being the Hebrew name of the land in the Fertile Crescent occupied by the Semitic people (the Arameans) who were the ancestors of the patriarch Abraham. Aramaic was the most widely spoken vernacular of West Asia until it was replaced by Arabic in the 7th century. **Jewish Aramaic** was the vernacular of most Jews in Babylonia and the Land of Israel until the beginning of the Diaspora. Some books of the Bible (Ezra, Daniel) have parts written in a Jewish Aramaic dialect. The Babylonian and Jerusalemite gemaras, parts of the Zohar, the various Targums, parts of the liturgy (as the kaddish and Kol Nidre), and numerous responsa of the Babylonian geonim, are written in various literary forms or dialects of Jewish Aramaic. Jewish Aramaic and Hebrew figured prominently in the formation of **Jewish languages.**

Aramic. A former name of **Jewish Aramaic.**

arba kanfos. See **tzitzis.**

ark. A word translating Hebrew *tevah* and *aron,* both meaning 'box, chest, case,' and applied to such disparate objects as Noah's Ark (*Genesis 6:14*), the Ark of the Covenant (*Exodus 25:10*), and the holy ark (Hebrew *aron*

According to students of Jewish languages, a modern form of Jewish Aramaic has survived among the Jews of Kurdistan and Azerbaijan, which their speakers call *Targum*. This form of Aramaic has several dialects and a large admixture of borrowings from Turkish, Arabic, and Persian. The self-name of this language, Targum, derives from the Aramaic word meaning 'translation,' which the Talmud uses to refer to the Aramaic versions of the Scriptures, such as Onkelos's and Yonasan ben Uziel's versions.

hakodesh or *heichal),* in which the Torah scrolls are kept in the synagogue. A*r*k goes back to Old English *earc, arc,* an early borrowing from Latin *arca,* 'chest, box, casket,' and is used in English exclusively in the senses listed above.

Ashkenazi, plural **Ashkenazim.** A name designating a Jew whose customs and traditions originated in Germany and spread into eastern Europe in the Middle Ages, as distinguished from a **Sephardi,** a Jew whose customs and traditions originated in Spain and Portugal. The name is also used as an adjective, along with **Ashkenazic,** as in *Ashkenazi* (or *Ashkenazic) Jews, the Ashkenazi* (or *Ashkenazic) Hebrew pronunciation.* See also *nusach Ashkenaz* (under **nusach**).

askan, plural **askanim.** A Jewish communal or social worker. The Yiddish-origin form is *asken,* plural *asko'nim.* From Hebrew, derived from *esek* 'business, occupation.'

atbash. A form of **gematria** in which the first Hebrew letter or number (א, aleph) is represented by the last letter or number (ת, tav), the second (ב, bet) is represented by the penultimate letter (ש, shin), and so on. A Biblical example of *atbash* is the name Sheshach (Jeremiah 25:26), which is another name for Babel (Babylonia). The word *atbash* is an acronym of *a*leph, *t*av, *b*et, *sh*in.

aufruf /ouf'roof/. The custom of honoring a bridegroom at the Torah-reading on the Sabbath before his wedding is known among Ashkenazim as an

---

Ashkenazi derives from *Ashkenaz,* a geographical designation identified in rabbinic literature since the 9th century with Germany, after the name of an ancient people mentioned in Jeremiah 51:27, and ultimately probably from the name of the second son of Gomer, the grandson of Noah (Genesis 10:3). Originally the term *Ashkenazim* referred to the Jews living in the German-speaking region of the Rhine Valley, many of whom had come from northern France and Italy. But as persecutions forced them to migrate eastward during the Middle Ages, their religious customs and traditions spread into the Slavic countries of eastern Europe. Thereafter the name *Ashkenazim* was broadly applied to all European Jews except those of Spanish and Portuguese descent.

aufruf. This honor is accompanied by the custom of showering the groom with raisins, almonds, and other confections (a custom called *bavarfns* in Yiddish). The word *aufruf* comes from German and is derived from the verb *aufrufen* 'to call up,' which German Jews use to designate the honor of being called up to the Torah during its public reading. *Aufruf* means literally 'call-up.' The corresponding Yiddish word is *ufrufns*, and the normal spelling in East European Ashkenazic English is *ufruf*. But the German spelling *aufruf* has taken root in American soil and, with occasional exceptions, this is how the word appears in synagogue announcements and bulletins. Bridegrooms and their families have a choice of either announcing the *aufruf* or the *ufruf*. Both forms are acceptable. What is unacceptable is the occasional splitting of this word into two (*Auf Ruf* or *Auf ruf*), an error that should be avoided. See also **wedding terms.**

auto-da-fé, plural **autos-da-fé.** From Portuguese, literally, 'act of faith.' The corresponding Spanish term is **auto de fe,** plural **autos de fe.** Both forms are often capitalized: **Auto-da-Fé** or **Auto de Fe.** Contextually, the term is sometimes shortened to **auto,** plural **autos,** as in "Between 1481 and 1826 approximately 2,000 autos took place in Spain and Portugal." The term refers chiefly to the ceremony at which the Inquisition authorities in Portugal and Spain passed sentence against heretics; but more popularly it refers to the public execution, usually by burning at the stake, of accused heretics, many of whom were crypto-Jews. See **marranos.**

An interesting, though now obsolescent, Ashkenazi custom related to the aufruf is the *Spinnholz*, known in Yiddish as *forshpil* (literally, 'prelude'). On the Sabbath afternoon following the aufruf, a reception is held in the home of the bride's parents, and at this reception the bride is formally presented with her trousseau. The name of this custom is an example of folk etymology, for *Spinnholz*, which is the German word for 'distaff' (an old symbol of feminine domesticity), is actually a popular alteration of Latin *sponsalia*, meaning betrothal. (The Latin word is also the source of the English word *espousal*.) The *Spinnholz* thus appears to be a medieval outgrowth of the traditional Jewish betrothal ceremony. The aufruf itself is a much older custom: its observance has been traced back to Solomon's Temple, which was built with a special gate through which bridegrooms were led ceremonially into the Temple on the Sabbath before their wedding.

Av. The eleventh month in the Jewish calendar, consisting of 30 days and occurring usually in July or August. In the Bible, where the year begins with the month of Nisan, Av is the fifth month. The ninth of Av (*Tisha B'Av*) is a fast day on which Jews mourn the destruction of both Temples in Jerusalem and, more recently, the destruction of European Jewry in the Holocaust. The nine days preceding Tisha B'Av, known by the Yiddish name *nayn teg*, 'Nine Days,' are treated traditionally as mournful days on which no meat and wine are consumed, no haircuts are taken, and no new clothes are worn, in accordance with the Mishnaic dictum (*Taanis 4:6*), "With the beginning of Av, rejoicings are curtailed." (Compare **Adar**). The fifteenth of Av (*Tu B'Av*) was a joyous holiday during the Second Temple period, in which young women danced in the vineyards of Jerusalem and young men chose wives from among them (*Taanis 4:8*).

av bet din or (*Ashkenazi*) **av bes din.** In current usage, the title of the head of a Jewish court of law; literally, the Hebrew term means 'father of the law court (house of judgment).' A *segan av bet din* is the deputy of an av bet din. Historically the term had various applications. In the period of the Second Temple, it was the title of the deputy or assistant of the president (*Nasi*) of the Sanhedrin. In the Talmudic and Gaonic periods, it was the title of the head of a yeshiva in Babylonia and the Land of Israel. In Eastern Europe, especially after the 16th century, it was the title of the chief rabbi of a city or town. See **bet din.**

avel, avelus. See under **mourning terms.**

ayen-hore. Variant of **eyn-hore.**

– B –

baal-. A productive prefix, meaning 'master, owner, possessor,' that appears in many words borrowed from Hebrew or Yiddish. Some examples are: *baal-kore* (literally, 'master reader'), or *baal-keriah* (literally, 'master of reading'), the person who reads from the Torah scroll at religious services; *baal-simchah* (literally, 'master of festivity'), the celebrant of a festive occasion, the host or sponsor of a circumcision, wedding, etc.; *baal-tefillah* (literally, 'master of prayer'), the person who leads the morning, afternoon, or evening prayers, or a reader or cantor; *baal-tekiah* (literally, 'master of the shofar sound'), the person who blows the shofar, as on Rosh Hashanah; *baal-tzedakah*(literally, 'master of charity'), a charitable person, philanthropist. The plural of all phrases with *baal-* is **baale-**, e.g., *baale-tefillah, baale-keriah, baale-simchah.* See also *bar.*

baal-shem. A term meaning literally 'possessor of the Name,' popularly applied since the Middle Ages, especially in eastern Europe, to a miracle worker or healer. Such a person presumably possessed secret knowledge of the Tetragrammaton and other Divine names, which were used in amulets and other ways to heal the sick and perform miracles.

The term has two variant plurals, **baale-shem** and **baale-shemos.** A variant of the singular form was **baal-shem-tov**, literally, 'possessor of the good name,' but after the rise of Hasidism this variant came to be applied exclusively to its founder, Israel Baal Shem Tov (c.1700–1760), also known by the acronym *Besht.*

baal-teshuvah or **baal-teshuva.** Literally, 'master of repentance,' this Yiddish- and Hebrew-origin term referred originally to a Jew who repented from wrongdoing and, after making genuine contrition, proceeded to observe all the commandments of the Torah. In the latter part of the 20th century, a change in the word's meaning occurred, as many Jews began to apply the term *baal-teshuvah* (pronounced *bal tshu' ve*) to a Jew who, lacking any foundation in traditional Judaism, seeks to learn about and follow the religious observances of his faith. The plural form is **baale-teshuvah.** The feminine form is **baalas-teshuvah.** A formal English equivalent sometimes used is *returnee.* A Yiddish equivalent, *bal-tshuvenik,* is also sometimes used. An informal abbreviation, *B.T.,* is a recent American innovation.

badchan or **badchen.** See under **music and dance terms; wedding terms.**

badekn. See under **wedding terms.**

bagel. See under **food terms.**

balebos. A Yiddish-origin word with various meanings, including: (1) the owner of a house or building; landlord; (2) the proprietor of a business; (3)

When not used in a phrase, the Hebrew word **baal** means 'husband' or 'master (of the house),' plural **baalim.** The capitalized form **Baal** (literally, 'Lord,' usually preceded by **the**) represents the name of a Canaanite deity or idol whose worship the prophet Elijah and other prophets condemned (I Kings 18, II Kings 10). The widespread worship of Baal is known as *Baalism* and its practitioners are called *Baalists.*

the head of a household, master of the house; (4) a member of a synagogue or congregation. The plural, **balebatim**, is used by English-speaking Ashkenazim chiefly in the sense of definition 4. The feminine form, **baleboste**, means primarily (1) a housewife, especially a very efficient one; (2) a landlady; and (3) an owner or proprietor. The adjective, **balebatish**, applied to a person or a home, signifies 'befitting a balebos; well-to-do, respectable, comfortable, genteel.' Historically, the Yiddish words *balebos* and *balebatim* derived from the Ashkenazi Hebrew *baal-bayis* and *baale-batim*, literally, 'master(s) of the house(s).' The feminine *baleboste* was formed with the Yiddish suffix *–te* (e.g., *shokhnte*, '(female) neighbor,' *khaznte*, 'cantor's wife').

balemer. See **almemar.**

bar. An Aramaic word meaning literally 'son of,' occurring as a part of names, such as *Bar Kamtza, (Eleazar) Bar Kappara, (Shimon) Bar Kochba, Bar Talmai* (the source of English *Bartholomew*), *(Shimon) Bar Yochai*. But the word also functions as a prefix meaning 'possesssor, master,' in such compounds as *bar daas*, 'possessor of reason, rational person;' *bar ulpan*, 'master of learning, scholar,' a meaning paralleled in the Hebrew prefix **baal-**; and also in the Hebrew *ben-*, as in *ben-torah,* '(one) learned in Torah,' *ben-daas* (= *bar daas*). See also **bar mitzvah** below.

barches. See **challah**, 26.

bar mitzvah. The proper translation of this universally known term is not 'son of the commandment' but rather 'possessor or master of the commandments,' as shown under **bar.** The term appears in the Talmud (*Bava Metzia 96a*) in the sense of 'one who is subject to all the commandments,' i.e., a Jew, as distinguished from a Canaanite slave; but in the sense of a boy who has reached thirteen (postulated in *Pirke Avos 5:25* as the age at which he is obliged to keep the commandments as an adult) the term is first found in the 15th century. See also **bat mitzvah.**

The term *bar mitzvah* means primarily a boy of 13 (and a day), i.e., a boy who has come of age for religious purposes, such as being included in a **minyan**, wearing tefillin (phylacteries), and fasting on Yom Kippur. Therefore, a boy is said *to be* or *become (a) bar mitzvah.* Extended uses of the term are: (1) the ceremony or celebration marking the event, as in *to have a bar mitzvah, to make a bar mitzvah, to attend a bar mitzvah;* and (2) the condition of becoming a bar mitzvah, as in *to celebrate one's bar mitzvah.* A nonstandard, informal Americanism is the phrase *to be* (or *get*) *bar mitzvahed,* coined on the model of such phrases as *to be* (or *get*) *cir-*

cumcised, married, divorced, etc. Though this informal phrase is often used instead of the standard *to become bar mitzvah,* careful speakers and writers avoid using it. *Bar mitzvah* has been also extended figuratively to mean '13th year,' as in "Our organization has recently reached its bar mitzvah."

bashert. This word, used to designate a future or predestined spouse, is an American Ashkenazi innovation derived from two related but different Yiddish forms. The term is used chiefly among American Ashkenazim in sentences like "She went to a shadchen to find her bashert." The term has found its way into books on dating and marriage, such as *Finding Your Bashert* (S. Stein, Judaica Press, 1999).

The source of this word is a shortening of the Yiddish masculine form *basherter,* meaning a predestined husband, and the Yiddish feminine *basherte,* meaning a predestined wife. In American Ashkenazic English, the masculine form first coalesced with the feminine due to the influence of varieties of Yiddish and English in which word-final *–r* is not pronounced. This resulted in *basherte.* Then, probably due to the influence of the Yiddish adjective *bashert,* 'destined, predestined,' the final *–e* was dropped, and the result was *bashert* as a noun.

The notion of a predestined spouse is based on the traditional concept of *zivug,* 'matching of couples, marriage,' especially the passage in tractate *Sotah (2a),* "Rav Yehuda said in the name of Rav: Forty days before the creation of a child, a heavenly voice proclaims [that] the daughter of so-

---

The high point of the bar mitzvah ceremony occurs when the boy is called up to read from (or recite the blessings over) the Torah, after which his father pronounces the blessing *boruch shepetarani,* in which he praises God for releasing him from responsibility for the sins of his son. The source of this custom is aggadic (*Bereshis Rabba 63:14*), and not found in the Talmud or codified in the *Shulchan Aruch.* Hence the validity of the blessing has been questioned since the 16th century, resulting in the Sephardic custom of pronouncing the blessing without the *shem umalkhus* (God's Name and His Kingship). While many Ashkenazim follow this custom, others accept the ruling of the Vilna Gaon and the Mishna Berura that the blessing should be recited in full. In Yiddish, *boruch shepotrani* is a popular facetious expression meaning 'Good riddance!'

and-so shall be for so-and-so"—implying that a first marriage is ordained even before a person is born. As this dictum appears to contradict the basic tenet of Free Will, various commentators have interpreted Rav's statement as referring to a spiritual union of two souls, or to the equal apportioning of a couple's possessions, rather than to the conjugal union of a man and a woman.

batlan. A Hebrew-origin term, usually used in the plural **batlanim**, that literally means 'man of leisure,' and was historically an honorific title applied to any Jew who refrained from ordinary work to devote himself to study, prayer, and community service. In the Talmud (*Megillah 3b*) a city is defined as one that had at least ten batlanim. The function of these men ranged from serving as a permanent *minyan* of ten men at synagogue services to rendering decisions on religious, legal, and ethical questions. In later times, as the value of men who lacked a job or trade depreciated, the term became pejorative. Thus in Yiddish, a **batlen** (plural **batlonim**) came to mean first an idle person, a loafter, and later any clumsy or ineffectual person, a clod. This sense passed from the Yiddish to the Hebrew word. The literal meaning of *batlan* is 'one who ceases doing;' the root is *batel,* 'to cease, stop, be idle.'

bat mitzvah or (*Ashkenazi*) **bas mitzvah.** This term appears in the Talmud (*Bava Kamma 15a*) as the feminine of **bar mitzvah** (in the sense of one who is subject to all the commandments), with Hebrew **bat**, literally, 'daughter (of),' substituting for Aramaic **bar.** In its current sense, the term first came into popular use among Conservative and Reform Jews in the mid-1950s, though the notion of a ceremony that included girls who have come of age existed among German Reform Jews since the 1800s. In practice, this took the form of a collective *Confirmation* ceremony, usually held during or near the festival of Shavuos, at which a group of adolescent boys and girls (usually older than thirteen) recite Scriptural passages and affirm their adherence to Judaism. Confirmation, however, did not succeed in replacing the bar mitzvah ceremony even among liberal Jews, and a call for a ceremony for girls parallel to that of boys led to the introduction of the *bat mitzvah* ceremony.

Among Orthodox Jews, the concept of a bat mitzvah started to gain acceptance in the 1970s. With the growth of the religious education of girls through day schools and yeshivas, and with bar mitzvahs becoming increasingly elaborate affairs, Orthodox parents felt the need to celebrate their daughters' coming of age with a party or reception similar to that accorded a bar mitzvah. This celebration has taken various forms, depending on the family and the community, but it is always held at or about the time a girl reaches the age of twelve years and a day, which in Jewish law defines the onset of a girl's adulthood. Among the traditional Orthodox, a bat mitzvah is celebrated as a birthday party at the girl's home or in a reception hall, but not in the synagogue. Modern Orthdox parents, on the other hand, tend to treat the celebration more as a religious rite, as by having the bat mitzvah deliver a learned discourse in the synagogue after the services, or, among the more liberal ones, allowing her to lead prayers or read from the Torah at a prayer service consisting exclusively of women.

The term *bat mitzvah* is used in standard English exactly as *bar mitzvah* is: *to be* or *become (a) bat mitzvah, to have* or *make a bat mitzvah, to attend a bat mitzvah, to celebrate one's bat mitzvah.*

bavarfns. See **aufruf** and **wedding terms**.

B.C.E. Abbreviation of *Before the Common Era.* Until the late 20th century it was a common practice among Jewish writers and editors to use the Christian abbreviations A.D. (for Latin A*nno* D*omini;* 'in the Year of the Lord') and B.C. (for 'Before Christ') or B.C.E. (for 'Before the Christian Era') in indicating a particular year or century in the Gregorian calendar. Thus a Jewish historian, in a book about the history of the Jews, would write: ". . . in A.D. 38, he [Apion] headed a delegation of Alexandrians . . . ," "In 39 B.C. Herod arrived in Palestine," and even such a self-contradictory phrase as "Jesus was born about 4 B.C."

More recently, a new awareness of the Christian character of these abbreviations have led many Jewish writers and editors to replace them with the abbreviations **C.E.** (for 'Common Era') and **B.C.E.** (for 'Before the Common Era'). These abbreviations are not offensive to Christians, since the letter C can stand for "Christian" as well as for "Common." Even some gentile writers have chosen to use these abbreviations in order to avoid the religious overtones of A.D. and B.C.

becher. See **kiddush cup**.

beis midrash, bet midrash. See under **synagogue terms**.

bekeshe. See under **clothing terms**.

belaaz. A Hebrew- and Yiddish-origin adverb meaning 'in a foreign language,' used to indicate the equivalent of a Jewish (Hebrew, Aramaic, Yiddish, etc.) term in a non-Jewish language, as in *a Talmud Torah, or Hebrew*

School belaaz. It is sometimes humorously applied to a pair of Jewish terms of different origins: *Chanukah, or Feast of Lights belaaz.* An extended meaning, also humorous, is 'otherwise called, alias': *Yosef, or Joey belaaz; Jacob, or James belaaz.*

The root form *laaz* (plural *leazim*) is a variant of Hebrew *loez,* 'strange (or foreign) language,' found in the Biblical phrase *am loez,* 'a people of strange language' (*Psalms 114:1*). The Mishna (*Megillah 2:1*) calls one who speaks a foreign language and no Hebrew a *loez,* and uses the word *belaaz* to mean 'in his language.' In early medieval times, *loez* or *laaz* became identified with Latin and the Romance languages into which Latin evolved, especially Old Italian and Old French. (see **Loez.**) In rabbinical sources, *loez* or *laaz* came to mean a Latin or Romance translation rendered in Hebrew letters. Hence in most of the commentator Rashi's glosses on the Talmud, the formula *belaaz* has the meaning 'in Old French.'

A popular but unfounded etymology is that the Hebrew *loez* (or the variant *laaz*) is an acronym of *leshon am zar,* 'language of an alien nation.' This etymology is not given by Rashi, Radak, Ibn Ezra, or any other early commentator on the Tanach.

beli neder. A Hebrew- and Yiddish-origin phrase meaning 'without a vow' or 'no vow intended,' used when speaking of some future action, in order to avoid being bound by a promise that one may not be able to keep. Loosely, the phrase is equivalent to "God willing" (*"Will you come to the wedding?" "I will, beli neder."*) The usage, common among observant Jews, is based on the Torah law (*Numbers 30:3*) prohibiting violation of a vow or oath. Compare **shnoder.** See also **exclamations and interjections.**

bendel. A slender red ribbon or thread worn on the wrist as a bracelet or wound around the finger of an infant to deflect or prevent an **eyn-hore** or evil eye. From Yiddish *bendl,* literallly, 'ribbon,' diminutive of *band,* 'band, string, tape.'

bentsh. The common Ashkenazi English verb *to bentsh,* meaning literally 'to bless,' comes from Yiddish *bentshn,* which is one of the oldest words in the Yiddish language. It was formed in Yiddish by combining an Old Italian form of Latin *benedicere* 'to bless, praise' with the Germanic verb suffix *–(e)n.* The common meaning of *to bentsh* is 'to recite the after-meal blessings (often called *the bentshing*).' In Ashkenazic English the word receives the regular English inflections: (I, you, he, she, we, they) *bentshed,* (he, she) *bentshes,* (am, is, are) *bentshing.* The word also appears in various phrases adopted from Yiddish: *to bentsh mezumen* (in which three adult males recite the after-meal blessings by invitation); *to bentsh likht* (to light the Sabbath or holiday candles with a blessing, a ritual called either *likhtbentshn* or *candlelighting*); *to bentsh rosh chodesh* (to recite the blessing of the New Month), *to bentsh gomel* (to recite the thanksgiving blessing after surviving a dangerous illness, journey, or accident). Except for *to bentsh likht* ('to light the candles') there are no English equivalents to these usages. The spelling *bentsh* is preferable to *bensh* or *bench*, since the former does not reflect the pronunciation, and the latter overlaps with the unrelated English word *bench*.

bet din or (*Ashkenazi*) **bes din.** A Jewish court of law or tribunal. From Hebrew, literally, 'house of judgment.' The plural is **battei din** or (*Ashkenazi*, from Yiddish) **bes dinim.** The minimal number to constitute a bet din is three men. A rabbinical high court of law is called a **bet** (or **bes**) **din tzedek,** literally, 'righteous court of law,' often called by its acronym **bedatz** (בד״ץ). The archaic spelling **beth din** is still used, chiefly in official names, such as *Beth Din of America.* See also **av bet din.**

bet knesset. See under **synagogue terms.**

bimah. A raised platform or pulpit in the men's section of the synagogue on which the table or desk (*shulchan*) for reading the Torah or chanting the prayers stands. The Sephardim call the platform **tevah.** Traditionally, the bimah was located in the center of the synagogue, but in the early 19th century Reform temples moved the bimah to the front of the synagogue. Conservative synagogues and some Modern Orthodox ones in the United States followed suit. From Hebrew, borrowed from Greek *bēma,* 'step,

---

It is customary at bar and bat mitzvahs, weddings, and other religious occasions to hand out pocket-size booklets containing the after-meal blessings, and often other blessings, Sabbath songs, and even various prayers. These booklets are called **bentshers,** derived from the Yiddish diminutive *bentsherl,* meaning a booklet used for bentshing and derived from Yiddish *bentshn,* 'to bentsh.' The spelling *bentsher* is preferable to *bensher* or *bencher.* The modern Hebrew coinage corresponding to *bentsher* is **birchon,** a word derived from *birkat (hamazon),* 'after-meal blessing.'

Betar: a tale of two names

Betar (also spelled Bethar) was the name of the last stronghold of Simeon Bar Kochba (d.135 C.E.), who led the revolt in Judea against Roman rule in 132–135 C.E. It was in Betar, a small town in the Judean hills southwest of Jerusalem, where Bar Kochba and his small band of followers defied the Roman legions at the cost of their lives. Their defense of Betar became an enduring symbol of heroism in Jewish history.

Almost two thousand years later, in 1925, Betar was reborn as the name of a militant Zionist youth movement founded by Zev Jabotinsky (1880–1940). The name was chosen by Jabotinsky because it conveyed a double meaning. First, it was the abbreviation of the movement's official name, B(*'rit*) T(*rumpeldo*)r, "Covenant of Trumpeldor," in honor of Joseph Trumpeldor (1880–1920), a hero of World War I who died heroically as a pioneer defending the settlement of Tel Hai in northern Eretz Israel. Second, it was the name of Bar Kochba's last stronghold. Thus, to the members of the movement, it was a double symbol of supreme Jewish heroism in defense of the Holy Land.

platform,' derived from the verb *bainein*, 'to go.' Compare **almemar**. See also *shulchan* under **synagogue terms**.

birchon. See **bentsh**, 20.

blatt. See **daf**.

blech. A Yiddish-origin word for a metal sheet, used in English by Orthodox Ashkenazim in the specialized sense of a metal sheet for keeping a lighted gas range covered on the Sabbath. Jewish law prohibits cooking on the Sabbath but permits keeping cooked dishes hot as long as they are placed on the blech and do not come into contact with the fire. From Yiddish *blekh*, derived from German *Blech*, 'sheet metal, tin plate.' The Yiddish plural is *blekhn*, but English-speaking Jews have innovated the plural **blechs** and (less commonly) **blecher**.

blintz. See under **food terms**.

bobe mayse. A Yiddish-origin phrase used derisively to mean an old wives' tale, a fairy tale, a pure fantasy. The assumption that the literal meaning is 'grandmother tale' (presumably from *bobe*, 'grandmother') is false. The original Yiddish phrase was *bove mayse*, meaning the story of *Bove*, referring to a famous Yiddish romance of chivalry in poetic form called *bovebukh*, 'Bove book,' composed about 1507–08 by Elye Bokher (1469–1549). This Yiddish book was based on the Italian version (*Buovo d'Antona*) of a popular 13th-century English romance (*Sir*) *Bevis of Hampton*. The change from *bove mayse* to *bobe mayse*, along with the generalized meaning of 'old wives' tale,' may have come about through association with *bobe*, 'grandmother.'

bobkes. In Yiddish, this word is an interjection meaning 'rubbish! nonsense!,' derived from *bobke*, which means 'sheep or goat dung.' The word was borrowed from the Polish noun *bobki*, of the same meaning. Nevertheless, many have confused this word with the Yiddish words for beans, *bobes*, a confusion that has led Jewish English speakers to equate *bobkes* with the American English slang use of "beans," as in *He don't know beans* (attested in English since 1833), and *I don't care beans about that.* So sentences like "I got bobkes for all my efforts," "He made bobkes this year on the market," and "Even if you win the case, the damages you'll get will be worth bobkes" are examples of Jewish English usage (see **Jewish English**). Also Anglicized as **bupkes.**

borsht. See under **food terms.**

bris or **brit.** The circumcision ceremony; in full **bris milah** or **brit milah.** The form *bris* is from Yiddish, in which the plural is *brisn.* The form *brit*

---

brouhaha: a word history

The English noun *brouhaha*, meaning 'noise, hubbub, uproar, confusion,' originated in French and came into English in the late 1800s. The origin of the French word was unknown until the linguists Oscar Bloch and Walther von Wartburg proposed as a plausible source the Hebrew phrase *baruch habba*, 'welcome!' (literally, 'blessed is he who comes'), found in the *Hallel* prayer (Psalms 118:26) and commonly used as a greeting at public gatherings such as weddings and synagogue services. As evidence, Bloch and von Wartburg cite dialectal Italian (Arezzo) *barruccaba*, meaning 'uproar, disorder,' which is clearly a rendering of the Hebrew phrase.

comes from Hebrew and its plural is *britot*. But the preferred plural in English is **brisses,** as in "Today I went to a bris, and tomorrow I will attend two brisses" (not *britot*). Literally, the term means 'pact or covenant (of circumcision),' but in actual usage it means the ceremony of circumcising a male child (usually) on the eighth day after birth. Some related terms are **milah, mohel, kvater, sandek,** and **vachnacht.**

– C –

cabala. A Medieval Latin spelling of Hebrew **kabbalah.** The Medieval Latin word was first recorded in English in 1521, with the meaning 'mystical interpretation of the Hebrew Scriptures.' A later (1665) meaning of the word was 'a secret doctrine or art.' (The related English word *cabal*, meaning 'a secret group,' was borrowed from French *cabale*, which took the word from the Medieval Latin.) In the current sense of 'Jewish mystical teachings' or 'Jewish mysticism,' the preferred spelling in Jewish English is **kabbalah,** with the derivatives *kabbalist* and *kabbalistic*. However, due to the influence of Medieval Latin, especially in Christian theology, English dictionaries treat the form *cabala* as a main entry (with the derivatives *cabalist* and *cabalistic*) and cross-refer *kabbalah* to *cabala* without considering the differences in usage between the two forms.

camps. See under **Holocaust terms.**

candlelighting. In standard English, this word has long been obsolescent, since its meaning, 'the time for lighting candles; twilight; dusk,' puts it in a period before the invention of gaslight. Most dictionaries have stopped recording the word. Uniquely, however, Jews have reintroduced it into English, because lighting candles before the Sabbath and holidays and lighting the menorah on the eight days of Chanukah are almost universal rituals among Jews. The term *candlelighting* is not an adoption of the old English word but a new coinage translating Yiddish *likht-tsindn* or Hebrew *hadlokas neros*. Jewish calendars often include a *candlelighting chart*, which lists the times for lighting candles before the Sabbath in various cities or countries. Since a blessing is recited before candlelighting, the ritual is also often called *likhtbentshn* (literally, 'candle blessing') among Ashkenazim. See **bentsh.**

Lighting candles is not limited to the eves of the Sabbath and holidays and the eight days of Chanukah. A candle is lit in the havdalah ceremony at the end of Sabbath. It is also customary to light yahrzeit candles on the anniversary of a close relative's death and on the eve of the day on which the yizkor memorial is recited. Memorial candles are also lit daily in a house where mourners sit shivah. At many weddings, the parents of the bride and the groom carry lit candles as they lead their offspring to the chuppah. The term *candlelighting*, however, refers exclusively to the kindling of Sabbath, holiday, and Chanukah candles.

Canaanites: A tale of two names

The original Cannanites were the indigenous inhabitants of Canaan, a strip of land extending north and south along the eastern Mediterranean. Canaan was the land promised by God to the Children of Israel (Exodus 6:4) and conquered under the leadership of Joshua. The Canaanites were descendants of *Canaan*, the fourth son of Ham, who was cursed by his grandfather Noah (Genesis 9:25).

The name *Canaanite* was revived in midst of World War II (about 1942) by a group of young Jewish nationalists, mostly poets and artists, born in Palestine and seeking to establish a new kind of society based on their shared Hebrew language, culture, and historical ancestry. Their main goal was to distinguish themselves from the Jews of the Diaspora. They called themselves Canaanites rather than Jews (though they did not object to being called Hebrews or Israelites), and sought to integrate the Arab population into the new nation they hoped to create. The ideas of the Canaanites (Hebrew *kenaanim*) exerted considerable influence on the literature, education, and secular policies of the State of Israel.

cantor. See **chazzan.**

C.E. Abbreviation of *Common Era.* See **B.C.E.**

Chabad. See under **Hasidic terms.**

chacham, plural **chachamim.** From Hebrew, literally, 'wise man, sage.' Among Sephardim, *chacham* is a title given to the elected rabbi of a community. In the Ottoman empire and its successor states, the title *chacham bashi* ('chief chacham') was accorded to the highest-ranking Sephardic rabbi of a province. The **chachamin** were the rabbis and sages cited in the Talmud. The acronym **chazal,** denoting the rabbis of the Talmud, stands for *chachomeynu zichronom livrochoh,* 'our sages of blessed memory.' TheYiddish-origin form, **chochom,** plural **chachomim,** is often used sarcastically or derisively, as in *chochom eyner,* 'smart one, wise-acre, fool.' The related Yiddish-origin word **chochme,** literally, 'wisdom,' is commonly used to mean a joke or witticism.

chag, plural **chagim.** From Hebrew, '(Jewish) festival or holiday.' Specifically, *chag* refers to the festivals of Sukkos, Pesach, and Shavuos, which in the Bible are called *chag hasukkos, chag hapesach,* and *chag shavuos.* In popular usage, however, *chag* is also used for other holidays, especially Purim (*chag purim*). Ashkenazim who refer to the Jewish festivals as *chagim* usually greet one another with *chag sameach!* ('Joyous Festival!'); those who refer to the festivals by the Yiddish-origin term *yon-toyvim* (from Hebrew *yomim tovim,* literally, 'good days') usually use the Yiddish-origin greeting *gut yon-tef!* (Many Ashkenazim alternate both greetings.) A **chagiga** is a holiday festivity or celebration, as in *a Chanukah chagiga.* Compare **choge.** See also **yom tov.**

chai. In Hebrew, this word is an adjective meaning 'alive, living.' But Yiddish adopted the word as a noun in the specialized sense of 'eighteen,' or more particularly, 'a donation of 18 (crowns, rubles, dollars, etc.).' This meaning results from the fact that the two Hebrew letters forming the word, namely *ches* (ח) and *yod* (י), are numerically equal to 18 (*ches* = 8; *yod* = 10), whence the idea that the number 18 symbolizes living or 'life,' a notion reinforced by the traditional concept that charity wards off death. As prosperity in America stimulated almsgiving in the Jewish community, the Yiddish usage passed into English. Standard amounts of charitable donations rose from *chai* ($18) to *twice chai* ($36) to *three times chai* ($54), and beyond, reaching at times *a hundred times chai* and even *a thousand times chai.* The word's popularity led to its use in gold and silver charms in the shape of the Hebrew word חי, the necklaces becoming known as 'chai pendants.' The word is also used figuratively to mean '18th,' as in "We are celebrating the Community Center's chai anniversary."

chalaka. See **opsherenish.**

chalitzah. See **yibbum.**

challah, plural **challas** or **challot.** Also spelled **hallah.** The basic meaning of this Hebrew- and Yiddish-origin word is a portion of dough from each baking that was set aside for a gift to the kohen, as prescribed in the Torah (*Numbers 15:20*). In the Diaspora, the rabbis ordained that in order that the law of challah should not be forgotten, a piece of the dough used in baking should be separated and symbolically burned in the oven. This precept was specifically prescribed for women, who usually did the baking, with a special blessing to be recited before setting aside the portion of dough for burning. From this precept it became customary to refer to the ceremonial white loaf of bread, usually in braided form, that is baked for the Sabbath and holidays as a *challah*. Such loaves are also baked for the meal at a religious ceremony such as a wedding, circumcision, *pidyon haben*, or *siyyum*. See also **food terms**.

Chanukah. See under **holiday terms**.

Chanukiyah, plural **Chanukiyot**. Also spelled **Hanukiyah**. A Hebrew term for the eight-branched candelabrum used on Chanukah. The more widely used term, especially in America, is *Chanukah lamp* or *Chanukah menorah*, or *menorah* for short.

chasan, chasene. See **wedding terms**.

Chasid, Chasidic, Chasidism, Chasidus. See **Hasid**.

chaver, plural **chaverim**. A Hebrew- and Yiddish-origin term meaning a companion, associate, or friend. In yeshiva usage, it refers to a companion in Talmudic study, the companionship being called a *chavrusa* or *chavruta* (from Aramaic). In the period of the Second Temple, the term *chaver* referred to a member of a **chavurah**, an association of scholars noted for their punctilious observance of the laws of purity and tithes, as distinguished from the unobservant *amei-haaretz* of the time (see **am-haaretz**).

At least three distinct Yiddish-origin terms are used by Ashkenazim for the braided loaf of white bread eaten on the Sabbath, holidays, etc. The most widespread is **challah**, from Eastern Yiddish *khale*, derived from the Hebrew *challah*. Another is **barches** (sometimes **berches**), the standard term in Western Yiddish, derived from a variant of *broches*, 'blessings.' A third term is **koyletsh**, borrowed from Polish *kolacz*, 'twisted loaf,' and used mainly by Polish Jews and their descendants.

In western Europe, especially in Germany, it became customary since about the 16th century to confer the honorary title of *chaver* to distinguished scholars who were not ordained rabbis. See also **chevra.**

chazal. See **chacham.**

chazer, plural **chazerim.** Literally, a pig or its meat, pork, but chiefly used figuratively by Ashkenazim to mean a filthy or uncouth person. This pejorative meaning is common in Yiddish, whereas the original Hebrew was more literal and less expressive. The pejorative usage is unrelated to the fact that the eating of pork is prohibited to Jews, since in many languages, including English, the pig is regarded as a creature of filthy habits (consider English *pigsty*) and its name is used derogatorily. The derivative **chazerai,** also from Yiddish, can refer to trashy food or to anything filthy, messy, or obscene.

chazzan or **chazan,** plural **chazzanim.** The Hebrew- and Yiddish-origin word for a cantor, or religious functionary who chants the prayers and leads the congregation in the synagogue prayers. In Talmudic times, the *chazzan* served as a synagogue caretaker who taught young children and read publicly from the Torah. By the time of the Geonim, the *chazzan* chanted the prayers, often accompanied by a boys' choir. The early Sephardi communities in America raised the status of the "*hazzan*" to that of community leader, bestowing upon him the title of Reverend. In Europe the role of the rabbi always superseded that of the cantor, who was nevertheless held in high esteem as a *sheliach tzibbur,* 'deputy for the congregation' (a designation commonly abbreviated to *shatz,* ץ"ש, as in *chazoras ha-shatz,* 'repetition of the amidah by the *sheliach tzibbur*'). The Ashkenazim who immigrated to the United States at the turn of the 20th century created a cult of cantorial music that gave rise to a "Golden Age of Chaz-

In the late 20th century, the term *chavurah* (plural *chavurot*), also spelled *havurah* (plural *havurot*), was adopted among Conservative Jews and Reconstructionists to denote any informal group of Jews who gather regularly in various homes or other locations for the purpose of prayer, study, and fellowship. The reason for organizing these groups was to create an alternative to synagogue services, which some members regarded as too formal.

zanim," which lasted into the 1950s. Though professional cantors continue to serve in Conservative and Reform synagogues, most Orthodox synagogues rely on volunteers to lead prayers. These individuals are often loosely called chazzanim: "*Who's going to be the chazzan this morning?*" More accurately they are designated as *shelichei tzibbur* ('deputies of the congregation'), and specifically as *baale-tefillah* ('masters of prayer'), which may include a *baal-shacharis*, who leads the morning prayers, and a *baal-musaf*, who leads the additional Sabbath or holiday prayers. Also spelled **hazzan** or **hazan.**

cheder. Also spelled **heder.** A private religious elementary school for boys prevalent especially in Eastern Europe before World War II. The word derives from Yiddish and Hebrew, where it literally means 'room,' because the school consisted usually of a room in the house of the teacher (*melamed*). The teacher, as well as his assistant (the *belfer*, variant of *bahelfer*, 'assistant'), were paid by the pupil's parents. A type of school for children whose parents could not afford a cheder was the **Talmud Torah**, which was maintained and supported by the community. In the United States, community Talmud Torahs became **Hebrew schools**, with daily afternoon classes for both boys and girls following the public-school sessions. The Hebrew school declined as an institution after the advent of the Jewish **day school** or **yeshiva ketanah** ('little yeshiva'), where both religious and secular subjects are taught. The word's plural form is **cheders,** though the Yiddish-origin plural **chadorim** is occasionally used.

cherem. See **herem.**

chevra, plural **chevras.** Literally, an association, fellowship, or society. From Yiddish and Hebrew-Aramaic, related to **chaver.** In strictly Orthodox communities, the term denotes two types of associations; one religious, the other philanthropic. Religious *chevras* consist of study groups devoted to a particular text, such as *chevra mishnayos* (Mishnah) and *chevra tehillim* (Psalms). Philanthropic *chevras* include such associations as *chevra bikkur cholim* (visiting the sick) and notably the ancient institution of **chevra kadisha**, literally, 'holy fellowship,' whose members prepare the dead for burial. The word *chevra* is also used informally for any close-knit group of friends, as members of an organization or a kibbutz or yishuv in Israel. The term **chevraman** (from Yiddish *khev'reman*) means a tough, tricky, or roguish fellow.

chiloni. See **dati.**

choge. A non-Jewish religious holiday or festival, such as Christmas or Easter, as distinguished from a **chag.** The word comes from Yiddish, which took it through Hebrew from Aramaic, where it means any holiday or festival. The plural form, **choges,** is from Yiddish *khoges,* although Yiddish has a variant plural, *khago'es.*

cholent (tsho'lent). See under **food terms.**

chuppah or **chuppa,** plural **chuppahs, chuppas,** or (*Sephardi*) **chuppot.** Also spelled **huppah.** The canopy under which a bride and groom are wedded, representing the bridal chamber or tent in which originally the marriage was consummated. The word also means wedding ceremony or, loosely, a wedding. From Yiddish and Hebrew, literally, 'covering, canopy.' The term **open chuppah** refers to a wedding ceremony performed outdoors or under an open skylight. The custom of having the wedding ceremony outdoors arose in the Middle Ages, when weddings were held outside or in the courtyard of the synagogue as an omen that the offspring of the union may be as numerous as the stars in the sky. See also **wedding terms.**

Churban. See **Holocaust.**

chutzpah. This Yiddish-origin word has two senses in English, one negative and one positive. The negative sense is 'brazen effrontery or impudence, arrogance, gall,' which is its recorded meaning in the original Yiddish. The positive sense is 'great boldness or daring, nerve,' a meaning probably influenced by the English *nerve,* which can be both negative and positive, as in "You've got some nerve!" (negative); "It takes nerve to start a business from scratch." It should be pointed out, however, that Aramaic, from which Yiddish borrowed the word, already had both negative and positive senses in the Talmud. For example: "In the footsteps [i.e., at the advent] of Messiah *chutzpah* will increase and honor dwindle" (*Sotah 49b*). "*Chutzpah* is sovereignty without a crown [i.e., it has great power and lacks only a crown]" (*Sanhedrin 105a*). It is therefore likely that Yiddish encompassed both senses, though dictionaries have recorded only the negative one because of its predominance.

clothing terms. Jews have worn distinctive apparel since Biblical times, mainly to comply with the precept of not following the customs of gentiles

(Leviticus 18:3). Most of the special garments worn by Jews in history, as well as the garments' names, have become obsolete. At present, the only garment by which Jews are recognized are the hats or skullcaps which the observant wear in public. Strictly Orthodox and Hasidic men (and boys over thirteen) are recognized by their black hats (and are often facetiously referred to as "blackhats"); modern Orthodox men and boys are recognized by their knitted, colored, or decorated skullcaps. Some well-known clothing terms, such as **kippah, kittel, tallis,** and **yarmulke,** are listed as main entries. The following is a list of terms for other garments still used by some strictly Orthodox or Hasidic groups:

bekeshe. A man's long silken or satin cloak, often with pockets in the back. From Yiddish, borrowed from Polish *bekiesza,* 'long fur-lined coat,' which may have come from Hungarian *bekecs.*

biberhit. A man's black hat made of beaver fur, with a short crown and wide round brim, worn on weekdays by Hasidim. From Yiddish, 'beaver hat.'

chalat. A man's lightweight silk or woolen robe worn as a housecoat, especially on the Sabbath and holidays. From Yiddish, borrowed from Polish *chlat,* 'blouse.'

gartel. A black sash or girdle of silk or wool, often with tassels, tied by Hasidim around the waist before prayer to separate symbolically the heart from the lower part of the body. From Yiddish *gartl,* 'belt, girdle,' from Middle High German, cognate with Old English *gyrdel,* 'girdle' (from *gyrdan* 'to gird').

kaftan. A man's long overcoat, usually black. From Yiddish *kaftn,* ultimately from Persian.

kapl. A skullcap, same as **yarmulke.** From Central and Western Yiddish, a diminutive of German *Kappe,* 'cap.'

kapote. Same as **kaftan.** From Yiddish, ultimately from French *capote,* 'long cloak,' derived from *cape,* 'a cape.'

sheytl. A wig worn by strictly Orthodox and Hasidic women as a head covering. Anglicized as *sheitel.* From Yiddish, from Middle High German *scheitel,* 'crown of the head.'

shtrayml. A hat trimmed with fur pieces, usually sable, worn by Hasidim on the Sabbath and holidays. Anglicized as *shtreimel.* From Yiddish, derived from Polish *stroj,* 'fancy dress.'

shubitze. A warm cloak worn in winter, often over a bekeshe. From Yiddish, borrowed from Polish *zupica,* a kind of peasant cloak.

spodek. A high fur hat trimmed with plush, worn usually on weekdays. From Yiddish, borrowed from Polish, 'saucer.'

tichel. A kerchief worn by strictly Orthodox or Hasidic women as a head covering. From Yiddish *tikhl*, 'women's shawl,' diminutive of *tikh*, 'cloth,' a dialectal variant of *tukh*, 'cloth, kerchief,' from German *Tuch*.

Confirmation. See **bat mitzvah.**

congratulatory terms. The universal Jewish phrase, uttered at weddings, brisses, bar mitzvahs, and other festive occasions is ***mazel tov!*** (from Yiddish *mazltov!*) or ***mazal tov!*** (from Hebrew), meaning 'congratulations!' or 'good luck!' See **mazel.**

Other congratulatory terms are:

(be)siman tov! '(May it be) for a good omen!' Literally, '(for a) good sign!' From Hebrew, used by Sephardim at most personal celebrations except on the occasion of a daughter's birth, when *mazal tov* is used. (Sephardi girls are often named Mazaltov.)

chazak (u)varuch! '(May you be) strong (and) blessed!' From Hebrew, used by Sephardim to congratulate someone who has received an honor. It corresponds to the Ashkenazi *yasher koakh.* The response is ***baruch tiye!*** 'May you be blessed!'

mazel (un) broche! 'Success!' Literally, 'Luck (and) blessing!' From Yiddish *mazl(un)brokhe*, used especially by Ashkenazim formally when sealing a business transaction, usually with a handshake. The Sephardi equivalent is *mazal uvracha!*

yasher koach! or ***shekoach!*** 'Congratulations!' 'Well done!' From Yiddish *(ya)sher-koyekh*, derived from Hebrew *yeyasher kochacha*, literally, 'May (God) increase your strength!' Used by Ashkenazim to congratulate someone who has received an honor.

See also **greetings and salutations.**

Conservative. This term, adopted from the vocabulary of politics, arose in the United States in the 1880s to designate the form of modern Judaism whose goal was to *conserve* "historical Judaism," as opposed to the "radical" ideology of Reform Judaism that had prevailed in America since the early 19th century. The term is always capitalized and usually functions as an adjective: *Conservative Judaism, Conservative Jews, the Conservative movement, Conservative synagogues.* It is sometimes also used as a noun, especially in the plural: *The Jews in this town are mainly Conservatives.* The philosophy or ideology of the Conservative movement is called **Conservatism.** Conservative synagogues that practice Orthodox rituals are sometimes referred to as ***Conservadox.*** See also **Masorti.** Compare **Orthodox, Reform.**

conversos. See **marranos.**

crypto-Jews. See **marranos.**

– D –

daf, plural **dafim** or **dapim.** A folio or leaf of a Talmudic tractate, with a page on each side. The word comes from Hebrew and Aramaic, and means literally 'plank' or 'board.' The synonymous Yiddish-origin word **blatt** (plural **bletter**) means literally 'leaf.' The standard daf, established in the Bomberg edition (1520–23), is numbered according to the letters of the Hebrew alphabet, beginning with the second letter, ב. (This is due to the fact that the preceding folio, containing the tractate's title page, was counted as the first daf.) Each side of a daf is called an **amud** (*Ashkenazi* o'med). In citing a particular page in a tractate, one gives the daf or folio number followed by the amud, which is shown either as *a* and *b* or as a period for the first amud (**.**) and a colon for the second amud (**:**). Thus the citation *Nedarim 30a and 30b* (or *Nedarim 30. and 30:*) refers to the tractate *Nedarim*, leaf number 30, sides *a* and *b*.

dati. A Hebrew-origin adjective meaning 'religious, observant, devout,' applied to Orthodox Jews in Israel, as distinguished from secular (**chiloni**)

The **daf yomi** (from Aramaic, literally, 'daily daf') is a worldwide system of Talmud study initiated by Rav Meir Shapira (1887–1934) of Lublin at the first International Congress of Agudath Israel in Vienna in 1923. The system enables Jews everywhere to study the same folio of the Babylonian Talmud every day, making it possible for all participants to complete in a 7-1/2-year cycle the entire Talmud simultaneously. The term *daf yomi* also denotes the daf assigned for study on a particular day of the cycle; this is often called **the daf**, as in "I'm going to learn the daf tonight." The popularity of the daf yomi has also stimulated the creation of other daily study cycles, such as *mishna yomit* (daily Mishna), *Rambam yomi* (studying the code of laws of Maimonides), and *Tanach yomi* (studying the Tanach, or Hebrew Bible). There is also a daily study cycle for the Jerusalemite Talmud (*Talmud Yerushalmi*), but it is not as popular as the *daf yomi* of the Babylonian Talmud (*Talmud Bavli*).

Jews. The adjective is usually predicative: *Hillel is not dati. That kibbutz is dati.* Compare **frum, haredi.** As a noun, the term means a religious or Orthodox Jew and takes the plural **datiyim,** as opposed to a **chiloni** (plural **chiloniyim**). The word **dati** derives from Hebrew *dat,* 'religion, faith; custom, law,' which is etymologically related to *din,* 'judgment, law' (see **din**) and *dayan,* 'judge' (see **dayan**). In colloquial Israeli Hebrew, a somewhat disparaging word for an Orthodox Jew is **dos** (plural **dosim**), from Yiddish *dos,* 'religion, faith,' derived from Hebrew *dat.*

daven. This common Ashkenazic English verb (from Yiddish *dav(e)nen*) is often improperly translated as 'to pray.' It actually means 'to recite the prescribed daily, Sabbath, or holiday prayers,' and this is the sense in which Jews use it in English: *Did you daven already? He davened at the early minyan. I'm davening at home today.* Perhaps a closer (though somewhat archaic) translation would be 'to worship.' Ashkenazim who regularly worship at a synagogue (*shul*), i.e., congregants, are called either *daveners* or *mispallelim* (from Ashkenazi Hebrew, plural of *mispallel,* 'one who prays'). The Ashkenazi English equivalent of 'to pray' is *to be mispallel* (from Yiddish *mispalel zayn*). Yiddish also has a German-origin word for 'to pray,' namely *betn,* 'to beg, beseech, pray,' as in *betn Got,* 'pray to God.' The Yiddish noun *gebet* (from German *Gebet*) means 'prayer, plea' and is a doublet of *tfile* (from Hebrew *tefillah*).

dayan (*Ashkenazi* da′yen; *Sephardi* dayan′), plural (*Ashkenazi*) **dayo′nim,** (*Sephardic*) **dayanim′.** The word's basic meaning is 'one who renders judgment at a trial, a judge.' The word is related to **din,** 'judgment, law.' A dayan is usually a member of a court of law or **bet din.** In Europe, the dayan was often the rabbi of the community. In Israel, a dayan is appointed by the Chief Rabbi. In Sephardic communities, a dayan is an assistant of the **av bet din** (head of the court) or of the chief rabbi of a community.

day school. See **cheder.**

decisor. Formal English term for a **posek.**

derasha or **derashah** (*Ashkenazi* dro′she; *Sephardi* derasha′). This word, from Hebrew and Yiddish, generally means a discourse, sermon, or oration. Specifically, it denotes a scholarly discourse or sermon delivered by a rabbi, a *darshan* ('preacher'), or a bridegroom at his wedding. Near-synonyms include **devar Torah** (literally, 'word of Torah'), plural **divrei Torah,** which is usually shorter than a derasha and is delivered by anyone

davening: an etymological mystery

Though over a dozen different theories have been proposed by Yiddish scholars to account for the ultimate origin of the word *daven* and its derivatives, not one has been substantiated so far.

The immediate source of the word is of course Yiddish *dav(e)nen*. Modern scholarship has established that this word arose in Eastern Europe some time in the early 1500s and by the end of that century had spread over the entire territory where Eastern Yiddish was spoken. Amazingly, it quickly displaced the entrenched earlier Yiddish word, *oren*, which derived ultimately from Latin *orare*, 'to speak, pray' (the source of English *oration, orator,* etc.). Why this major displacement occurred is unknown.

Among the most common (and commonly discredited) theories put forth to explain the origin of *davenen* are the following:

1. Aramaic *d'avhonon*, meaning 'from our (fore)fathers,' based on the Talmudic tradition (*Berachos 26b*) that the three daily prayers were instituted by the three Patriarchs.
2. The Hebrew verb *da'av*, 'to grieve,' and its noun, *d'avon*, 'grief, sorrow' (especially in *d'avon-lev*, 'grieving heart'), based on the idea that the truest prayer comes from a broken heart.
3. Lithuanian *dovana* and Latvian *davana* 'gift,' based on the notion that that the Hebrew word for the afternoon prayer is *mincha*, which literally means 'gift.'
4. Latin *devovere*, 'to devote, offer, consecrate.'
5. French *divin* (presumably shortened from *service divin*, 'divine service').
6. Arabic *dawwana* 'to record, set down' or the related word *diwan*, 'anthology of poems.'

The most elaborate, yet linguistically most credible, etymology traces the word *dav(e)nen* back to an earlier Yiddish form, *doynen*, which originally referred to the chanting of prayers by a cantor in the synagogue and that may have been later transferred to the chanting of prayers by any Jew. The form *doynen* derives from Middle High German *doenen, toenen* 'to chant, intone,' apparently ultimately from Latin *tonus*, 'tone.' This is a plausible theory, but how the form and meaning of *doynen* evolved into *dav(e)nen* has not been satisfactorily explained. So the definitive story of the word's origin has yet to be written.

---

delta: a word history

This word is best known as the name of the triangle-shaped alluvial plain at the mouth of the Nile River (*the Nile Delta*) or of any similar place. The Egyptian delta was so named because it resembles the triangular fourth letter of the Greek alphabet (Δ), which is named *delta*. The Greek letter and its name are of Semitic origin, probably Hebrew *dalet*, the fourth letter of the Hebrew alphabet, which anciently resembled a triangle without a base, like a reverse V (∧). The Hebrew *dalet* was derived from *delet*, 'door,' and was originally formed from the hieroglyph of a tent door.

---

on any occasion; **pshetl** (from Yiddish, diminutive of *pshat*, 'literal meaning'), which involves an analytical interpretation of the plain meaning of a text; and a **vort** (from Yiddish, literally, 'word'), which is a short devar Torah.

derech eretz. From Hebrew and Yiddish, literally, 'way of the land.' The term has various meanings. The commonest meaning, 'respect for elders and teachers, and especially for parents,' was the last to appear, probably in Yiddish. The earliest meaning, found in the Mishnah (*Pirke Avos 2:2*), is 'worldly occupation or trade, means of livelihood.' In the Gemara and Midrash, the phrase is usually used in the sense of 'good manners, proper conduct, politeness,' as for example in tractate *Yoma 4a:* "The Torah teaches us *derech eretz*, that a man should not address his neighbor without first calling him (by name)." Two of the minor tractates, *derech eretz rabba* and *derech eretz zuta*, deal in detail with the rules of good behavior and etiquette, often based on verses from the Pentateuch. In the 19th century, Rabbi Samson Raphael Hirsch (1808–1888), extended the Mishnaic meaning of worldly occupation or trade to include the idea of worldly (i.e., secular) knowledge, summarizing his philosophy in the phrase *Torah Im Derech Eretz,* 'Torah (combined) with wordly knowledge' as the guiding principle of enlightened Orthodoxy; see **Neo-Orthodoxy.**

Deuteronomy. See **Pentateuch.**

Diaspora, the. The term used for the extensive settlement of Jews outside the Land of Israel following the Babylonian Exile in 586 B.C.E. It is sometimes used as a synonym of Hebrew **galut** and **golah**, though the latter mean 'exile' and emphasize the banishment of Jews from their land, whereas *Diaspora*, which means 'scattering, dispersion,' emphasizes the widespread settlement of Jews in places like Persia, Arabia, North Africa, and Spain as a result of their exile. A Hebrew word corresponding to Diaspora is *tefutsos* (also *nefutsos*), found in the Prophets and derived from the verb *lehafits*, 'to scatter, disperse.' Since the establishment of the State of Israel, *the tefutsos* (Sephardi *tefutsot*) has been the preferred term for the Jewish communities outside Israel. Historians use the word *Diaspora* also in referring to any part or segment of Jewry living in the Diaspora, as for example *the Moroccan Diaspora, the Ashkenazi Diaspora*; this usage takes a plural, as in *Among the Diasporas, perhaps the greatest was the Spanish Diaspora.*

The word *Diaspora* came into English from Greek in the 1870s. The Greek word derived from the verb *diaspeirein*, 'to scatter about.' When capitalized, it usually refers to the Jewish dispersion; when used in lowercase, it may refer to the dispersion of any population from its traditional homeland or habitat, as in "the African diaspora."

dietary laws. See **kashrus.**

din, plural **dinim.** A Hebrew-origin word meaning 'Jewish religious law or judgment,' and, by extension, '(in a Jewish court) lawsuit, verdict, justice.' The word appears in many widely used legal, religious, and theological terms, such as the following (from Hebrew and Yiddish):

baal din. A party to a lawsuit in a Jewish court; a litigant.

bet din or *bes din.* A Jewish court of law. See the main entry.

dinei mamonos. Jewish civil law. Literally, 'monetary laws.'

dinei nefashos. Jewish criminal law. Literally, 'laws of persons (who had committed capital crimes).'

din Torah. A lawsuit in a Jewish court. Literally, 'Torah justice.'

din vecheshbon. A statement of accounts; an accounting. Literally, 'judgment and reckoning.'

midas hadin. Stringent Divine justice (as opposed to *midas horachamim,* Divine leniency). Literally, '(God's) attribute of justice.'

pesak din. A judgment or verdict, as of a law court.

tzidduk hadin. Prayer recited during the burial service acknowledging God's judgment. Literally, 'justification of the Divine decree.'

yom hadin. Day of Judgment. Used especially in reference to Rosh Hashanah.

See also **dayan.**

dreidel, plural **dreidels** or (Yiddish) **dreidlech**. The common name and spelling for the four-sided spinning top played with on Chanukah. The word came from Eastern Yiddish *dreydl*, a diminutive of *dreyen*, 'to turn, twist' (from Middle High German *drehen*). A less common name is **trendl**, from Western Yiddish, which came from Middle High German *trendel*, 'disk, spinning top,' and is related to English *trundle*. Since the emergence of Modern Hebrew, another popular name of the dreidel is **sevivon** (plural **sevivonim**), a translation of Yiddish *dreydl* based on Hebrew *sevuv*, 'circle, spin, turn.'

duchen (said of a kohen or kohanim). To recite the *birkat kohanim* or blessing of the kohanim (*Numbers 6: 23–27*) during the reader's repetition of the shemone-esrei or amidah (daily in Israel, during the holidays in the Diaspora). This Ashkenazi English verb is from Yiddish *dukh(e)nen*, derived from the Hebrew-Aramaic *duchan*, 'platform, specifically the platform or pulpit upon which the kohanim recite their blessing.' The Ashkenazi English verb is regularly inflected as *duchened, duchens, duchening*. See also ***nesias kapayim*** under **ritual terms.**

– E –

Ebri. A Persian dialect containing many Hebrew words and written in Hebrew characters, used by the Jews of Persia (Iran). Formerly called **Judeo-Persian.**

erev. The eve of (the Sabbath or of a holiday), *erev* always preceding the name, as in *erev Shabbos* (= Friday), *erev yom tov* (= the eve of a holiday), *erev rosh chodesh* (= the eve of Rosh Chodesh). From Hebrew, 'evening, eve,' and Yiddish, preposition 'on the eve of.' Compare **motz(o)e**, the close or outgoing of (the Sabbath or a holiday), as in *motz(o)e yom kippur* (= the close of Yom Kippur, the night on which Yom Kippur ends).

The four sides of the dreidel are marked with the four Hebrew letters *nun, gimmel, hei,* and *shin,* which traditionally stand for the words *Nes Gadol Haya Sham,* 'A great miracle happened there.' In Israel it has become customary to replace the last letter, *shin,* with the letter *pei,* to form the phrase *Nes Gadol Haya Po,* 'A great miracle happened *here.*'

eruv, plural **eruvs** or (from Hebrew and Yiddish) **eruvim.** The term commonly used for a rabbinical means by which objects may be carried on the Sabbath through an amalgamation or fusion of public and private domains. The eruv is usually a wire fixed to poles that encircles an area of dwellings or a town or neighborhood. From Hebrew, literally, 'blending, fusion, amalgamation,' a shortening of *eruv chatzeros,* 'blending of courtyards.'

esnoga. The Judezmo term for a synagogue. It is a variant of Spanish *sinagoga,* from Late Latin, from Greek *synagoge,* 'place of assembly' (part translation of Hebrew *bet haknesset),* from *synagein,* 'to bring together, assemble.'

exclamations and interjections. Common phrases used as exclamations or interjections in colloquial Jewish speech include the terms below. Unless otherwise indicated, the terms come from Hebrew and Yiddish.

> *aderabe.* 'On the contrary; not at all; by all means.' From Yiddish, derived from Hebrew-Aramaic, contraction of Aramaic *al deraba,* 'turn to the stronger side.'
>
> *beezras Hashem.* 'God willing.' Literally, 'with the help of God.'
>
> *beli ayin hara.* 'May no evil eye befall.' Literally, 'without the evil eye.' Compare below *kanehore, kan eyn-hore.*
>
> *beli neder.* 'God willing.' Literally, 'without (making) a vow.' See **neder.**
>
> *boruch habo!* 'Welcome!' Literally, 'Blessed be he who comes!'
>
> *boruch Hashem.* 'Thank God.' Literally, 'Blessed be the Name.' Most often used in response to the question, "How are you?"
>
> *chas vesholem!* or *chas vecholile!* 'Heaven forbid!'

The Talmudic tractate *Eruvin* deals with the common eruv as well as with two other forms of rabbinical amalgamation: *eruv techumim,* 'blending of boundaries,' whereby the prescribed Sabbath boundary of 2,000 cubits may be extended so as to allow movement from one area or town to another; and *eruv tavshilin,* 'blending of dishes,' whereby preparation of food on a holiday for the immediately following Sabbath is permitted by setting aside two dishes on the eve of a holiday for consumption on the succeeding Sabbath. However, when the term *eruv* is used in the singular, it always refers to the common eruv permitting the carrying of necessary articles on the Sabbath.

cholile! or *cholile vechas!* 'Heaven forbid!'

davke. Precisely; necessarily; purposely, as in *Why did you pick davke me?* or *Davke today, when I'm so busy, I have to report to jury duty.* In negation, one might use the phrase *lav davke,* 'not exactly, not quite, not necessarily.' From Yiddish and Hebrew.

halevay. 'Would that it be so!' Also spelled *alevay.* From Yiddish and Hebrew-Aramaic.

im yirtze Hashem. 'God willing.' Often pronounced *myertseshem,* from the Yiddish contraction.

kanehore or *kan eyn-hore.* 'May no evil eye befall.' Literally, 'no evil eye.' A phrase used after speaking words of praise about someone or something and intended to avert the evil eye. From Yiddish. See the main entry **eyn-hore.**

kavyochl. As if; as it were; as though possible (used especially when attributing to God typically human actions). The word is also sometimes used as a euphemism for God. From Yiddish *kavyokhl,* derived from Hebrew *kivyachol.*

keyn yirbu! 'So may they increase in numbers!' (used in reference to someone's offspring or to any group whose growth is desirable).

lemaan Hashem! 'Definitely; without fail!' Literally, 'for the sake of God.'

lehavdl. To differentiate; distinguish (between two things, usually one sacred, the other not), as in *the study of the Torah and, lehavdl, of secular subjects.*

nebech! 'A pity! How unfortunate! Poor thing!' From Eastern Yiddish *nebekh,* borrowed from a Slavic word akin to Polish *nieboze.* The related form *nebbish,* which entered American English slang as an adjective meaning 'pitiful' and as a noun meaning 'a pitiful or ineffectual person,' came from the Western Yiddish equivalent of Eastern Yiddish *nebekh.*

olev (or *oleho*) *hasholem,* plural, *alehem hasholem.* 'May he (or she) rest in peace.' Literally, 'Peace be upon him (or her).' Used after mention of a person or his name, as in *my father, olev hasholem.*

tischadesh! (tis-cha'-desh) 'Wear it (new clothing) in good health!' Literally, 'May you be renewed!'

yimach shemo! 'May he be cursed!' Literally, 'May his name be blotted out!' Also, *yimach shemo vezichro!,* plural, *yimach shemom (vezichrom).* (Literally) 'May his name and memory be blotted out!' Used after an individual's name, as in *Haman yimach shemo!*

zichrono livrocho, plural, *zichronom livrocho.* 'Of blessed memory.'

Literally, 'May his (or her) memory be blessed.' Used after mention of a person or his name, as in *our revered rebbe, zichrono livrocho.*

Exilarch. A scholarly name for the **resh galuta**, the Jewish civil ruler during the Babylonian Exile, from the 6th century B.C.E. to the 10th century C.E. Formed from English *exile* + the suffix *–arch*, 'ruler.'

Exile. See **galut.**

Exodus. See **Pentateuch.**

eyn-hore or **ayen-hore.** The "evil eye" of tradition and folklore, referring to the glance of an evil person that may cause harm to another, or to any harm that may come from praising or boasting about someone or something, or for being so conspicuously beautiful, wealthy, or lucky as to invite spite, jealousy, and ill-wishes toward oneself, and especially towards one's children. From Yiddish, derived from Hebrew *ayin hara,* 'evil eye.' The expression **to give an eyn-hore** (from Yiddish *tsu gebn an eyn-hore*) means to harm with the evil eye, or, by extension, to cause a person to be harmed by giving him or her too much praise or honor. See also *kanehore* under **exclamations and interjections.**

– F –

fast, fasting. "To fast" is one of several English verbs that have become specialized in Jewish (chiefly Orthodox) usage as a result of contact with Yiddish near-homophones. The like-sounding words in this case are English *to fast* and Yiddish *tsu fastn,* both usually meaning to abstain from both food and drink during a public religious fast. (Other examples of such verbs are *to learn,* as in *He learns in a yeshiva*; and *to wash,* as in *If we're going to eat bread, we'll have to wash*; influenced by Yiddish *lernen* and *vashn (zikh)* respectively). Two of the public fasts, Yom Kippur and Tisha B'Av, are observed for 24 hours; all other fasts last one day, from dawn to nightfall. Examples of Jewish usage are: *If you're a firstborn, you'll have to fast on erev Pesach. Is she old enough to fast? When is the fast over?* (In this example, the noun "fast" translates Yiddish *tones* or *taynes.*) *He is too sick to be fasting. Some religious Jews fast every Monday and Thursday.*

fast days. The major fast days are **Yom Kippur** and **Tisha B'Av.** The minor fast days are *asara beteves* (10th of Teves), commemorating the besieging of Jerusalem by the Babylonians (Kings II, 25); *shiva asar betamuz* (17th of Tamuz), commemorating the breaching of the walls of Jerusalem three weeks before the destruction of the Temple (see **Three Weeks**); *taanis ester* (13th of Adar), commemorating the fast of Queen Esther preceding Purim; and *tzom gedaliah* (3rd of Tishri), commemorating the assassination of Gedaliah ben Ahikam, the governor of Judah (Kings II, 25:25).

fleishig. (of food) made of meat or meat products; (of utensils) used only for meat or meat products. From Yiddish *fleyshik,* literally, 'of meat,' derived from *fleysh,* 'meat, flesh.' Contrasted with **milchig.** See also **parve, kashrus.**

food terms. Some Jewish food terms are found as main entries in the dictionary, as, for example, **adafina, afikoman,** and **challah.** Other common ones are given below.

    arbes. Boiled chick peas, often salted and peppered, served as a snack at various festivities. From Yiddish, 'peas.'

    ayngemachts. Any jam or preserves, as one made by boiling minced beets and carrots in sugar. From Yiddish *ayngemakhts,* from German *Eingemachtes.*

    babka. A spongy coffee cake, usually with marbelized chocolate. From Yiddish *babke,* of Slavic origin; compare Polish *babka,* diminutive of *baba,* 'old woman, grandmother.'

    bagel. The popular doughnut-shaped bread roll. Borrowed from Yiddish *beygl,* a diminutive derived from *beygn,* 'to bend, bow.'

    bialy. An onion roll with a depression in the middle and a crusty bottom. Shortened from Yiddish *bialistoker (kukhn),* 'Bialystok (cake),' after the city of Bialystok, in northeastern Poland, where this bread roll was originally made.

    blintz. Also, *blintze.* A folded-over thin pancake with a filling of cottage cheese, fruit, or potato. From Yiddish *blintse,* from Russian *blinets,* diminutive of *blin,* pancake.'

    bokser. The pod of the carob tree, a long, flat, hard fruit with seeds, eaten traditionally on Tu Bishvat (Jewish arbor day). From Yiddish.

    borsht. Also spelled *borscht.* A beet soup, often served cold with sour cream or hot with cabbage and meat. From Yiddish *borsht,* borrowed from Russian *borshch.*

    burekas. A Sephardi pastry of Turkish origin, with a filling of spinach, eggplant, potatoes, and sometimes meat or cheese.

chremzlech. Fritters made from matzo meal. Singular, *chremzl.* From Yiddish *khremzlekh.*

chreyn. Horseradish sauce, served as a relish with gefilte fish and boiled beef. From Yiddish *khreyn,* 'horseradish.'

cholent (tsholnt). An Ashkenazi Sabbath dish of slowly cooking meat, potatoes, beans, and other vegetables, covered on Friday and left to simmer until the next day. From Yiddish *tsholnt,* borrowed from Old French *chalent-,* 'warming,' derived from Latin *calentem,* present participle of *calere,* 'be warm.'

derma. Another name for *kishke.* From Yiddish *derme,* plural of *darm,* 'intestine,' from Middle High German.

eyer kichlech. Egg cookies, usually in the shape of a bowtie. Also called *bowties.* From Yiddish *eyer kikhlekh.*

falafel. An Israeli pita sandwich made with fried ground chick peas, chopped vegetables, mixed spices, and a dressing of humus or tahina. From Hebrew, borrowed from Arabic *falafil,* a derivative of *filfil,* 'pepper.'

farfel. An Ashkenazi dish of small granules of noodle dough. From Yiddish *farfl,* from Middle High German *varveln,* 'crumbs of dough.'

gefilte fish. Chopped fish mixed with egg, matzo or bread crumbs, seasoning, etc., and boiled in the shape of cakes or balls. From Yiddish, literally, 'stuffed fish.'

gribenes. Goose or chicken cracklings. From Yiddish *grivenes,* variant of *grivn.*

hamantashen. Purim cookies, usually three-cornered, with poppy seed, prune jam, or other sweet filling. Singular, *hamantash.* From Yiddish *homentash(n),* literally, 'Haman pockets.'

holeptses or *holishkes.* An Ashkenazi dish of sweet-and-sour cabbage leaves, rolled up and stuffed with rice and ground meat. From Yiddish, of Slavic origin.

humus or *hummus.* A purée of ground chick peas and sesame seeds, also used as a spread or dip. From Israeli Hebrew *chumus,* borrowed from Arabic.

kasha. Coarse, cracked buckwheat, or any cereal or porridge made from it. From Yiddish, borrowed from Russian.

kishke. A casing of beef or fowl stuffed with fat, flour, onions, etc., and roasted. From Yiddish, literally, 'gut, intestine,' of Slavic origin; compare Polish *kiszka,* 'sausage.' Also called *derma.*

kneydl, plural, *kneydlech.* A boiled or roast dumpling made of matzo meal, eggs, and chicken fat, eaten in soup. From Yiddish, derived from Middle High German *knödel.*

knish. A baked or fried square of pastry dough filled with potatoes, kasha, sweet cottage cheese, etc. From Yiddish, of Slavic (probably Russian) origin.

kreplech, singular, ***krepl.*** Small, three-cornered pieces of dough filled with chopped meat or cheese, boiled and eaten in soup or as a side dish. From Yiddish *kreplekh*, derived from dialectal German.

kugl. A baked pudding or casserole made of noodles, potatoes, or vegetables. Often spelled ***kugel.*** From Yiddish *kugl* (plural *kuglen)*, derived from Middle High German *kugel*, 'ball, sphere.'

latke. A crisp fried pancake usually made with grated potatoes customarily eaten on Chanukah. From Yiddish, of Slavic origin.

lekech. Cake, especially honey cake. From Yiddish *leykekh*, of uncertain origin. Folk etymology traces the word to Hebrew *lekach*, 'portion,' in allusion to the Biblical phrase (Proverbs 4:2) *ki lekach tov nosati lochem*, "for a goodly portion have I given you."

lokshn. Noodles, as in *lokshn kugl*; pasta. Often spelled ***lokshen.*** From Yiddish (singular *loksh*), of Slavic (Polish or Russian) origin.

lox. Smoked salmon. From Yiddish *laks,* derived from Middle High German *lahs,* 'salmon.'

mamaliga. A Romanian-Jewish dish of thick cornmeal mush. From Yiddish *mamelige*, borrowed from Romanian.

mandelbrot. A crunchy almond cake. From Western Yiddish, literally, 'almond bread.'

matzo. A crisp, square wafer of unleavened bread, especially of the kind made for Passover with carefully protected flour and cooled water, with continuous kneading and baking in less than eighteen minutes to prevent fermentation. From Yiddish *matse* and Hebrew *matsa*. A ***matzo ball*** is a round kneydl or dumpling made of matzo meal, usually eaten with chicken soup. A ***matzo bray*** (or ***matzo braye***) is a dish of fried crumbled matzo with eggs and grated onion. From Yiddish *matse bray.*

mern. A sweet carrot dish eaten by Ashkenazim on Rosh Hashanah. From Yiddish, literally "increase," to symbolize the wish to increase one's merits in the new year.

petcha. Calves' foot jelly or jellied chicken, served with garlic and spices as an appetizer. From dialectal Yiddish, of Slavic origin.

pirogen, singular ***pirog.*** Small dumplings filled with meat or vegetables. From Yiddish *pirogn,* plural of *pirog*, borrowed from Russian.

pita. A round, thin bread with a pocket, eaten plain or with a filling as a sandwich. From Israeli Hebrew, ultimately from Greek, 'cake, pie.'

pletzl. A flat baked roll. From Yiddish, related to German *Plätzchen,* 'cracker.'

rugelech. A pastry usually made with curd cheese and sour cream and filled with nuts, raisins, and cinnamon. Singular, *rugele.* From dialectal Yiddish *rugelekh.*

schav or *tschav.* A cold cream-of-sorrel soup. From Yiddish *shtshav,* of Slavic origin.

shashlik. A dish of skewered and grilled lamb or beef meat, usually eaten with humus, tehina, and various salads. From Israeli Hebrew, of Slavic origin.

strudel. A pastry made by rolling up a thin sheet of dough with a fruit or cheese filling and baking it. From Yiddish *shtrudl* (plural *shtrudlen*), literally, 'whirlpool.'

sufganiyot. Jelly doughnuts popular in Israel during Chanukah (presumably because they are fried in oil, alluding to the miracle of the oil that lasted eight days). From Hebrew, plural of *sufganit,* 'doughnut, sponge cake.'

tahina or *tehina.* A paste made from ground sesame seeds, used as a dip or spread. From Israeli Hebrew *techinah,* from Arabic, from Turkish *tahin,* 'ground sesame.'

tayglech. Small spicy cakes dipped in honey. From Yiddish *teyglekh,* literally, 'bits of dough,' derived from *teyg,* 'dough.'

tschav. Variant of *schav.*

tzimes or *tzimmes.* A sweet, fruit-and-vegetable stew made usually with carrots, plums, apples, and sweet potatoes. From Yiddish *tsimes,* of uncertain origin.

varenikes. Cheese dumplings. From Yiddish, of Slavic origin.

forshpil. An Ashkenazi custom of entertaining the bride on the Sabbath afternoon or evening preceding the wedding. From Yiddish (plural *forshpiln*), literally, 'prelude,' from German *Vorspiel.* See also **Spinnholz, aufruf, wedding terms.**

frum. A Yiddish-origin adjective meaning 'religious, observant, devout,' applied among Ashkenazim to Jews who adhere to Orthodox practices such as strict Sabbath and holiday observance, maintenance of kosher homes, and use of the mikveh for ritual purity. Compare **dati, haredi.** The Yiddish word derives from German *fromm.* A common variant form of the word is **frim,** reflecting the Central and Southeastern Yiddish dialects. A derivative term for the state of being strictly Orthodox is **frumkayt,** from Yiddish, literally, 'religiousness, piety.' Typical usage: *Josh comes from a frum* *family. Are her parents frum?* The term usually denotes a male Jew who wears a black skullcap in private and public, dons a black hat on the Sabbath and holidays, and often exposes the ritual fringes (tzitzis) outside his shirt; it denotes in turn a female Jew whose dress cover her arms and legs and who, if she is married, covers her hair. Some Modern Orthodox Ashkenazim use the term more broadly to encompass anyone who is Orthodox, as distinguished from one who is Conservative or Reform. See also **ultra-Orthodox.**

–G–

gabbai, plural **gabboim** or (Anglicized) **gabbais.** In common usage, a gabbai is an appointed or elected officer of a synagogue whose function is the orderly running of the services and the distribution of honors. The gabbai decides who will receive *aliyahs* and who will serve as *chazzan.* In Hasidic usage, a gabbai (*gabe* in Yiddish) is a trustee who manages the affairs of a *rebbe.* In the Middle Ages, the term referred to a congregational official in charge of collecting and allocating funds for the support of the community. From Hebrew, literally, 'collector (of dues, taxes, etc.),' from *gavah,* 'to collect.'

galut or (*Ashkenazi*) **golus.** Jewish exile; specifically, all the countries in which Jews lived after being exiled from the Land of Israel. Compare **Diaspora.** From Hebrew, literally, 'exile,' derived from the verb *galah,* 'to wander, go into exile.' A synonym of *galut,* from the same Hebrew root, is **golah.** Typical usages: *The law of Shemita (Sabbatical Year) can only be observed in Israel, not in the galut. Jews have been in galut (or golus) for over two thousand years.* The major Jewish **galuyot** or exiles have their own names, such as *galut bavel,* 'the Babylonian Exile (or Captivity),' *galut edom,* 'the Roman Diaspora (or Captivity),' *galut seforad,* 'the Spanish Exile (or Expulsion).' On a cosmic level, Jewish mystics speak of the *galut haShechinah,* 'the exile of the Divine Presence,' that took place alongside the exile of the people of Israel. In Jewish law, *galut* is the penalty prescribed for one who unintentionally but neglectfully kills another. In Hasidism, *golus* often refers to self-imposed exile by a tzaddik to atone for sins known or unknown. See **Hasidic terms.**

ganef. A common Ashkenazi word for a thief, crook, rascal, or scoundrel, sometimes used jocularly or as a mild rebuke. The plural is **ganovim.** From

Yiddish, derived from Hebrew *ganav*. The word entered British slang in the 1830s in the form *gonnof* and the meaning 'a thief, especially a pick-pocket.' In the mid-1900s it came into American slang in the form *gonnif*. Three Yiddish-origin derivatives used in Ashkenazi English are the feminine form *ganefte*, 'female thief,' the noun *ganeyve*, 'theft,' and the adjective *ganeyvish*, 'thievish, rascally.'

gaon, plural **geonim** or **Geonim.** Usually spelled **Gaon** in names. The title of any of the heads of the yeshivas of Sura and Pumbedita in Babylonia, such as Saadia Gaon, Hai Gaon, and Sherira Gaon, from 589 to 1038 C.E. (the dates of the first and last heads of the yeshiva of Pumbedita). The Hebrew-origin word means literally 'glory, excellence, majesty.' The word also has the generalized meanings of 'a brilliant person, a genius,' and especially 'a great Talmudic scholar, a genius in Torah learning.' The latter was specifically applied to Elijah of Vilna (Vilnius), 1720–1797, famed as the *Vilna Gaon*. English derivatives are *gaonate*, 'the position or office of a gaon,' and *gaonic* or *geonic*, 'pertaining to a gaon or geonim.'

gartel. See under **clothing terms.**

Gemara. The part of the Talmud which supplements the Mishnah and contains the explanation of and commentaries on the Mishnah by the amoraim. The uncapitalized form *gemara* often refers to a piece or section of the Gemara, as in *This gemara is very difficult.* The Gemara is written in Aramaic, and the word itself comes from Aramaic, where it means literally 'completion' (since it completes the Mishnah). In Talmudic usage, however, the word means 'learning, study, tradition,' as distinguished from a *sevara*, 'logical deduction, reasoning.' The Yiddish-origin form of the word is **gemore.**

gematria. The word *gematria* means either calculations based on the numerical value of Hebrew letters or the numerical value of a particular Hebrew word. The sages of the Talmud practiced this method of calculation to connect disparate words or phrases on the basis of their equivalent numerical values. This method came to be widely used to interpret words of the Bible for aggadic or homiletical purposes, e.g., in the Gemara (*Berochos 8a*), the statement that there are 903 causes of death is supported by the word *totsaot*, 'avenues' (of death), in Psalms 68:21, the gematria or numerical value of this word being 903.

The Hebrew plural *gematrios* is found in the Mishna (*Pirkei Avos 3:23*) in the general sense of calculations or mathematics, which suggests that

gehenna: a word history

The word *gehenna,* meaning the place where the souls of the wicked are damned to eternal suffering (broadly, 'the nether world, hell, Hades'), came into English in the late 1500s from Latin and Greek, which had taken it from a Hebrew place name mentioned in the Bible, *gei hinnom,* 'Valley of Hinnom.' This valley, situated outside Jerusalem, is mentioned several times in Scripture. It is unclear, though, why it became associated with the nether world. One possible reason is that since in II Kings 23:10 and Jeremiah 7:31 the valley is identified as the place where children were burned and sacrificed in rites dedicated to the pagan deity Moloch, the gruesomeness of these rites became a metaphor for the horrors awaiting sinners in a nether world similar to the Valley of Hinnom. Mention of *gei hinnom* as a place of punishment for the souls of evildoers first occurs in the Talmud (*Pirkei Avos 1:5, Rosh Hashana 17a*), the Midrash, and the Zohar. English *gehenna* in the sense of 'hell' had to come therefore from these post-Biblical sources, since the only word in the Bible referring to the nether world is *sheol,* which is usually translated as the realm or abode of the dead, the grave, and carries no suggestion of damnation or punishment. The Yiddish word **gehenem**, a cognate of English *gehenna* also meaning 'hell,' came directly from Hebrew *gei hinnom.*

the word *gematria* was borrowed from Greek *geometria,* 'geometry.' However, since geometry is concerned with measurement of lines and planes rather than the use of letters to signify numbers, some scholars have considered the Hebrew word to be a transposition of Greek *grammateia,* from *grammatos,* 'something written, letter of the alphabet,' derived from the stem of *graphein,* 'to write.' Possibly both Greek words influenced the formation of the Hebrew term.

Gematria, like **notarikon**, was incorporated in the thirty-two hermeneutic rules used in the aggadic interpretation of Biblical passages.

A form of gematria involving the substitution of letters or numbers has been widely employed by its practitioners. One of the earliest and best known ones is the *atbash*, an arrangement of Hebrew letters in which the first letter or number (aleph) stands for the last letter or number (tav), the second (bet) for the one before the last (shin), and so on. The word *atbash* is an acronym for the letters *a*leph, *t*av, *b*et, *sh*in. Another arrangement is called *albam* (acronym for *a*leph, *l*amed, *b*et, *m*em), in which aleph stands for the twelfth letter or number (lamed), bet for the thirteenth (mem), and so on.

Though excessive use of gematria has been criticized at various times, kabbalists and Hasidim continue to employ it as one of the traditional ways of plumbing the depth of the Torah.

gemilas chesed, plural gemilas chasodim. A loan of money without interest to help a needy person; more generally, a society dedicated to lending money free of interest to fellow Jews in need of financial assistance; more broadly, any assistance to the needy. Often abbreviated to **gemach** (e.g., *clothing gemachs*). From Ashkenazi Hebrew *gemilus chesed* (in Yiddish, *gmiles khesed*), literally, 'bestowal of lovingkindness.'

Genesis. See **Pentateuch.**

genizah. A storage room in a synagogue where disused sacred books and often-sacred articles are kept, since burning them or disposing of them otherwise is considered a sacrilege. Genizahs are no longer common; the custom is to keep disused sacred texts and objects in an unused place in the synagogue until they can be buried in a grave in the cemetery, often in a coffin alongside the remains of a pious Jew. Such texts usually consist of torn or stray pages of sacred books known in Yiddish as *sheymes* ('names') because they often contain the name of God. The most famous of the old genizahs is the one discovered in the Ezra synagogue in Cairo in the mid-1800s, containing fragments of thousands of ancient texts. From Hebrew *genizah*, literally, 'storage, archives,' derived from the verb *gonaz,* 'to store, hide.'

genocide. See **Holocaust.**

ger, plural gerim; the feminine is (*Ashkenazi*) **giyores,** (*Sephardi*) **giyoret.** A convert to Judaism; a proselyte. From Hebrew and Yiddish, originally meaning (in Hebrew) 'stranger, foreigner.' The formal English word for a *ger* is *proselyte,* from Greek *proselytos,* 'stranger,' a translation of Hebrew *ger* in the Septuagint. There are various types of *gerim* in Jewish law, but today the only acceptable one is a *ger tzedek,* a 'righteous convert (to Judaism),' that is, one who converts out of inner conviction, with no ulterior motive.

get, plural gittin. A Jewish divorce, as distinguished from a civil or secular one; a divorce according to Jewish law. Technically, a *get* is a written bill

gentile: a word history

Originally this word meant in English 'a non-Christian, a pagan.' In this sense, the word was adapted from the ecclesiastical Latin word *gentilis*, meaning foreign(er), heathen, pagan. Earlier, in classical Latin, *gentilis* meant a member of a particular race or nation, and was derived from *gent-, gens*, 'race, clan, nation' (related to such English words as *genus, gender,* and *kin).*

How did the English word come to mean 'a non-Jew'?

This meaning is found around 1380 in the first English translation of the Bible, instituted by the religious reformer John Wycliffe. The translation was from the Latin Bible (the Vulgate), and the word appears as a plural form taken directly from the Latin plural noun *gentiles,* meaning the (non-Jewish) nations. The classical Latin word was used here to translate Greek *ethnikos,* referring to *ta ethne,* 'the nations,' which in the Septuagint (the Greek Bible) was a translation of Hebrew *hagoyim.* The English singular form thus came to mean 'one belonging to the (non-Jewish) nations,' and hence 'a non-Jew.'

Essentially, then, English borrowed the word twice, from two different forms of Latin: once from ecclesiastical Latin, where the word referred to heathens; and once from classical Latin, where it referred to the non-Jewish nations. Curiously, English seems to be the only modern language that replaced the original pejorative meaning of *gentile* ('pagan, heathen') with the neutral meaning 'non-Jew.' In Latinate languages like Spanish and French, for example, this word has kept the original meaning of 'non-Christian, pagan, heathen.'

In modern English usage, the terms *gentile* and *goy* are synonyms and semantically equivalent, since both have the basic meaning of '(non-Jewish) nation.' But the two words differ in usage, since *gentile* is the standard term for a non-Jew, whereas *goy* is nonstandard, being a 19th-century borrowing from Yiddish and used mainly by Jews.

of divorcement signed by two competent witnesses and placed by the husband (or his proxy) into the wife's hands in the presence of a competent rabbinical court. The text of a get is in Aramaic. The capitalized form **Gittin** is the name of a Talmudic tractate dealing with the laws of divorce. From Hebrew, from Aramaic, *get, gito,* borrowed from Akkadian *gittu* 'bill or legal document.'

gezerah or **gezera.** In Jewish law, a prohibition enacted by the Sages as a measure to protect religious observance under changed conditions. But more commonly, the term refers to an evil decree or edict, especially an anti-Jewish decree or legislation, and is usually used in the plural: (*Ashkenazi Hebrew*) **gezeros,** (*Yiddish*) **gzeyres.** From Hebrew, literally, 'decree,' derived from the verb *gazar,* 'to cut, ordain, decree.'

ghetto: a word history. Among words of Jewish interest, *ghetto,* meaning a part of a city formerly assigned to Jews as a forced residential area, is one of the most intriguing. Its ultimate origin has eluded scholars for more than a hundred years, though theories about its roots have not been wanting. It is generally accepted that the immediate source of the word is Italian. The first document in which the word is used to describe a city quarter to which Jews are restricted is a Papal edict issued in Rome and dated February 27, 1562. In this edict, the then Pope allows Jews to have shops outside the Jewish quarter. The phrase used in the Latin text is *extra ghectum,* translated as 'outside the ghetto.'

The most widely believed theory is that the word developed in the Venetian dialect of Italian from the name *Geto Nuovo,* 'New Foundry,' referring to an area in Venice, once the site of the Venetian republic's state foundry, to which the Jews of that city were officialy restricted on April 10, 1516. As far back as the 1300s, the site of the foundry had been called *geto* or *getto,* though by 1516 the actual foundry had been closed for many years. There are a few difficulties with this theory. One is, how did the initial consonant of Italian *geto* (pronounced with a j-sound) change to the "hard" g of *ghetto*? Another is, how did the Papal edict's *ghectum* develop from *geto*? And lastly, where did the word *geto* or *getto,* presumably meaning 'foundry,' come from?

These problems gave rise to a number of other theories, the most common of which are:

1. *Ghetto* supposedly derived from the Hebrew *get,* meaning divorce or separation, since the ghetto separated Jews from the rest of a population;
2. It was abstracted from Italian *borghetto,* 'small section of a town,' a diminutive of *borgo,* 'town,' ultimately from Latin *burgus,* 'fortress';
3. It was a clipped and altered form of Italian *Egitto,* from Latin *Aegyptus,* 'Egypt' (though how this connects with a ghetto remains obscure);
4. It derived from Greek *geiton, geitonia,* 'neighbor, neighborhood';
5. It was a clipped form of early Yiddish or Middle High German *gehecktes ort,* 'fenced-in place';

6. It derived from Gothic *gatvo,* 'street';
7. It developed from Medieval Latin *iectus,* 'thrown,' ultimately from Latin *iacere,* 'to throw.'

None of these etymologies have convinced scholars. On the other hand, support has been gaining for the theory that the name of the Venetian foundry is the source of *ghetto.* For example, in an article in *The American Sephardi* (vol. VI, 1973), Ariel Toaff, a professor of history at the University of Pisa, adduced as proof of the theory two documents, one proving that as far back as 1300s, along with the spelling *getto,* there also appeared the form *ghetto,* the other proving that in the 1500s and 1600s, long after the Jewish quarter of Venice had been called *ghetto,* the spellings *geto, getto* were still current. These facts may put to rest the phonetic problem mentioned above. As to the ultimate source of the Venetian word for its state foundry, Toaff thinks that it probably derives from the Venetian Italian verb *ghettare,* 'to refine metal with peroxide of lead,' which in turn derives from *ghetta,* 'peroxide of lead.'

The rest of the word's history is well known. By the time Israel Zangwill published his famous novel *Children of the Ghetto* (1892), the word had expanded its meaning to any (nonrestricted) section inhabited by Jews. Though the Nazis reintroduced forced ghettos for Jews, such as the Warsaw Ghetto, during the Holocaust, the word has been applied since the early 1900s to any city quarter populated largely by blacks, hispanics, and other minority groups.

Jewish quarters existed in many countries before the ghetto of Venice came into being. However, these quarters or streets (e.g., *Judería* in Spain, *Jüdengasse* in Germany) were voluntary in character, based on the desire of Jews to live together in the vicinity of their synagogues, schools, ritual baths, etc. The establishment of the ghetto of Venice was the first known instance of an area into which Jews were isolated and segregated by government decree.

gilgul. See under **Hasidic terms.**

glatt. This adjective evolved from the phrase *glatt kosher,* meaning 'strictly or flawlessly kosher,' which Orthodox Ashkenazi Jews took from Yiddish *glat kosher,* referring to the flawless or "smooth" (Yiddish *glat* = 'smooth') condition of a slaughtered animal's lungs that makes the animal ritually clean by the most stringent standards. By shortening the phrase, *glatt* itself has come to mean 'strictly or flawlessly kosher,' and is today widely used in Ashkenazi English in such phrases as *glatt meat, a glatt* *cuisine, glatt meals,* and even predicatively, as in *Our meat is glatt. This restaurant serves only glatt.*

golah. See **galut.**

golem. See under **Hasidic terms.**

golus. See **galut.**

goy, plural **goyim.** The Jewish word for a non-Jew or gentile. The word came into English slang in the 1830s, borrowed from Yiddish and Hebrew. The meaning 'non-Jew' has existed in Hebrew since post-Biblical times, the Biblical and literal meaning of the word being 'nation, people.' In Yiddish, *goy* is also applied disparagingly to a Jew who is either not religious or ignorant of things Jewish; this usage has passed into general Jewish usage. The feminine **goya** (from Yiddish *goye*) means both a gentile woman or, disparagingly, an irreligious or ignorant Jewish woman; compare **shiksa.** A common adjective from Yiddish is **goyish,** meaning either 'non-Jewish, gentile,' or 'irreligious, nonobservant,' as in *the goyish world, a Jewish boy trying to look goyish, His family is more goyish than Jewish.* Less commonly, the adjective has variants that reflect Yiddish gender distinctions: *goyishe* (feminine), *goyisher* (masculine): *a goyishe family, a goyisher snob.*

Grand Rabbi. A title used for a Hasidic **rebbe.**

greetings and salutations. Some notable differences between Ashkenazim and Sephardim are found in the manner of their mutual greeting and saluting on various occasions. The following is an alphabetical list of commonly used greetings and salutations. Unless otherwise indicated, the words come from Ashkenazi or Sephardi Hebrew.

> *aleychem sholem!* 'Upon you, peace!' (The standard response to the greeting *sholem aleychem!* 'Peace upon you!').
>
> *an easy fast!* Used by Ashkenazim before a public fast day, such as Tisha B′Av. Translated from Yiddish *a laykhter tones.*
>
> *baruch tiye!* 'May you be blessed!' (said by Sephardim in response to *chazak (u)varuch!* '(May you be) strong (and) blessed!' See **congratulatory terms.**
>
> *beteavon!* 'Bon appétit!' Derived from Hebrew *teavon,* 'appetite.'
>
> *boruch tiye!* 'May you be blessed!' (said by Ashkenazim in response to

---

greenhorn: a word history

Used in English since the early 1900s as a term of disparagement for a newly arrived European, usually Jewish, immigrant, *greenhorn* has often been thought to be a borrowing from Yiddish. There is indeed an equivalent Yiddish word, *grinhorn*, on record, but this word was actually borrowed from English, not the other way around. English *greenhorn* is found attested as far back as 1650 in the sense of a raw or inexperienced soldier, a use extended by 1682 to any novice or inexperienced person. The original reference was apparently to a young, callow animal (i.e., one with a green horn). By the mid-1700s, *greenhorn* was applied disparagingly to a raw newcomer into a city, a country bumpkin. When European immigrants began arriving in masses to the United States just before the turn of the 20th century, they were soon tagged with the derisive word, which the immigrants themselves began to use among themselves both in Yiddish and English.

---

yasher koach! 'May (God) increase your strength!'). See **congratulatory terms.**

chag sameach! 'Joyous festival!' (A chiefly Ashkenazi greeting on holidays, including Purim).

chagim uzmanim lesason! 'Festivals and seasons for joy!' (A Sephardi response to the holiday greeting *moadim lesimcha!*). From the words in the evening kiddush recited on Sukkos, Pesach, and Shavuos.

chazak veematz! 'Be very strong and courageous!' (An occasional Sephardi response to *chazak (u)varuch!* '(May you be) strong (and) blessed!'). From the words in the book of Joshua (1:7).

gam atem! 'You too; the same to you' (a plural use, even where a single person is addressed, said by Ashkenazim in response to a greeting, such as *shana tova!* or *gut yor!* 'Good Year!')

gemar tov! 'Good conclusion!' A short version of *gemar chasima tova!*

gemar chasima tova! 'A good final sealing (in the Book of Life)!' (Ashkenazi greeting between Yom Kippur and Hoshana Rabbah).

gut chodesh! 'Good month!' (Ashkenazi greeting on Rosh Chodesh, the beginning of a new month). From Yiddish.

gut moed! 'Good festival season!' Used by Ashkenazim on Chol Hamoed, the intermediary weekdays of the Pesach and Sukkos holidays. From Yiddish.

gut shabes! 'Good Sabbath!' (Ashkenazi Sabbath greeting, often used on Friday before the actual onset of Sabbath). From Yiddish. Many Ashkenazim alternate between *gut shabes!* and *shabbat shalom!*

gut voch! 'Good week!' (Ashkenazi greeting at the conclusion of the Sabbath). From Yiddish *gut-vokh.* Many Ashkenazim alternate between *gut voch!* and *shavua tov!*

gut yontef! 'Happy holiday!' (Ashkenazi greeting used on any of the holidays, including Rosh Hashanah and Yom Kippur, but not on Rosh Chodesh, Chanukah, or Purim). From Yiddish.

gut yor! 'Good year!' (Ashkenazi greeting on Rosh Hashanah). From Yiddish. Many Ashkenazim alternate between *gut yor!* (also, *gute gebentshte yor*, 'Good blessed year!') and *shana tova!*

Hashem imahem. 'God be with you!' (Sephardi greeting given by one approaching the Torah-reading desk after being called up to the Torah, to which the reader responds *yevarechecha Hashem*, 'God bless you!'

kesiva vechasima tova! 'A good inscribing and sealing (in the Book of Life)!' (formal Ashkenazi greeting on Rosh Hashanah).

kol tuv! 'All the best!' (said on parting, equivalent to good-bye, farewell).

labriut! 'To (your) health! Bless you!' (said after someone sneezes).

lechayim! 'To life!' The customary toast made before drinking a glass of whiskey, wine, or other alcoholic liquor, especially in someone's honor; equivalent to "Here's to your health!" Also spelled **l'chayim.**

lehitraot! 'Till we see each other again! So long; au revoir.' (Used at parting and equivalent to farewell, good-bye).

leshono tovo tikosevu! '(May you) be inscribed for a good year (in the Book of Life)!' (A formal greeting exchanged by Ashkenazim on Rosh Hashanah). Though the greeting is plural, it is addressed to one or several individuals.

moadim lesimcha! 'Happy holiday!' Literally, 'Appointed festivals for rejoicing!' (Sephardi greeting on the holidays, to which the response is *chagim uzmanim lesason!*) From the words of the kiddush recited on the evening of the festivals.

refua shelema! '(I wish you) a complete recovery!' In Yiddish, *refue shleyme!*

shabbat shalom! 'Peaceful Sabbath!' (Used as a Sabbath greeting by both Ashkenazim and Sephardim).

shalom! 'Hello, good-bye'; literally, 'peace.' (A standard greeting exchanged on meeting or parting.)

shalom uveracha! 'Peace and blessing!' (A more emphatic greeting than *shalom.*)

shana tova! 'Good year!' From Hebrew, short for *leshana tova (tika-tevu)!* '(May you) be inscribed for a good year (in the Book of Life).'
sholem aleychem! 'Peace unto you!' (A standard greeting of welcome, to which the response is *aleychem sholem!* Unto you, peace.")
tizke leshanim rabot! 'May you merit (to live) many years!' (A Sephardi greeting on Rosh Hashanah, the response to which is *tizke ve-tichye vetaarich yamim!* 'May you merit and live and your days be lengthened!'
tzu gezunt! 'To (your) health! Bless you!' (said after someone sneezes). From Yiddish.
zay gezunt! 'Be well! Stay healthy!' (Used in parting and equivalent to farewell, good-bye.) From Yiddish.
See also **exclamations and interjections.**

– H –

haggadah or **haggada** (*Ashkenazi* hago'de; *Sephardi* hagada'). The book containing the seder service on the first night or (outside Israel) the first two nights of Passover. It consists essentially of the retelling of the story of the exodus from Egypt. From Hebrew, literally, 'telling, narrative.' Compare **aggadah.**

Hagiographa. The formal English name of *kesuvim* (Sephardi *ketuvim*), usually translated as **the Writings,** the last of the three divisions of the Tanach or Hebrew Bible, comprising the Psalms (Tehillim), Proverbs (Mishlei), Job (Iyov), Song of Songs (Shir Hashirim), Ruth (Rus), Lamentations (Eichah), Ecclesiastes (Koheles), Esther, Daniel, Ezra, Nehemiah, and Chronicles (Divrei Hayomim). From Latin and Greek, literally, 'sacred writings.' Though plural in form, the term is used in English with a singular verb. It should not be confused with **hagiography,** the biography of a legendary hero, martyr, or sage (or the biography of anyone who is idealized), which is singular in form and use. *The Hagiographa* comprises the sacred writings of the Bible; *a hagiography* is an account of the life of a holy or saintly personality.

halachah or **halakhah** (*Ashkenazi* halo'che; *Sephardi* halacha'). The body of Jewish law or tradition, especially the body of practical laws and legal decisions that have been passed down and codified by the rabbis since the Talmudic period. Also, the part of the Talmud and Midrash that deals with legal matters, as distinguished from **aggadah.** Also, a conclusive law, as

---

Hadassah: The story of a name

According to the Book of Esther (*Esther 2:7*), Queen Esther was also called Hadassah, a name derived from the Hebrew word *hadas*, 'myrtle,' an evergreen shrub whose branches are part of the four species (lulav, esrog, hadasim, arovos) used on Sukkos. The Talmud (*Megillah 13a*) asks why Esther was called Hadassah: according to Ben Azzai, it was because she was perfectly formed, neither too tall nor too short, like the myrtle; according to R. Yehoshua ben Korcha, because though her complexion was sallow like the myrtle leaf, she was endowed with great charm. (One notes in passing that English *myrtle* and the related word *myrrh* are both of Semitic origin—compare Hebrew *mor*, 'myrrh'—and that in tractate *Hullin 139b* the name Mordechai is derived from the phrase *mor deror*, 'flowing myrrh,' in Aramaic *mira dakhia*.)

Thanks to the popularity of the story of Queen Esther, the name Hadassah was often bestowed (sometimes in combination with Esther) to newborn girls. In Yiddish, the name was transmuted to *Hodes*, but, like the English name *Myrtle*, the Yiddish name fell into obsolescence early in the 20th century. On the other hand, the name *Hadassah* enjoyed a revival after an American women's Zionist organization called "Daughters of Zion" decided in 1914 to change its name to Hadassah, after the Hebrew name of the heroic Queen Esther.

---

in *The halachah is according to Rabbi Akiva.* From Hebrew, literally, 'way, path, road,' derived from the verb *halach*, 'go, walk.' The adjective is **halachic** or **halakhic,** as in *halachic principles, the halakhic contributions of the geonim.* The construct form is **hilchos** or **hilkhos** (*Sephardi, -ot*), as in *hilchos tefillin,* 'the laws of tefillin.'

halachic terms. While most legal systems are closed books to ordinary or lay people, Jewish law is familiar to many Jews who are neither rabbis nor teachers. Halachic terminology runs into the thousands, and is often extremely esoteric. However, certain basic terms have made their way into general Jewish usage, especially among the Orthodox. The following list contains a small sampling of such terms. Except where indicated otherwise, all the terms derive from Hebrew.

    asur. Prohibited; banned. Contrasted with *mutar.* See *isur.*

    bedieved. 'After the fact'; halachically acceptable or valid after one has performed an action, though not permitted initially. Contrasted with *lechatchilah.* From Aramaic.

bedikah or **bedika.** (1) Inspection or examination (of an animal after slaughter, of a witness in court, etc.). (2) Search for (bread or other forbidden food) on Passover eve.

chayav. Guilty, responsible; obliged, liable. Contrasted with *patur.*

chazakah or **chazaka,** plural **chazakos.** A legal claim of ownership based on its possession for a certain time. A *chazakah* is also a presumption or assumption based on probability. Literally, 'an overpowering, a seizing by force.'

chiyuv. A duty or obligation. See *chayav.*

chumrah or **chumra,** plural **chumros.** A restrictive ruling or measure, usually one that follows the stricter opinion in a dispute. Contrasted with *kulah.* See *machmir.*

eyd, plural **eydim.** A witness. A witness's testimony is called *eydus.*

gezerah, plural **gezeros.** A prohibition enacted by the Sages as a measure to protect religious observance under changed conditions. Literally, 'decree.'

hasraah. A formal warning given to a person who is about to commit a sin.

hefker. Ownerless, as a piece of unclaimed property.

heter. Permission to do something; license; permit. Contrasted with *isur.* See *mutar.*

isur. A prohibition, ban, or injunction. See *asur.*

kal vachomer. A logical inference from minor to major (i.e., from a more lenient case to a more stringent one). Literally, 'lenient and stringent.'

kenas. A fine paid as a penalty for wrongdoing.

kezayis. A halakhic measure for the minimum amount that may not be eaten of a prohibited substance or that must be eaten to fulfill a commandment. Literally, 'like an olive (in dimension).'

kinyan. The act or manner of legally acquiring or agreeing to something; a formal acquisition or agreement. Literally, 'act of buying.'

koras. Excision; Divine punishment by premature death.

kulah or **kula,** plural **kulos.** A lenient ruling or measure, usually one that follows the less strict opinion in a dispute. Contrasted with *chumrah.* See *meykil.*

lav. A Scriptural prohibition; any of the 365 prohibitions given in the Torah. From Aramaic, literally, 'no, not.'

lechatchilah. 'At first; before the fact'; (of an action) not halachically valid initially, though perhaps acceptable after the fact. Contrasted with *bedieved.* From Aramaic.

machmir. A decisor (posek) who follows a strict opinion and issues a *chumrah.*

maris ayin. The mere appearance of breaking the law even when doing something permissible, resulting either in arousing suspicion or in misleading others. Literally, 'appearance to the eye.'

meykil. A decisor (posek) who follows a lenient opinion and issues a *kulah.*

meyzid. One who commits a sin consciously and deliberately. Contrasted with *shogeg.*

mutar. Permitted; not prohibited. Contrasted with *asur.* See *heter.*

onesh. Punishment; penalty.

pasul. Disqualified; unfit; invalid (as a witness, a kohen, a divorce, etc.).

patur. Not guilty or responsible; not liable; free or exempt. Contrasted with *chayav.*

pikuach nefesh. The principle that the law of saving a person's life takes precedence over all other laws, with the exception of the laws prohibiting idolatry, incestuous relations, and the murder of an innocent person. Literally, 'saving a soul.'

safek, plural **sefekos.** A doubt or doubtful case.

shogeg. One who commits a sin unintentionally. Contrasted with *meyzid.*

shtar. Any legal document or writ, such as a bill of sale or a promissory note.

takkanah, plural **takkanos.** A rabbinical decree or ordinance, issued to improve religious life. Literally, 'improvement.'

tenai, plural **tenoim.** A condition, especially one made as part of an agreement.

hallah. Variant spelling of **challah.**

hamsa. A good-luck amulet in the shaped of an inverted hand, popular in Israel. It was originally made of painted plaster and placed near the front door of a house to ward off the evil eye or evil spirits, but later designed in various forms for use as jewelry and decoration. From Arabic, literally, 'five (fingers).' The word should not be confused with the technical term *hamza,* also from Arabic, used in phonetics for the sign of the glottal stop represented by the Arabic letter *alif.* Also spelled **khamsa.**

Hanukiyah. Variant spelling of **Chanukiyah.**

haredi (cha-rey'di), plural **haredim.** A Hebrew-origin word applied to an extremely observant or pious Orthodox Jew, one who is often described as 'ultra-Orthodox.' The word is also used as an adjective, as in *The yishuv he lives in is haredi. She comes from a haredi family.* Compare **dati, frum.** From Hebrew *charedi,* derived from the adjective *charad,* 'very pious, God-fearing,' literally, 'trembling (with fear).'

Hashem. The name commonly used for God by religious Jews. From Hebrew, literally, 'the Name.' It was abstracted from traditional phrases, such as *boruch Hashem,* 'praise God, thank God,' *beezras Hashem,* 'God willing,' *lemaan Hashem,* 'positively, without fail' (literally, 'for God's sake'), *kiddush Hashem,* 'sanctification of God's Name' (= martyrdom), and *chillul Hashem,* 'desecration of God's Name.' See also **Adonai.**

hashgachah or **hashgacha.** 1. (Divine) Providence. 2. Supervision. See **kosher.**

hashkamah or **hashkama.** See under **synagogue terms.**

hashkavah or **hashkava.** See under **mourning terms.**

Hasid, plural **Hasidim.** An adherent of a Jewish mystical religious movement founded in Poland by Israel Baal Shem Tov (c.1700–1760). From Hebrew *chasid* and Yiddish *khosed,* literally, 'gracious, benevolent, charitable (person),' derived from *khesed,* 'grace, kindness, charity.' The adjective is **Hasidic.** The Hasidic movement or its teachings are known as **Hasidism** (or, less frequently, **Chasidus).** Hasidism believes in the mystical teachings of the kabbalah and in the supernatural powers of Hasidic leaders, known as *rebbes* or *tzaddikim,* many of whom are often erudite scholars. While Hasidism stresses a simple faith in God, piety and ecstasy in prayer, and joy in fulfilling the commandments, it also values learning and intellect. Hasidism expressed itself in the mother tongue of East European Jews, Yiddish, which it transformed into a vehicle of fervent pietistic expression and which it formalized as the language of the Jewish masses. Some of the more famous surviving branches of Hasidism, corresponding to dynasties of rebbes (often known as "Grand Rabbis"), include *Belz, Bobov, Bratslav, Ger, Lubavitch, Sanz,* and *Satmar.* The traditional opponents of the Hasidim were known as **Misnagdim.** Variant spellings are **Chasid, Chasidic,** and **Chasidism.** The lower-case form *hasid* is occasionally used in the general sense of 'follower, devotee,' as in *The rabbi in our shul has many hasidim.*

Hasidic terms. The influence of Hasidism on Jewish customs and usage is in part reflected in the vocabulary it injected into mainstream Jewish culture. Some concrete examples of that vocabulary is listed under **clothing terms.** Below is a selection of other common terms associated with Hasidim and Hasidism.

> *admor,* plural *admorim.* A title of a rebbe or tzaddik, usually placed after the name, formed as an acronym from the Hebrew phrase *ad(o-nenu) mo(renu) (ve)r(abenu),* 'our master, teacher, and rabbi.' It is sometimes used as a common noun.

> *Chabad, Habad.* A philosophy of Hasidism evolved from the teachings of Rabbi Shneur Zalman of Liadi (1745–1812), the founding rebbe of Lubavitch Hasidim. The term is an acronym for the Hebrew words *ch(ochmah) b(inah) d(aas),* 'wisdom, understanding, knowledge,' three of the ten *sefiros* of the Kabbalah.

> *devekus.* A state of ecstatic attachment or adherence to God in one's everyday activities. From Hebrew, literally, 'a clinging, cleaving, adhering,' ultimately from the verb *davak,* 'to cling, cleave, adhere.'

> *dibbuk.* A spirit or soul that takes possession of a living person's body. From Yiddish *dibek* and Hebrew *dibbuk,* literally, 'an adhesion, attachment,' derived from Hebrew *davak,* 'to cling, cleave, adhere.'

> *eynikl,* plural *eyniklech.* A descendant of a Hasidic dynasty of rebbes. From Yiddish, literally, 'grandchild,' derived from Middle High German *Enkel.*

> *farbrengen.* A festive Hasidic get-together, especially among Lubavitch Hasidim. From Yiddish, noun use of the verb meaning 'to pass (time), amuse oneself.' The noun, in turn, has been Anglicized as a verb *to farbreng,* 'to hold a farbrengen,' with the usual English inflections: *farbrenged, farbrengs, farbrenging,* as in *We farbrenged at the rebbe's tish till midnight.*

> *gashmius.* Materiality; sensuality; earthly matters or concerns. From Hebrew, derived from *geshem,* 'matter, substance.' Contrasted with *ruchnius.*

> *gilgul.* The transmigration of souls; reincarnation; also the being into which a soul may pass to atone for sins committed in a previous incarnation. Literally, 'revolving.'

> *golem.* A human being created artificially by a mystical ritual usually involving God's secret name. In medieval legend, golems were created to serve their creator. Literally, 'shapeless form.'

golus. A life of wandering or exile emulating the exile of the Jewish people (and on a mystic level, the *golus haShekhina*, the exile of the Divine Presence) undertaken by a tzaddik for spiritual purification and atonement of sins. From Hebrew, literally, 'exile.' See also **galut.**

hisbodedus. Seclusion or isolation, especially of a tzaddik. From Hebrew, ultimately from *boded,* 'alone, solitary.'

hisgalus. Revelation or disclosure, especially the revelation of a tzaddik to the world after a period of obscurity. From Hebrew, ultimately from *gala,* 'to reveal, disclose.'

hislahavus. Enthusiasm, fervor, or ecstasy in the service of God. From Hebrew, ultimately from *lahav,* 'flame.'

hisorerus. Spiritual awakening. From Hebrew, ultimately from *orer,* 'to awaken or arouse.'

ibbur. The entry of someone's soul into the body of another, usually temporarily and to fulfill a Torah law. Literally, 'impregnation.' Distinguished from **gilgul.**

kamea. An amulet or charm, especially one with a mystical inscription or an appropriate Biblical verse, worn to ward off evil. From Hebrew-Aramaic *kamia.*

kavanah or *kavana.* Devotional intent; concentrated attention. Also, earnestness of feeling; zeal; fervor. From Hebrew, derived from the verb *kiven,* 'to direct, aim, intend.'

kefitzas haderech. A miraculous shortcut or abridgment of a long journey. From Hebrew, literally, 'a leap over the road.'

kloyz. A small synagogue and house of study. From Yiddish, probably borrowed from German *Klause,* a hermitage or monastery cell, ultimately from Latin *clausum,* 'closed space.' Compare **shtibl.**

kvitl. A written note submitted to a rebbe, petitioning his blessing, intercession, or advice. It contains an account of one's problems or the names of those requiring help, and is usually accompanied by a pidyon. From Yiddish, literally, 'note.'

lamedvovnik. One of thirty-six righteous men who, according to legend, live in every generation and in whose merit the world continues to exist. The legend is based on Abaye's statement in the Talmud (*Sukkah 45b*), "The world has never less than thirty-six righteous men who are vouchsafed a sight of the Shechinah every day." From Yiddish, coined from *lamed-vov,* two letters of the Hebrew alphabet numerically equivalent to 'thirty-six' + the agent suffix *–nik.*

maggid, plural *maggidim.* An itinerant Jewish preacher. The term is used among Hasidim as a title of certain great Hasidic preachers, such as Rabbi Dov Ber, the "Maggid of Mezritsch," (died about 1772), successor of the Baal Shem Tov, and Rabbi Yisroel, the "Maggid of Kozienice," (1733–1814). From Yiddish *maged* and Hebrew *maggid*, literally, 'one who tells, narrator.' See also the main entry **maggid**.

nigleh. The teachings of the Torah that can be revealed or made publicly known, as distinguished from the Torah's esoteric or mystical teachings. From Yiddish and Hebrew, literally, '(that which is) apparent, clear, or revealed.' Contrasted with *nistor.*

niggun, plural **niggunim.** A Hasidic melody or tune, sung without words, and believed to express the feelings of the soul. From Yiddish *nign* and Hebrew *niggun,* 'tune.'

nistor. The esoteric or mystical teachings of the Torah. From Yiddish *nister* and Hebrew *nistor,* literally, '(that which is) concealed.' Contrasted with *nigleh.*

pidyon. A monetary contribution accompanying a *kvitl.* From Yiddish *pidyen,* derived from Hebrew *pidyon,* literally, 'redemption, ransom.'

rebbe, plural **rebbes.** The title of a Hasidic master or spiritual leader. From Yiddish *rebe,* literally, 'master,' from Hebrew *rabbī;* see **rabbi.** An informal adjective is *rebbeish* or *rebbish.* Compare *tzaddik.*

ruchnius. Spirituality; spiritual matters or concerns. From Hebrew, derived from *ruach,* 'spirit.' Compare *gashmius.*

shed, plural **sheydim.** An evil spirit; a demon or devil. From Aramaic.

shirayim. Remainders of a rebbe's meal, distributed by the rebbe among the Hasidim after he has tasted or eaten parts of it. Yiddish *shiraim,* alteration of Hebrew *sheyorim,* 'remainders, leftovers.'

shtibl, plural, **shtiblech** or **shtiblach** or (Anglicized) **shtibls.** A small Hasidic synagogue and house of study. From Yiddish, literally, 'small room.'

tikkun. An improvement or rectification of a penitent soul. It is customary among Hasidim to drink a toast to the soul of a deceased person on his yahrzeit as a tikkun. The brandy or other alcoholic liquor served is informally also called a tikkun. From Yiddish *tikn* and Hebrew *tikkun,* literally, 'improvement, repair.'

tish. A rebbe's table, at which he delivers Torah discourses and sings niggunim with the Hasidim. From Yiddish, literally, 'table.'

tzaddik, plural *tzaddikim.* A title for a charismatic and holy Hasidic spiritual leader, commonly applied by the early Hasidim to their rebbes. Also, a synonym for a *rebbe.* From Yiddish *tsadek* and Hebrew *tsaddik,* literally, 'righteous man.'

yechidus. A private audience with a rebbe to obtain his advice or blessing. From Yiddish *yekhides* and Hebrew *yechidus*, literally, 'aloneness, privacy.'

havurah. Variant spelling of **chavurah.** See **chaver.**

hazzan or **hazan.** Variant spellings of **chazzan** or **chazan.**

Hebraica. See **Judaica.**

Hebraisms. A Hebraism (from Greek *Hebraismos*) is a word or expression taken from Hebrew into another language. Due to the influence of Bible translations, many Hebraisms came into English since Anglo-Saxon times. Early Hebraisms in English include such familiar words as *amen, babel, behemoth, camel, cherub, gehenna, leviathan, manna, rabbi, Sabbath, shekel, shibboleth.* The Hebrew Bible also popularized in English many personal names and place-names, such as *David, Sarah, Joseph, Rebecca, Israel, Bethlehem, Canaan, Jerusalem, Shiloh, Zion.*

Starting with the 16th century, a number of cultural and religious terms were introduced into English through scholarly works, e.g., *Cabala* (1521), *Talmud* (1532), *Sanhedrin* (1588), *Mishnah* (1610), *mezuzah* (1650). With the revival of Hebrew during the 19th and 20th century, modern Hebraisms were introduced into English through the writings of British and American Jews. Among the well-known Hebraisms emerging from the Jewish experience in Israel before and following Statehood are such terms as *aliyah* 'immigration' (literally, 'ascent'), *oleh,* 'immigrant,' *chalutz,* 'pioneer' (literally, 'vanguard'), *chug (ivri),* '(Hebrew) circle or club,' *hora,* 'Israeli round dance,' *kibbutz,* 'cooperative settlement,' *Knesset,* 'the Israeli parliament,' *moshav,* 'cooperative village,' *pita,* 'oriental bread,' *sabra,* 'a native Israeli' (from Arabic, 'cactus'), *shalom,* 'hello; good-by' (literally, 'peace'), *ulpan,* 'Hebrew language class,' *yishuv,* 'settlement.' Compare **Yiddishisms.** See also **Israeli terms.**

Hebrew. The northern Semitic language of the ancient Israelites and modern Israel, closely related to Aramaic and Phoenician. The word *Hebrew* came through Greek *Hebraios* from Aramaic *Evrai,* which corresponds to Hebrew *ivri,* an epithet applied in the Bible to the patriarch Abraham (Genesis 14:13) and his descendants. (*Ivri* is traditionally thought to derive either from the Hebrew word *eiver,* meaning 'the other side' (of the Euphrates, where Abraham came from) or from *Eber,* the name of one of Abraham's ancestors.) In the Bible (II Kings 18:26, Isaiah 36:13), the Hebrew language is called *yehudit* (literally, 'Judean') and in the Talmud (Baba Kama

83a) *lashon hakodesh,* 'holy tongue.' The sanctity accorded to Hebrew is reflected in the Yiddish word *ivre* (from Hebrew *ivri*), meaning the sacred Hebrew texts. In Yiddish, *kenen ivre,* 'to know *ivre,*' means to be able to read the Hebrew words. Yiddish itself was formerly called *ivre-taytsh,* literally 'Hebrew-German,' when referring to the Yiddish translations of sacred Hebrew texts.

Scholars have divided the development of Hebrew into four distinct periods: Biblical (c.12c. B.C.E.–c.70 C.E.); Mishnaic (c.70–500); Medieval (6c.–13c.); and Modern (late 19c.–present). Modern Hebrew is a revived form of the language developed chiefly in Eretz Yisrael by European Jewish settlers. It is called *ivrit.* In English it is often referred to as Israeli Hebrew.

Except for long-established English borrowings from Hebrew (e.g., *amen, babel, cherub, manna, mezuzah, Sabbath, sanhedrin*), more recent borrowings are marked by variant spellings. For example, an English dictionary of record, *Webster's Third New International,* gives as many as seven variants for the holiday of Shavuos: *shabuoth, shabuot, shavuoth, shavuot, shavuos, shevuoth, shevuos.* These variants reflect actual spellings collected from a number of Jewish-English printed texts. The standardization of English spellings of Hebrew-origin (and Yiddish-origin) words is a goal that editors and publishers of Jewish books and periodicals have yet to address. See also **Israelite and Hebrew.**

Hebrew alphabet. English-language dictionaries customarily define the Hebrew alphabet as consisting of 23 letters. This error resulted from mistakenly counting *shin* (ש) and *sin* (ש) as two distinct letters, the 21st and 22nd, thereby counting the last letter, *tav* (ת), as the 23rd. In fact, the same letter, *shin,* has always represented two distinct sounds, as it still does in all non-punctuated texts, from a Torah scroll to books written in Hebrew. The placement of right and left dots over this letter to indicate the sounds *sh* and *s* was the work of the Masoretes, who also added diacritical marks to Hebrew words to indicate their correct pronunciations and fixed the spellings and cantillations of the Biblical text. But no Hebrew scholar ever regarded the phonological dots as indicating two different letters. An obvious proof that the shin is a single letter is the fact that its numerical value is 300, while the numerical value of tav is 400, and no intervening numerical value exists for the variant form *sin.* Jewish alphabet is a better name for the *aleph-bet* (Yiddish *alef-beys*) than "Hebrew alphabet" since it is used not only for Hebrew but all Jewish languages. When referring to the Hebrew language, however, "Hebrew alphabet" is appropriate.

heder. Variant spelling of **cheder.**

heichal. The Sephardi term for the *aron hakodesh*, or holy ark, the cabinet or chest in which the Torah scrolls are stored in a synagogue. See **ark.** In the Bible, the term refers to the Holy Temple (e.g., Ezekiel 41:1–25), and especially the inner part of the Holy Temple containing the altar of incense (*mizbeakh haketores*), the menorah, and the table of the shewbread (*shulchan hapanim*). From Hebrew, 'palace, shrine, tabernacle.'

herem. A solemn rabbinical ban issued either as a punishment for a serious transgression or to enforce obedience to a decree. The term "excommunication," often used to translate the term, is inexact, as only one type of a *herem* involves exclusion or isolation of a person from the community. "Ban" is probably a more accurate translation. For example, the *herem derabenu gershom*, a famous *herem* imposed by Rabbenu Gershom ben Judah (960–1040), banned polygamy and divorcing a woman without her consent. The *herem* is the most stringent ban, lasting indefinitely. A less severe ban is the **niddui,** a form of ostracism usually lasting thirty days. A person who has been placed under **niddui** but fails to show remorse may be condemned to a more severe ban known as **shamta,** 'curse' (*Moed Katan 16a*). From Hebrew *cherem*, derived from the verb *charam*, 'to vow, consecrate; ban, outlaw.' Also spelled **cherem.**

holekrash or **hollekreisch.** A ceremony among German Jews, held usually on the afternoon of the fourth Sabbath after the birth of a child, at which the infant is lifted three times in the air, with the guests present calling out "Holle kreisch!" each time. The purpose of the ceremony, which has lasted well into the 20th century, is to ward off evil influence, and the usual explanation given for the term is that *Holle* refers to an evil witch of German folklore (*Frau Holle*) and *kreisch* derives from the German verb *kreisen*, 'to encircle,' in reference to the protective encircling of the child. Several variations of the ceremony have been reported, such as the custom of the child's father shouting three times, "Holle kreisch, what shall this child be called?" followed by the guests shouting the child's name. See also **vachnacht.**

holiday terms. Jewish holidays and observances are associated with traditional terms, a list of which may run into the hundreds. The following terms represent the most common or familiar usages connected with the holidays.

aseres yemei teshuva. The "Ten Days of Penitence" between Rosh Hashanah and Yom Kippur, during which special *selichos*, or penitential prayers, are recited. See also *yomim neroim.*

Chanukah, Literally, 'dedication, consecration (of the Temple),' is a rabbinically ordained festival celebrated for eight days by lighting candles or oil-dipped wicks in an eight-branched *menorah*, or candelabrum, also called a **Chanukiyah**. A **shammes** or **shammash** is an extra candle used to light the eight candles or wicks. The hymn of praise **Hallel** and the prayer **Al Hanissim** are recited each day. A popular game is the four-sided spinning top (**dreidel** or **sevivon**), though formerly it was also customary among Ashkenazim to play **kvitlech** (from Yiddish, literally, 'notes, slips'), a card game similar to twenty-one. Children are given **Chanukah gelt** (from Yiddish, 'Chanukah money') or presents. Traditional foods are **latkes** or **levivot** (pancakes) and, in Israel, **sufganiyot** (jelly doughnuts). Chanukah is often called the **Feast** (or **Festival**) **of lights.**

Chol Hamoed. Also spelled **Hol Hamoed.** The intermediary days between the first and last days of the festivals of Pesach and Sukkos, having a partly weekday and a partly holiday status. The **Hallel** hymn and the holiday prayer **Yaale Veyavo** are recited each day. From Hebrew, literally, 'weekday of the festival.'

high holy days. Also capitalized **High Holy Days.** This spelling is preferred to *high holidays* or *High Holidays,* since Rosh Hashanah and Yom Kippur, to which this term refers, are especially *holy* days in which judgment is rendered upon mankind.

Hoshana Rabbah. The seventh day of Sukkos (fifth day of Chol Hamoed), literally, 'the Great Hosanna,' is traditionally regarded as the culmination of the days of penitence and prayer that begins on Rosh Hashanah. In the synagogue, all the Torah scrolls are removed from the ark and the *hoshanos*, special Sukkos prayers beginning with the word *hoshana*, 'O save,' are recited while performing seven circuits (*hakafos*) around the Torah-reading desk, each circuit ending with a single sounding of the shofar. Afterwards a bundle of five willow twigs, also called *hoshanos,* are beaten against the desk (or to the ground), following the custom in the ancient Temple of throwing them against the altar (Mishnah *Sukkah 4:5*). The devout stay up the night before Hoshana Rabbah, and recite passages from the *tikkun leyl hoshana rabbah* ('order of service for the night of Hoshana Rabbah'), which includes the reading of the book of Deuteronomy, the Psalms, and parts of the Talmud, Midrash, and Zohar.

Isru Chag. The day after the end of Pesach, Sukkos, and Shavuos, regarded as a semi-holiday on which mourning is curbed and fasting prohibited. From Hebrew, literally, 'bind the festival offering,' from Psalm 118:27, part of the *Hallel* hymns recited on Pesach, Sukkos, and Shavuos.

Lag B'omer or **Lag Baomer.** A minor holiday observed on the thirty-third day of the *sefiras haomer* ('counting of the omer') between Pesach and Shavuos (see **omer**). It corresponds to the 18th of Iyar. The *sefira* customs of mourning are suspended on that day and weddings and haircuts are permitted. Various reasons are given for the holiday. The most common reason, based on the Talmud (*Yevamos 62b*), is that on that day the plague that had killed 22,000 students of Rabbi Akiva came to an end. Another tradition holds that the day is the anniversary of Bar Kochba's victory over the Romans. Kabbalists commemorate it as a feast day in memory of the tanna R. Simeon ben Yochai, believed to be the author of the Zohar, whose grave in Meron, a village near Safed, is the setting of many celebrations on Lag B'omer, such as giving first haircuts to boys who have reached the age of three (see **opsherenish**). From Hebrew, a phrase formed from the numerical value of the Hebrew letters *l(amed)* and *g(immel)*, "33" ($l = 30 + g = 3$) and *B'omer*, 'of (the counting of) the omer,' referring to the counting of the 49 days from the second day of Pesach until Shavuos.

Pesach, Literally, 'Passover' (from God's "passing over" the houses of the Israelites to spare them from the plague of the firstborn), is called in the Bible **chag hapesach** (Exodus 34:25), as well as **chag hamatzos** (Leviticus 23:6), 'the festival of matzos.' It is also called **chag haaviv**, 'the festival of spring,' for its occurrence in springtime (Deuteronomy 16) and the beginning of the barley harvest (see **omer**). Pesach is the first of the **shalosh regalim**, the three pilgrimage festivals. The **haggadah**, narrating the Exodus from Egypt, is recited at the **seder** or 'order (of service)' on the first two nights (in Israel, only the first night). *Arba kosos*, four cups of wine (or grape juice), are drunk at the seder, and besides matzos, *maror* ('bitter herbs'), *charoses* (a mixture of apples, nuts, and wine), and *karpas* (a boiled potato, celery, or parsley) are eaten as parts of the seder ritual. Any food made with leaven (*chometz*) is forbidden on Pesach. See also **afikoman.**

Purim, Literally, 'lots' (from the lots cast by Haman to choose the day of the destruction of Persian Jewry), is a rabbinically ordained festival celebrated mainly by reading in public the *megillah* (full name, *megillas ester*, the Book of Esther) from a parchment scroll on the evening of the 14th of Adar and on the following morning. During the reading, noisemakers called **graggers** (from Yiddish *grager*, 'rattle') or **raashonim** (from Hebrew *raashon,* 'noisemaker') are sounded at mention of Haman's name. As on Chanukah, the prayer *Al Hanissim* is recited, but in a version appropriate to Purim. Other customs include the exchanging of gifts between friends and neighbors (Hebrew *mishloach manos,* literally, 'sending of gifts,' Yiddish **shlakhmones**), giving food or money to the poor (**matonos loevyonim**), eating **hamantashen** (named after Haman), and partaking of a Purim *seudah* or banquet, at which a satiric Purim play (**Purimspiel**, from Yiddish *Purimshpil*) may be shown, often (especially in yeshivas) featuring a **Purim rabbi**, who delivers a mock Torah discourse. See also **adloyada.**

Rosh Chodesh. The first day (or first two days) of the Jewish month. Literally, 'head (or beginning) of the month.' It is a semi-holiday on which part of the **Hallel** hymn ("half-hallel") and the prayer *Yaale Veyavo* are recited and a **musaf** service is added. On the preceding Sabbath, known as **shabbos mevorchim**, a special blessing for the new month is recited and usually the **molad,** the appearance ('birth') of the new moon in Jerusalem, is announced.

Rosh Hashanah or **Rosh Hashana**, The New Year, literally 'head (or beginning) of the year,' is called in the Bible (Numbers 29:1) *yom terua,* 'the day of shofar-sounding.' Based on the Talmud, it is traditionally also called **yom hadin**, 'Day of Judgment,' and **yom hazikaron**, 'Day of Remembrance.' As the beginning of the **yomim neroim** ('Days of Awe') and the **aseres yemei teshuva** ('Ten Days of Penitence'), Rosh Hashanah is marked by the repeated sounding of the **shofar** or ram's horn (except on the Sabbath) to call worshipers to repentance. The custom of **tashlich**, of going near a body of water and reciting there appropriate penitential verses (especially Micah 7:19), is observed in the afternoon. See under **ritual terms.**

shalosh regalim. Literally, 'three pilgrim festivals' (Exodus 23:14), these are the three festivals of Pesach, Shavuos, and Sukkos, on each of which all male Jew were obliged to make a pilgrimage to Jerusalem to bring sacrifices and redeem tithes.

Shavuos, Literally, 'Weeks,' so called for its celebration seven weeks after Pesach. In the Bible it is called **chag shavuos** (Exodus 34:22), 'festival of weeks,' **chag hakatzir** (Exodus 23:16), 'festival of the harvest,' and **yom habikkurim** (Numbers 28:26), 'day of the first fruits.' The Talmud refers to it simply as **atzeres**, '(solemn) assembly,' a term used in the Bible for the seventh day of Pesach and the eighth day of Sukkos. Shavuos is the second of the **shalosh regalim**, the three pilgrimage festivals. In English it is known as the **Feast of Weeks** or, anciently, as **Pentecost,** a word borrowed ultimately from Greek *pentekostet*, 'fiftieth,' in reference to the fifty days between Pesach and Shavuos. The Talmud (*Shabbos 86b*) declares the first day of Shavuos as the *zeman matan torasenu*, 'the season of the giving of our Torah' on Sinai, and the day is commemorated by reading the Ten Commandments in the synagogue.

Shemini Atzeres, Literally, 'eighth (day) of assembly,' so called from the clause in the Bible (Numbers 29:35) "The *eighth* day shall be an *assembly* for you," referring to the eighth day of Sukkos as an independent holiday, different in various ways from the preceding seven days. During the Musaf (additional) service of Shemini Atzeres, the prayer for rain (*geshem*) is chanted. See also **Simchas Torah.**

Simchas Torah, Literally, 'rejoicing of the Torah,' a holiday observed on Shemini Atzeres (on the second day outside Israel) to celebrate the completion of the year-round reading of the Torah or Pentateuch and the immediate beginning of a new cycle of Torah-reading. Before the reading, all the Torah scrolls are removed from the ark and carried around the synagogue in seven **hakafos** (circuits). Everyone receives an **aliyah** to the Torah during the reading, including a collective one for all the young children (**kol haneorim**, 'all the youngsters'), with the last aliyah in *Devarim* (Deuteronomy) given to the **chasan Torah** ('bridegroom of the Torah') and the first aliyah in *Bereshis* (Genesis) given to the **chasan Bereshis.**

Sukkos or **Succos** or (*Sephardi*) **Sukkot**. Literally, 'Booths,' known in English as the **Festival of Tabernacles**, Sukkos is called in the Bible **chag hasukkos** (Deuteronomy 16:13), 'festival of booths,' as well as **chag haasif,** 'festival of the harvest." It is the third of the **shalosh regalim**, or three pilgrimage festivals, and it is marked by building a **sukkah** or temporary booth in which meals are eaten during the eight days of the festival. In addition, the **arba minim** or **four species**, consisting of an **esrog** (citron), a **lulav** (palm branch), three **hadasim** (myrtle twigs), and two **arovos** (willow branches) are carried and shaken during the recital of the **Hallel** hymn. The last day of **Chol Hamoed**, or intermediary days of Sukkos, is **Hoshana Rabbah,** followed by **Shemini Atzeres.**

Tu Bishvat, Also called **New Year of Trees** and **Jewish Arbor Day**, a minor festival celebrated on the 15th of Shevat (*Tu* is numerically equivalent to 15: the letter *t(es)* = 9 + vocalic *v(av)* = 6). The first Mishna in tractate *Rosh Hashanah* calls it **Rosh Hashanah Leilon**

('New Year for the Tree') and states that according to Beth Hillel it is observed on the 15th of Shevat.

Yom Haatzmaut. A celebration on the 5th of Iyar to commemorate the establishment of the State of Israel on 5 Iyyar, 5708 (May 14, 1948); Israel's Independence Day. From Modern Hebrew, literally, 'Day of Independence.'

yomim neroim (*Ashkenazi*) or **yamim noraim** (*Sephardi*). The 'Days of Awe,' encompassing the period each year when God passes judgment upon individuals and decrees their fate. This period includes mainly the 'Ten Days of Penitence' (*aseres yemei teshuva*) between Rosh Hashanah and Yom Kippur, but it may begin as early as the month of Elul, when the shofar is sounded each day; or the days before Rosh Hashanah when the **selichos** penitential prayers are begun; or continue until **Hoshana Rabbah.**

Yom Kippur, Literally, 'Day of Atonement,' is called in the Bible **yom hakippurim** (Leviticus 23:27), from the Hebrew verb *kipper*, 'to atone (for a sin), expiate.' Though it is a Biblically ordained fast day marked also by not bathing or wearing leather shoes, it is regarded as a **yom tov** or holiday. The strictly Orthodox observe the ritual of giving **kapparot** (Ashkenazi Hebrew **kaporos**), or expiatory offerings, on the morning of erev Yom Kippur by waving a chicken (a rooster for a male, a hen for a female) over the head while reciting a formula offering the chicken's life as an expiation for one's sins. In Yiddish, this ritual is called **shlogn kapores**. The alternative custom is to give money (Yiddish **kapore-gelt**) for charity instead of sacrificing the rooster or hen. The evening prayers on Yom Kippur begin with **Kol Nidre** (Aramaic, 'all vows'), a declaration by which all the vows made to God during the year are nullified. Among Ashkenazim, many men wear a **kittel,** the white garment symbolizing purity. A unique service, the **Neilah** (literally, 'closing,' referring either to the closing of the Temple gates or of the heavenly gates), concludes the day, with the sounding of the **shofar** signaling the end of the holiday. See also **fast days.**

Holocaust. It is not clear how the term Holocaust came to mean the systematic mass murder of Jews by the Nazis during World War II. The English word *holocaust* originally meant a burnt offering or sacrifice and came into the language about 1250 from Greek *holokaustos* 'burnt whole.' Its first appearance is in a song describing Abraham's readiness to sacrifice Isaac as a burnt offering to God. The poet John Milton used the word, (in his 1671 epic poem *Samson Agonistes*) in the wider sense of 'complete destruction by fire.' The specific application of the term to the mass murder of Jews, though sporadically found before the 1960s in such a phrase as "the Nazi holocaust" (e.g., the psychoanalyst A. A. Brill in 1938), was first recorded as a capitalized word in a 1963 book about the Warsaw Ghetto by Alexander Donat, entitled *The Holocaust Kingdom.*

The earlier term **genocide** (literally, 'race killing'), which was coined by the scholar Raphael Lemkin in 1944 to describe the mass murder of Jews, had a detached, scientific sound and failed to suggest in a meaningful way the slaughter of millions of Jews. A more appropriate coinage, by Arno J. Mayer, was **Judeocide** (*Why Did the Heavens Not Darken?*, 1988) but the term did not catch on. Hence the adoption of Holocaust as a term more closely descriptive of the immense tragedy. But as this term came to be applied to other forms of genocidal killings (e.g., Cambodia and Bosnia), Jews looking for a term unique to them began to use the Hebrew-origin word **Shoah**, meaning 'destruction, catastrophe.' (In Modern Hebrew, *ha-shoah* means 'the Holocaust.') This term was popularized by Claude Lanzmann's nine-hour documentary film dealing with the Holocaust, which appeared in 1985 and was entitled *Shoah.* Nevertheless, some writers have found the term *Shoah* inadequate, partly because it has been applied in Hebrew to natural catastrophes, and formerly to pogroms, which, however tragic, could never be compared to the immense cataclysm of the Holocaust.

The Yiddish-origin term **Churban,** literally, 'destruction, ruin' (from Hebrew), was used by Holocaust survivors after the war to refer to the tragedy, and is still used in Yiddish as a standard term for the Holocaust. But it was not generally adopted, since *Churban* traditionally referred to the destruction of the First and Second Temples and was therefore not evocative of the mass destruction of European Jewry.

For lack of a more appropriate term, then, *the Holocaust* is still the only phrase that is able to evoke in most people's minds the horrors perpetrated by the Nazis against the Jewish people.

Holocaust Day or **Holocaust Memorial Day.** Another name for **Yom Hashoah.**

Holocaust terms. The vast literature dealing with the Holocaust that has been published since the 1950s has introduced many special terms into the vocabulary of Jewish writers and readers. A sampling of the most common ones follows.

Aktion. Any operation for rounding up Jews to deport them to ghettos or concentration camps. From German, literally, 'campaign, project.'

Appell. A roll call of concentration camp inmates for the purpose of making a head count. The **Appellplatz** was a parade ground where roll calls were regularly made. From German, short for *Zählappell*, literally, 'roll-call count.'

Arbeitslager. A concentration camp where Jews (*Arbeitsjuden*) were sent to do forced labor. From German, literally, 'labor camp.'

Aussenkommandos. Groups of immates located outside the **Stammlager** (main camp). From German, literally, 'outside squads.'

Aussiedlung. A euphemism for the transportation of Jews to extermination camps. From German, literally, 'resettlement.' Also called **Umsiedlung.**

Ausweis. A work certificate issued in a ghetto. From German, 'identification card, certification.'

Blockältester. An inmate assigned to be the head of each block of prisoners' barracks. From German, literally, 'block eldest.'

camps, the. The Nazi concentration and extermination camps. Translation of Yiddish *di lagern.* The phrase "the lagers" is also used as a synonym.

concentration camp. Any of the Nazi internment centers where Jews were imprisoned, tortured, starved, or killed. Three of the most notorious German concentration camps were Bergen-Belsen, Buchenwald, and Dachau. Translation of German *Konzentrationslager.*

death camp. Another name for an **extermination camp.**

Desinfektion. A euphemism used by the Nazis for herding inmates into gas chambers. From German, literally, 'disinfection.'

Einsatzgruppe. Any of the mobile units of SS men who operated in the rear of the German army (**Wehrmacht**) to rid conquered areas of Jews. *Einsatzgruppen* varied from 500 to 1000 men and enlisted local police and auxiliary units to carry out the program of extermination. An **Einsatzkommando** was a subunit of an Einsatzgruppe. From German, literally, 'operational group.'

Endlösung. German name for the **Final Solution.**

extermination camp. A concentration camp where the mass destruction of Jews was systematically carried out by the Nazis, chiefly by means of gas chambers and crematoria. Among major extermination camps were Auschwitz, Belzec, Birkenau, Majdanek, Sobibor, and Treblinka. Translation of German *Vernichtungslager.*

Final Solution. A euphemism used by the Nazis for their plans to exterminate the Jews of Europe. Translation of German *Endlösung.*

genocide. See **Holocaust.**

Judenältester. A Jew assigned by the Nazi authorities to serve as head or president of a Judenrat. From German, literally, 'Jewish eldest.'

Judenfrei. Another term for *Judenrein.* From German, literally, 'free of Jews.'

Judenrat, plural, *Judenräte.* A Jewish communal body established by the Nazis in a city or town to carry out Nazi orders affecting Jews, such as settling them in ghettos, administering community affairs, calling up workers for forced labor, and selecting people to be sent to concentration camps. From German, literally, 'Jewish council.'

Judenjagd. The term used by the Nazis for the tracking down and killing of Jews in hiding. From German, literally, 'Jewish hunt.'

Judenrein. The term used by the Nazis for a town, city, or other area emptied of Jews. From German, literally, 'clean of Jews.' Also, *Judenfrei.*

Judenstern. The identification badge that Jews were forced to wear under Nazi rule, consisting of a star of David, usually yellow, with the word "Jude" or the letter "J" in the middle. From German, literally, 'Jewish star.'

Kapo. A concentration camp trustee in charge of a work detail and directly responsible to the SS command leader (*Kommandofuehrer*). From German, of uncertain origin but likely to come from Italian *capo,* 'chief, head.'

katzenik. A concentration camp inmate. Formed in Yiddish from *Ka Tze* (a pronunciation of *KZ*, abbreviation of German *Konzentrationslager,* 'concentration camp') and the agent suffix *-nik.*

Kommando. A work unit in a concentration camp. From German, literally, 'command, (military) detachment.'

Lager. Short name for a concentration camp. From German, short for *Konzentrationslager.*

Lagerältester. An inmate appointed by the camp commandant to be responsible for the administration of prisoners. From German, literally, 'camp eldest.'

musulman. A sick and debilitated concentration camp inmate who was mere skin and bones and had lost the will to live. From Yiddish, literally, a Muslim (the connection is unclear).

organizator. A concentration camp inmate who managed to supply by legal or illegal means his immediate needs. From Yiddish, literally, 'organizer.'

prominent. A privileged inmate in a concentration camp, especially an administrative official, such as a Kapo. From Yiddish, from German *Prominente,* 'prominent person.'

Schutzstaffel. The political police force of the Nazi state, better known as the *SS.* From German, literally, 'defense echelon.' See *Einsatz-gruppe.*

Selektion. The act of choosing of victims to be deported or killed in gas vans, gas chambers, or by other means. From German, literally, 'selection.'

Sonderbehandlung. A euphemism for the killing of inmates in a concentration camp. From German, literally, 'special treatment.'

Sonderkommando. A group of inmates working in the gas chambers. From German, literally, 'special squad.'

Stubendienst. A room orderly, serving to assist a Blockältester. From German, literally, 'room servant.'

Umschlagplatz. An assembly point for the mass deportation of Jews to concentration camps. From German, literally, 'transshipment place.'

Umsiedlung. Another term for *Aussiedlung.*

Zyklon B. Poison gas containing prussic acid that was used in the gas chambers.

– I –

ibbur. See **Hasidic terms.**

interjections. See **exclamations and interjections.**

Israel Independence Day. Another name for **Yom Haatzmaut.** See under **holiday terms.**

Israelite and Hebrew. As ancestral names of the Jews, these two terms are not interchangeable. The name *Israelites* (from Latin *Israelita* and Greek *Israelites*) designates the twelve tribes descended from the patriarch Jacob, who was renamed *Israel* (Genesis 32:29). *Israelite* is also the name sometimes given to an inhabitant of the ancient northern kingdom of Israel, as distinguished from a *Judean,* who inhabited the southern kingdom of Judea or Judah. In English usage, the name *Israelite* is confined to Biblical references. By contrast, various European languages, such as German, French, and Spanish, have been using respectively *Israelit, israélite,* and *israelita* in place of the somewhat pejorative names for "Jew" (*Jude, juif, judío*) since the period of the Emancipation (late 18th century). Compare **Jew.**

In Jewish religious usage, *Israelite* is sometimes applied formally in English to a Jew who is neither a kohen nor a levite, and is thus the third in

---

iota, jot: a word history

These two words derive from the same ultimate source, a Semitic word akin to Hebrew *yod*, the name of the tenth and smallest letter of the Hebrew alphabet, related to the word *yad*, 'hand.' English *jot*, meaning 'something of little value, a little bit,' was borrowed before 1500 from Latin *jota*, a variant form of *iota*, from Greek *iota*, the name of the ninth and smallest letter of the Greek alphabet. English *iota*, meaning 'something very small, a bit,' was separately borrowed later (1630s) from Latin *iota*. Thus, the English doublets *jot* and *iota* are figurative uses of the ninth and smallest Greek letter, which in turn is traceable to the tenth and smallest Hebrew letter.

---

line to be called up to the Torah-reading desk in the synagogue during the public reading of the Torah.

The name *Hebrew* is used chiefly by historians to designate any of the Semitic people descended from the patriarch Abraham, who is called in the Bible (Genesis 14:13) an *Ivri*, or Hebrew. Though in the past it was not uncommon among English-speaking gentiles to refer to Jews as Israelites or Hebrews, mainly as euphemisms to avoid using "Jew," which was often considered derogatory or offensive, the practice went out of fashion toward the end of the 20th century. (The derogatory American slang terms 'Hebe' or 'Hebie,' however, are still current.) Today the term *Hebrew* refers primarily to the Semitic language of the ancient Israelites and modern Israel. See **Hebrew.**

Since the creation of the State of Israel in 1948, the name ***Israeli*** has been applied to any citizen or inhabitant of Israel, regardless of religion ("Israeli Arabs"). It is a national designation, not a religious one. But because most Israelis are Jews, and Jews are generally viewed both as a nation ("the Jewish people") and as a religious group ("Americans of the Jewish faith"), to many people the distinction is without a difference.

Israeli terms. Since the establishment of the State of Israel, hundreds of Hebrew terms associated with Israeli life and culture have passed into the vocabulary of Jews in the Diaspora. Many of the terms hark back to pre-State times, but familiarity with Israel has given them present-day currency. The following is a sampling of some common terms. Unless indicated otherwise, the terms are all from Hebrew. The romanized spellings follow the system of the American National Standard Romanization of Hebrew, in which the letters ח and כ,ך are transcribed as *ch.*

abba. Father; daddy.

adon. Sir; mister.

balagan. (Slang) Big fuss or confusion; mess; muddle. Hebrew, from Persian *balachane,* 'noise, disorder.'

betach. 'To be sure; certainly.'

beteavon! 'Bon appétit!'

bevakashah. 'Please; if you please.' When used in response to *Todah* ('Thank you'), it means 'You're welcome.'

bituach. Insurance.

chalutz or ***halutz.*** A Jewish pioneer who went to the Land of Israel in the 19th and 20th centuries to build up the Jewish homeland. Literally, 'advance guard, vanguard.'

chalil or ***halil.*** An Israeli flute or recorder.

chozrim. Returnees to Israel from abroad. Literally, 'returnees.' Compare *olim, yordim.*

chug, plural ***chugim.*** A circle or club, as of Hebrew speakers or of prospective emigrants to Israel. Literally, 'circle.'

Eretz Yisrael, (Anglicized) **Eretz Israel.** The Land of Israel.

ganenet. A nursery or kindergarten teacher. Literally, '(female) gardener.'

gan yeladim. A nursery school or kindergarten. Literally, 'children's garden,' translation of German *Kindergarten.*

garin. A group or unit organized for a specific purpose, such as forming a settlement. Literally, 'kernel, nucleus.'

garinim. Seeds, especialy sunflower or pumpkin seeds, processed for eating.

geveret. Madam; Mrs.

hachsharah or ***hachshara.*** A training camp (or training period) for Zionist youth. Literally, 'preparation, training.'

hasbarah or ***hasbara.*** Information or propaganda; public relations.

hesder. A program combining military service with yeshiva study. Literally, 'arrangement, settlement.'

imma. Mother; mommy.

kefar. A village, especially as distinguished from a moshav, kibbutz, and the like.

kevutzah or ***kevutza.*** An agricultural collective. Literally, 'group, team.'

kibbutz, plural ***kibbutzim.*** A cooperative settlement, chiefly agricultural. Literally, 'gathering, group.'

kibbutznik, plural *kibbutzniks* or *kibbutznikim.* A member of a kibbutz.

kinus. Gathering; conference; convention.

klitah or *klita.* Absorption, especially the absorption of new immigrants.

knesset. Assembly. A *bet (ha)knesset* (literally, 'house of assembly') is a synagogue. The *Knesset* is Israel's Parliament.

kol hakavod. All honor to (a person or persons); well done.

kumzits, plural *kumzitsim.* A get-together, especially a campfire picnic. From Yiddish, from the phrase *kum zits,* 'come sit.'

kupat cholim. A fund for the sick, especially a workers' health insurance.

labriut! 'To (your) health!'

lehitraot! 'So long! Au revoir!'

malon. A hotel.

madrich. A leader or guide, as of a youth group.

mechanech. An educator or pedagogue.

Medinat Yisrael. The State of Israel.

menahel. A director or administrator, as of a school; a principal or headmaster.

mesibah. A reception, gathering, or party.

metapelet. A nursemaid or nanny.

metzuyan. Excellent; outstanding.

M.K. Member of Knesset.

moadon. A club or meeting place.

morah. A female teacher.

moreh. A male teacher.

mosad. An institution or establishment; an institute.

moshav. A cooperative village or smallholders' settlement.

moshavah or *moshava.* A settlement or colony.

nachon. Correct; true; right.

olim. Immigrants to Israel; literally, 'those who ascend (make aliyah).' Singular, *oleh* (masculine), *olah* (feminine). Compare *chozrim, yordim.*

protektzia. Influence; pull; favoritism.

sabra. A native Israeli.

sava. Grandfather; grandpa.

savta. Grandmother; grandma.

shabbaton. Sabbath rest and relaxation; Sabbath social gathering.

shalom! 'Hello!' 'Good-bye!' Literally, 'peace (be with you).'

sheket! Silence! Quiet!

sherut. A service, as a car service.

sherutim. A public lavatory; toilet.

shikun. A planned housing development or project.

shuk. A street bazaar or marketplace.

shvitzer. (Slang) An overaggressive, pushy person; a braggart. From Yiddish *shvitser*, literally, 'sweaty man.'

sichah or *sicha*, plural *sichot.* A talk; lecture.

tafsik! 'Stop it!'

teudah or *teuda.* A diploma.

tiyul. A stroll or walk; hike; excursion.

tochnit. Program; plan.

Todah! 'Thank you! Thanks!' Also, *Todah rabbah!* 'Many thanks!'

Tzahal. The Israel Defense Forces (IDF). Acronym for *Tzava Hagana Leyisrael.*

ulpan, plural *ulpanim.* A class or course in the Hebrew language, especially in conversational Hebrew.

yafe. Beautiful; well, right, appropriate.

yahadut. Judaism; Jewishness.

yishuv. A Jewish settlement or community in Israel. *The Yishuv* is the name given to the Jewish community in Eretz Yisrael before the establishment of the State of Israel in 1948.

yofi. A beauty; something splendid.

yordim. Emigrants from Israel; literally, 'those who descend.' Compare *chozrim, olim.*

ivre-taytsh. A formal written variety of Yiddish, formerly used to translate sacred Jewish texts. From Yiddish, literally, 'Hebrew-German.' Compare **Ladino.** See also **Hebrew.**

Ivrit. The Hebrew language. Though the term *Ivrit* is found in the Mishna (e.g., *Gittin 9:8*) in the sense of the Hebrew language, it was rarely used in the Diaspora until the revival of Hebrew as a spoken language in the 19th century. The term has thus come to mean specifically Modern Hebrew or the Hebrew spoken in Israel (as for example in the expression "to teach *ivrit beivrit*," meaning to teach Hebrew in spoken Hebrew). See also **Hebrew; lashon kodesh.**

–J–

Jehovah. Since the 1500s, *Jehovah* has been the representation in English and most European languages of the Tetragrammaton or sacred four-letter name of God. Partly because of its Christian origin and partly because it

---

Jabez: The story of a name

The name Jabez, a Latinate rendering of the Hebrew name *Yaavetz*, has an unusual history. Its first appearance is in the Bible, in Chronicles I, 2:55, as the name of a place inhabited by scribes. The commentators Rashi and Radak suggest that the place was named after their leader, a man called Jabez, who is described in Chronicles I, 4:9–10, as an honorable man whose mother called him *Yaavetz* because she had given him birth in pain (Hebrew *beotzev*, derived from *etzev*, 'pain, sadness'). Jabez prayed movingly to God that he may not be afflicted with pain or sadness, and God granted his request. (Jabez's short prayer was popularized with great success in 2000 in an English book, *The Prayer of Jabez*, published by a Christian minister, Bruce H. Wilkinson.) The Talmud (*Temurah 16a*) identifies Jabez with Osniel ben Kenaz, the first judge of Israel, because "God answered him," the name *Osniel* being a combination of the Hebrew words for 'answer' and 'God.' The next time Jabez turns up is as the name of a distinguished 16th century family of scholars of Spanish origin, notably Joseph Jabez (d. 1507), the author of *Or ha-Chaim* and other homiletic and exegetic works. In the 17th century the name appears in its Hebrew form *Yaavetz* in a list of verses for common given names compiled by the *Shelah*, the great kabbalist Isaiah Horowitz (d. 1630). Finally, *Yaavetz* became widely known as the pseudonym of the German halachic authority Rabbi Jacob Emden (1697–1776). The pseudonym was formed from an acronym of his Hebrew name, *Yaakov ben Tzvi*, but was probably influenced by the name in Chronicles I.

---

is intended to render a pronunciation of the unpronounceable Divine name, Jews do not use this word in speech or writing except in the name of the Christian sect *Jehovah's Witnesses*. The earliest known use of the word in English is in William Tyndale's Bible of 1530, where it appears in the form *Iehova*, borrowed from Latin. The Latin form was a transliteration of יהוה (the Tetragrammaton) that erroneously applied to this unpronounceable name the vowel points of Hebrew אֲדֹנָי (*Adonai*); these vowel points had been added by the Masoretes to יהוה as a direction to the reader to substitute *Adonai* ('my Lord') for it, the Tetragrammaton being too sacred for utterance. In contrast to Tyndale's Bible, John Wycliffe's earlier Bible translation (about 1324–1384) used the word *Adonai* to represent the Tetragrammaton, following the example of the Latin Vulgate Bible (400s C.E.), which also used *Adonai* in accordance with the Masoretes. See also **Adonai.**

Like *Jehovah*, other specifically Christian names are often avoided in Jewish usage. Examples are the names *Jesus, Christ, Jesus Christ, Jesus H. Christ!* (slang), the names of saints (*Saint Christopher, Saint Jude*), or the papal title *Holy Father*. The name *Christmas* is often avoided by circumlocution, as in replacing the greeting *Merry Christmas!* with *Happy Holiday!* These avoidances may be due as much to religious scruples as the fear that by using some of these words (perhaps inappropriately) they may offend the sensibilities of non-Jews. Avoidance of phrases or expressions related to, or presumed to be related to, Christianity is less common, probably owing to ignorance of their origin. Such phrases include: *It's the gospel truth! Let's keep our fingers crossed. Knock on wood* (presumed to be Jesus's wooden cross). *Cross my heart (and hope to die). Hers is a heavy cross to bear.*

Jew. Whether this word is derogatory or offensive, especially when used by a non-Jew, is a question that crops up regularly in language columns and usage books. The reason for this uncertainty is that *Jew* and its cognates (e.g., German *Jude*, Italian *giudeo*, Spanish *judío*, Polish *Żyd*, Hungarian *Zsidó*) have been used pejoratively through much of history, mainly because of the early association of Latin *Judaeus* (the source of the above names) with the name of the despised *Judas* Iscariot, who betrayed Jesus for money and was the only *Judean* among Jesus's twelve disciples (the others were Galileans, like Jesus). Thus the name *Jew* came to be equated in popular usage with deception, rapacity, and other villainous practices, as illustrated in literature by characters like Shylock and Fagin. It was not until after the Emancipation, especially in the 19th century, that Jews in many countries tried to improve their reputation by referring to themselves as *Israelites* and *Hebrews*. (See also the entry **Israelite and Hebrew.**) This change in nomenclature did little, however, to eradicate the widespread Judeophobia rampant in Europe that culminated in the Holocaust.

After the Holocaust, the word *Jew* and its cognates began to lose some of their pejorative connotations, but only superficially. In English, for example, many non-Jews are still uncomfortable using the word and prefer to say "He's Jewish" rather than "He's a Jew." Even some Jews are inclined to say "We're Jewish" instead of "We're Jews" in social situations. Another tendency, common in journalistic writing, is to avoid the word altogether and refer to Jews by their nationality; thus a Jewish Hollywood director is described as "German-born," and an artist as "born in Russia of Jewish parents."

As an adjective, *Jew* is now considered derogatory. Usages like "a Jew lawyer" or "a Jew holiday" are offensive to Jews, and sensitive non-Jews avoid using them. Some slang phrases, such as *Jewboy* (attested since 1796), *Jew flag* ('dollar bill,' 1932), *Jew buggy* ('a Cadillac,' 1960), and *Jew York* ('New York City,' 1931), are clearly meant to be contemptuous and are therefore unquestionably offensive.

By far the most offensive use of *Jew* is as a verb, first recorded in 1818. It means 'to haggle or bargain with; beat unfairly in price; cheat,' is written sometimes in lower-case, as in *to out-jew someone*, and is often used in the phrase *jew down*. Most dictionaries warn readers to avoid using this verb, but evidence shows that even today the usage persists, if mostly in speech.

Another related derogatory name for a Jew found in English slang since the 1880s is *yid* (rhyming with English "rid"). The word was taken from Yiddish *yid*, 'Jew' (derived from Middle High German *jude*), whose plural is *yidn*. The fact that the English slang name often uses the English plural *yids* may partially account for its offensiveness.

Etymologically, the word *Jew* came into English through two routes. It first appeared in Old English (before 1100) in the form *Iudeas*, borrowed directly from Latin *Judaeus*, as was Old High German *judo* (Modern German *Jude*). Later (about 1200), it reappeared in the forms *Jeu, iew* as a borrowing from Old French *juieu, jueu*, which derived from Latin *Judaeus*. The Latin word came from Greek *Ioudaios*, which was borrowed from Aramaic *yehudai*, a form corresponding to Hebrew *yehudi*, found in the Bible (*Kings II 16:6, Esther 2:5*) and meaning literally 'of or from the southern kingdom of *Yehuda* (Judah).' The kingdom was named after the tribe of *Yehuda*, which in turn was named after the tribe's ancestor, the fourth son of Jacob. The Latin name *Judea* for the southern region of the Land of Israel was derived from the name of the southern kingdom.

Jewess. This word for a Jewish girl or woman has been in English since the Middle Ages and has generally been used in a neutral manner. Noted American writers, among them Saul Bellow, Philip Roth, and John Updike, have used *Jewess* in their books without suggesting disparagement. Since the advent of the civil rights and feminist movements in the 1960s, however, the word has often been regarded in the United States as disparaging, along with certain other words ending in *–ess*, notably *Negress* (now practically obsolete), *actress* (commonly replaced by *actor*), and *poetess* (replaced by *poet*). *Jewess* may be appropriate in other Anglophone countries and in certain contexts, but the discriminating writer or speaker would best think twice before using it.

Jewish alphabet. See **Hebrew alphabet.**

Jewish Aramaic. The vernacular of most Jews in Babylonia and the Land of Israel until the beginning of the Diaspora. Formerly called *Targumic* or *Aramic.* See **Aramaic, Jewish languages.**

Jewish English. A cover term for the varieties of English spoken and written by Jews. Though the term itself is of recent coinage, Jewish English has existed in one form or another for as long as Jews have been speaking English. Currently the most widespread varieties are the Yiddish-influenced forms of English used chiefly by American and British Jews of Ashkenazi (Central and East European) descent. This variety has introduced into colloquial American and British English many Yiddish-origin words, such as *chutzpah, maven, nebbish, nosh, schlep,* and *shtick.* (See **Yiddishisms.**) An informal and facetious name for this variety of Jewish English is **Yinglish.**

Another variety of Jewish English is influenced by Modern (Israeli) Hebrew. This variety has introduced into mainstream English such terms as *kibbutz, moshav, sabra, aliyah,* and *Knesset.* (See **Hebraisms.**) Other varieties include a lesser known Judezmo-influenced English used by Jews of Sephardi descent, and a formal variety that replaces Yiddish- and Hebrew-origin religious and cultural terms with general English words, such as *skullcap* (for Yiddish-origin *yarmulke* or Hebrew-origin *kippah*), *ritual bath* or *ritualarium* (for *mikveh*), *dietary laws* (for *kashrus*), *sanctuary* (for *shul*), *sidecurls* (for *peyes*), *returnee* (for *baal-teshuvah*), *decisor* (for *posek*), *novellae* (for *chiddushim*), *responsa* (for *shayles-tshuves*), *Sabbath observer* (for *shomer Shabbos*), *Grand Rabbi* (for *rebbe,* 'Hasidic leader'), *ritual slaughterer* (for *shochet*), and so on.

A prominent stylistic feature of Ashkenazi Jewish English is a conversational style marked by a fast rate of speech, a tendency of interlocutors to overlap, and an abrupt shifting of topics with corresponding shifts in pitch and amplitude—all reflecting the influence of Yiddish conversational style of earlier immigrant generations. A remarkable pronunciation feature of Ashkenazi English is the replacement of Yiddish-origin word-final *–e,* as in *pastrame, shmate, tate, Sore, bobe* with word-final *–i,* as in *pastrami, shmati, tati, Sori, bobi.*

Grammatical features of Ashkenazi Jewish English include: (1) integration of Yiddish and Hebrew loanwords into English, as by dropping infinitive endings (*daven,* 'to pray the prescribed Jewish prayers,' from Yiddish *davenen*) and giving the verb English inflections (*davens, davened, davening*); (2) use of English plurals to supplement Yiddish and Hebrew plural forms (*shtetls* supplementing Yiddish-origin *shtetlekh, Shabbatons* supplementing Hebrew-origin *shabbatonim*); (3) formation of new derivatives with English endings (*shleppy, shleppiness, klutzy, klutzily, klutzish*); (4) changes in parts of speech (*nebbish* used as an adjective and noun, whereas the Yiddish word functions mainly as an interjection); (5) the use of inversions for emphasis (*Brilliant he is not. A living he makes.*); (6) the use of Yiddish-origin constructions (*I want you should do this. Don't be a crazy. Again with the complaints! Enough already!*); (7) the use of Yiddish-origin idioms (*From your mouth to God's ears. We need it like a hole in the head*); (8) the use of rhetorical questions, usually loan translations from Yiddish or Hebrew (*Who needs it? What's to forgive?*); (9) the use of new productive formatives taken from Yiddish forms, such as the dismissive suffix *shm-* used in reduplications (*money-shmoney, value-shmalue*), the originally Slavic agent suffix *–nik* (*allrightnik, real-estatenik*), and the diminutive suffixes *–ele* (*checkele*, 'little check') and *–chik* (*boychik*, 'little boy').

Ashkenazi Jewish English also includes many compounds formed with Yiddish and Hebrew loanwords and English words, such as *matzo balls, kiddush cup, chai pendant, tzedakah box, seforim store, challah cover*; semantic shifts in English words, often due to their being identical in sound and similar in meaning to a Yiddish loanword, e.g., *by*, 'with' (from Yiddish *ba*), as in *The money is by him*; and numerous abbreviations and acronyms peculiar to Jewish life and culture, e.g., *BT* (for *baal-teshuvah*, 'returnee to Judaism'), *JAP* (for 'Jewish American Princess').

A typical feature of Ashkenazi Jewish English is the use of "preventive" or "wishful" interjections, such as *kanehore*, 'may no evil befall,' *lehavdl*, 'no comparison intended,' *halevay*, 'would that it be so,' *keyn-yirbu*, 'may they increase in numbers.' Another characteristic is the avoidance of terms with un-Jewish, especially Christian, connotations, such as *Christian name* (the preferred terms are *first name* or *given name*); *B.C.* and *A.D.* (for the preferred abbreviations, see **B.C.E.** and **C.E.**); idioms alluding to Christian themes (*cross one's fingers, knock on* (or *touch*) *wood, the gospel truth, Christ!*); and terms with anti-Jewish denotations or connotations, such as the verb *jew down*, the noun *Jew* used as an adjective (as in *Jew town*), and the offensive names *Shylock* and *Hymie* (especially in the epithet *Hymie-town*).

Before *Jewish English* came into use as a cover term, "Judeo-English" was used to designate the vernacular of English-speaking Jews. This term is now archaic.

Jewish French. Another name for **Zarfatic.**

Jewish Italian. The vernacular used by Jews in central and southern Italy from the early Middle Ages until the twentieth century. It contained many

Hebrew elements and was at times written with Hebrew characters. It also retained many archaic terms from Old Italian. Some examples of Jewish Italian are: *scuola*, 'synagogue' (literally, 'school'), analogical to Yiddish *shul; malmazalle*, 'bad luck' (Italian *mal-*, 'bad' + Hebrew *mazal*, 'luck'), analogical to Yiddish *shlimazl*. See also **belaaz, Jewish languages, Loez.**

Jewish languages. In the course of their wanderings and dispersion among the nations, Jews developed more than thirty vernaculars. These have come to be known as Jewish languages because they were distinctively Jewish forms or correlates of the national languages spoken in the territories where the Jews lived. All Jewish languages have at their core a Hebrew-Aramaic component and have usually been written in Hebrew characters and read from right to left; nevertheless, these languages were considered by their users secular vernaculars, sharply distinguished from the sacred Hebrew tongue that was the medium of religious and communal activities. Typically, Jewish languages have served as everyday means of communication within Jewish communities, intermediate in holiness between Hebrew-Aramaic and non-Jewish languages.

The two most widely known and investigated Jewish languages are *Yiddish*, a Germanic language developed and used by Ashkenazi Jews, and *Judezmo*, a Romance language used by Sephardic Jews. Other Jewish languages of historical importance include *Yevanic (Judeo-Greek), Yahudic (Judeo-Arabic), Ebri (Judeo-Persian), Zarfatic (Judeo-French)*, and *Kenaanic (Judeo-Czech)*. See **Judeo-.**

Probably the earliest of the post-exilic Jewish languages was a Hebrew-influenced form of Aramaic known as *Jewish Aramaic* (formerly, *Targumic* or *Aramic*), used by the Jews of the Middle East after the Babylonian Exile in the sixth century B.C.E. The Babylonian and the Jerusalemite versions of the Talmud (*Bavli* and *Yerushalmi*) are written in Jewish Aramaic, each in its own variety of the language. Jewish Aramaic and Hebrew became the foundation of all succeeding Jewish languages, not only becoming a basic part of the vocabulary of each language but integrated into its sound system, word-formation, and sentence structure. However, since the speakers attached little or no significance to their speech, Jewish languages tended to be replaced by other languages acquired through immigration or conquest. This pattern of adoption and replacement characterized, for example, several Jewish languages (e.g., Jewish Italian and Zarfatic) that were the prelanguages of Yiddish in western Europe. Yet, for a variety of reasons, certain languages, including Yiddish and Judezmo, have managed to endure for an exceptionally long time.

Jewishness. See **Judaism.**

Jewry. See **Judaism.**

Judaica. This plural noun, meaning 'historic, literary, and other materials relating to Jews and Judaism,' was formed in the 1920s on the adjective *Judaic*, which is a Latinate synonym for 'Jewish.' Basically, then, *Judaica* means 'things Jewish.' It should not be confused with a more recent term, **Hebraica,** which is used chiefly by librarians as a cover term for 'Hebrew books or texts.' *Hebraica* was coined on the model of *Judaica* from the adjective *Hebraic*, which refers to the ancient Hebrew people and their culture, as well as to Hebrew script and literature.

Judaism. This word means 'the religion of the Jews,' and is used in such phrases as *the teachings of Judaism, the essence of Judaism, Judaism and medicine, the history of Judaism.* Nevertheless, it is often modified to specify a variety of the Jewish religion, as in *Hellenistic Judaism, Rabbinic*

---

jubilee: a word history

When this word first came into English (in John Wycliffe's Bible of about 1324–1384), it referred to the Biblical year of *yovel*, the fiftieth year when all land reverted to the original owners and all Jewish slaves were emancipated (*Leviticus 25:8–15; 3–43*). The *yovel* was proclaimed on Yom Kippur with the sounding of the shofar throughout the land. According to various commentators, the literal meaning of Hebrew *yovel* is 'ram,' and the word was used in allusion to the sounding of the ram's horn (shofar) to proclaim the fiftieth year. The English word *jubilee* did not come directly from Hebrew *yovel*; rather it was borrowed from Old French *jubilé*, which was derived from Latin *jubilaeus*, a form influenced by the unrelated Latin word *jubilare*, 'to shout for joy,' which added to the meaning "the fiftieth year" the idea of a joyful celebration or fiftieth anniversary. The source of Latin *jubilaeus* is Greek *iobelaos*, 'of the fiftieth year,' from *iobelos*, 'the fiftieth year'; it is this word which comes directly from the Hebrew *yovel*. Eventually English *jubilee*, as well as Hebrew *yovel*, came to mean the celebration of certain major anniversaries, such as a 50th wedding anniversary (English *golden jubilee*, Hebrew *yovel-hazahav*) or a 75th anniversary (English *diamond jubilee*, Hebrew *yovel-hayahalom*).

Judaism, normative Judaism, traditional Judaism, Torah-true Judaism, Orthodox Judaism, Conservative Judaism, Reform Judaism. Though dictionaries tend to break up the word's meaning into various subsenses, such as 'the way of life or culture of the Jews' and 'the whole body of Jews, the Jewish nation,' *Judaism* rarely means anything except 'the religion or beliefs of the Jewish people,' as contrasted with, for example, Christianity and Islam. The standard term for 'the whole body of Jews, the Jewish people' is **Jewry.** The standard term for 'the state or condition of being a Jew' is **Jewishness**, which also connotes an attachment or devotion to being Jewish. In contrast, the corresponding Yiddish term *yidishkeyt* means both Jewishness and Judaism (the Yiddish equivalent of the word Jewry is *yidn*), while the corresponding Hebrew word *yahadut* means all three: Judaism, Jewishness, and Jewry. See also **Yiddishkeit.**

Judaize. This verb, applied to non-Jews and meaning 'to follow the religious practices or beliefs of Jews,' came into English before the 1500s, along with the noun **Judaizer**, meaning a non-Jew who follows or causes others to follow Jewish practices and beliefs. In the Middle Ages the Christian Church persecuted Christians found to engage in the so-called "Judaizing heresy" by keeping the Jewish Sabbath or celebrating Passover. Judaizing sects have been found since then in many countries, such as Czarist Russia and 19th century Hungary, and among various peoples in Africa and Latin America.

Judengasse. Formerly, especially in the Middle Ages, the street in a German village, town, or city where Jews lived; by extension, a Jewish neighborhood. The Judengasse of Frankfort is described in George Eliot's *Daniel Deronda* (1876). From German, literally, 'Jews' street.' Similar Jewish streets or neighborhoods were called *judería* (in Spain), *juiverie* (in France), *giudecca* (in Italy), *Jewry* (in England). These terms should not be confused with a **ghetto**, where Jews were forced to live.

Judeo-. A learned combining form meaning 'Jewish,' derived from Latin *Judaeus*, Jew. Formerly used to create numerous compounds, such as *Judeo-Christian, Judeo-Roman, Judeo-German,* and *Judeo-Greek,* this combining form is found occasionally in compounds such as *Judeophobia* and in descriptive adjectives, as in *Judeo-Arabic society, Judeo-Greek history.* The names of **Jewish languages** in which the form *Judeo-* appears are now usually considered archaic, though these names still serve a historical purpose in emphasizing the distinctively *Jewish* character of the vernaculars.

Judeo-Arabic. Former name of **Yahudic.**

Judeo-Czech. Former name of **Kenaanic.**

Judeo-French. Former name of **Zarfatic.**

Judeo-German. Obsolete name of **Yiddish.**

Judeo-Greek. Former name of **Yevanic.**

Judeo-Persian. Former name of **Ebri.**

Judeophobia. See **Anti-Semitism.**

Judeo-Spanish. See **Judezmo.**

Judezmo. Formerly the chief Jewish vernacular of Sephardic Jewry, Judezmo arose in Castile, spread to other parts of the Iberian Peninsula, and, with the persecution of the Jews in the 15th century (culminating in their expulsion from Castile and Aragon in 1492), was taken to other Mediterranean countries and the Balkans. Judezmo is mostly of Hispanic (largely Spanish) origin, with an admixture of Hebrew-Aramaic, Arabic, Jewish Greek, and Jewish Latin. Outside the Iberian Peninsula, other languages influenced Judezmo, including Turkish, French, and Italian. Like most Jewish languages, Judezmo was traditionally written in a form of the Jewish alphabet, but since the 19th and 20th centuries it has come to be written mostly in the Roman alphabet, especially in publications whose readers are no longer familiar with the Hebrew letters. Some examples of Judezmo words adopted from Hebrew are *mazalado*, 'lucky' (compare Yiddish *mazldik*), from Hebrew *mazal*, 'luck'; *xavransa*, 'friendship, partnership,' from Hebrew *chaver*, 'friend'; *darsár*, 'to preach,' from Hebrew *darash*.

The English word *Judezmo* (formerly spelled *Judesmo* or *Dzhudezmo*) comes from *ǧudézmo*, a Judezmo name for the language whose literal meaning is 'Jewishness, Judaism.' The Judezmo name for the written variety of Judezmo used to translate sacred Jewish texts is *ladíno*, rendered in English as **Ladino.** The name of this variety derives through Old (Castilian) Spanish from the Vulgar Latin *Ladinum*, a variant of the classical Latin name *Latinum* for the language of the Romans. Ladino contains words not found in other varieties of Judezmo; for example, *paskwár*, 'celebrate Passover,' modeled on the Hebrew verb *pasach*, with the same meaning. Ladino follows Hebrew-Aramaic word order as closely as possible. Often Judezmo is mistakenly called *Ladino*. The mistake arose among certain non-Sephardic researchers who, finding the words *lašón i ladíno*, 'Hebrew-Aramaic and Ladino,' on the title pages of books containing the Hebrew-Aramaic original of a sacred text and its Ladino translation, erroneously thought that *ladíno* was the name of Judezmo as a whole. **Judeo-Spanish** is a descriptive term coined on the analogy of former names of older Jewish languages, such as Judeo-Arabic, Judeo-Greek, and Judeo-French. Unlike the latter terms, *Judeo-Spanish* still has some currency, especially as an adjective, e.g., "Judeo-Spanish ballads." Scholars often use *Judeo-Spanish* as a cover term for all varieties of Judezmo. The obsolescent names *Spaniolic* or *Spaniolish* were borrowed from German *Spaniolisch*, a term derived from Spanish *Español*, 'Spanish.'

Judezmo is still used in various parts of the world, although its speakers are few. Unlike its Ashkenazi counterpart, Yiddish, Judezmo does not have a devout constituency to promote its use, though attempts have been made to revive it in Israel. Yet it has a considerable literature that continues to be studied by scholars.

– K –

kabbalah. The mystical or esoteric teachings of Judaism; Jewish mysticism. From Hebrew, literally, 'a receiving; reception,' and, in a transferred sense, 'received (teaching); tradition,' derived from the verb *kibbel*, 'to receive.' The earlier form of this word, **cabala,** came into English through Medieval Latin and carries a different meaning or connotation, namely, 'a secret doctrine or art,' a meaning related to English *cabal*, 'a secret group.' It is therefore preferable to use the Hebrew-based spelling *kabbalah* for the sense of 'Jewish mysticism' rather than the Latinate form *cabala*. Most English dictionaries mistakenly treat the two words as spelling variants, with *cabala* as the main entry.

When used with the definite article, *the kabbalah* (often with an initial capital, as *the Kabbalah*) the term refers to the body of Jewish mystical or esoteric knowledge developed since the 1200s. Without the article (and usually without the initial capital), *kabbalah* refers to Jewish mystical and esoteric teachings in general, especially as found in popular lore, in Hasidic literature, and in ethical works. Hence there is a difference between studying or teaching *the Kabbalah* and studying or teaching *kabbalah*.

The present meaning of Hebrew *kabbalah* did not appear until the 1200s, when the mystical or esoteric teachings of Judaism took on the form of a movement. While mystical traditions are found already in the Talmud and Midrash, they are not referred to as *kabbalah*. In the Talmud and Midrash, the word *kabbalah* is used in the specific sense of the Prophets and the Writings (Hagiographa), as distinguished from the Torah or Pentateuch (see, for example, *Rosh Hashana 7a* and *Bava Kama 2b*). However, the Talmud also uses a verbal form, *mekubbol* and *kibbel*, 'have (received) a tradition' (see *Peah 2:6*), which may have been the basis of the new meaning attached to *kabbalah*. This meaning was introduced by the early **kabbalists** (known in Hebrew as *mekubbalim* or *baale kabbalah*), which included Isaac the Blind (c.1160–1235), Eleazar of Worms (c.1165–1238), Abraham Abulafia (1240–1290s), Moses ben Nachman (Nachmanides, 1194–1270), and Moses de Leon (1250–1305). The **kabbalistic** movement reached its highest form with the school of Safed, which included Moses Cordovero (1522–1570), Isaac Luria (the "Ari Hakadosh" or "Holy Lion," 1534–1572), and the latter's disciple, Hayim Vital (1543–1620). The main literary source of kabbalah is the **Zohar**; other sources are the *sefer haBahir* ("Book of the Shining"), the *sefer yetzirah* ("Book of Creation"), and the *sefer raziel hamalach* ("Book of the Angel Raziel"). **Hasidism** was profoundly influence by the kabbalah. (See **Hasidic terms.**)

kabbalistic terms. The following is a small sampling of the terminology used in the kabbalah. The central doctrine of the kabbalah, especially in its Lurianic form, is that prior to Creation, there was but God as the *En-Sof*, the Infinite. The process of Creation began with *tzsimtzum*, the self-contraction of the En-Sof that brought about a primordial space (*chalal*) in which a finite, physical world could exist. Divine light from the En-Sof formed the ten *sefiros* that facilitated the creation of the finite world. All the terms listed below come from Hebrew or Aramaic.

> *Adam Kadmon.* The first and highest emanation of the Divine light flowing into primordial space by the process of *tzimtzum*. Adam Kadmon, also called *Keser Elyon* ('Supreme Crown'), preceded the four worlds of of *atzilus*, *beriah*, *yetzirah*, and *asiyah* through which the *sefiros* came into being. Literally, 'Primordial Man.'
>
> *asiyah.* The fourth and lowest of the four worlds intermediate between the *En-Sof* and the physical world. Literally, (world of) 'action' or 'making.'
>
> *atzilus.* The first and highest of the four worlds, from which the ten *sefiros* emanated. Literally, (world of) 'emanation.'
>
> *beriah.* The second of the four worlds intermediate between the *En-Sof* and the physical world. Literally, (world of) 'creation.' The third is the world of *yetzirah.*

chalal. The primordial space formed as a result of *tzimtzum.* Literally, 'empty space, void.'

chitzoniyus. The lowest and most external level of a sefirah, as opposed to *pnimiyus.* Literally, 'outwardness.'

En-Sof. The Infinite God, conceived without His attributes, and made manifest to the material world by means of the *sefiros.* Literally, 'Infinite, (the one) Without End.'

kelipah. One of the shells or husks (*kelipos*) that captured the *nitzotzos* or Divine sparks after the breaking of the vessels (*sheviras hakelim*) and that represent evil and corruption. Literally, 'shell.' In Yiddish, a *klipe* is an evil spirit.

nitzotz, plural, *nitzotzos* or *nitzotzim.* Any of the sparks of the Divine light that broke away from their source during the *sheviras hakelim* and that can only be restored through *tikkun.* Literally, 'spark, gleam.'

partzuf. Any of the various configurations of the *sefiros* in which they lose their individuality. Literally, 'face, visage.'

pnimiyus. The core or essence of a sefirah, and hence its deepest level, as opposed to *chitzoniyus.* Literally, 'inwardness.'

sefirah or *sefira.* Any of the ten emanations (*sefiros*) of Divine light from the *En-Sof.* The sefiros include the following qualities: *Chochmah* ('Wisdom'), *Binah* ('Understanding'), *Daas* ('Knowledge'), *Chesed* ('kindness'), *Gevurah* ('Strength'), *Tiferes* ('Beauty'), *Netzach* ('Triumph'), *Hod* ('Majesty'), *Yesod* ('Foundation'), and *Malchus* ('Kingdom'). Hebrew *sefirah* means literally 'count, number,' and is not related to the word *sphere* or the word *sapphire,* as some commentators have conjectured.

sheviras hakelim. The 'breaking of the vessels,' a cosmic catastrophe by which the holy sparks (*nitzotzos*) which were spilled over from the *En-Sof* after *tzimtzum* were captured by the *kelipos.*

sitra achra. The realm of evil or demonic powers and emanations; the domain of Satan. Aramaic, literally, 'the other side.' In Yiddish, *sitre akhre* means the devil or Satan.

tikkun. The restoration of the holy sparks that were captured by the *kelipos* after the breaking of the vessels (*sheviras hakelim*). *Tikkun* can occur only through man's total devotion to God and performance of His commandments. Literally, 'repair, reparation.'

tzimtzum. The self-contraction of the *En-Sof* to allow room for the Creation. Literally, 'reduction, limitation.'

yetzirah. The third of the four worlds intermediate between the *En-Sof* and the physical world. Literally, (world of) 'formation.'

kaddish, plural **kaddishim** or (Yiddish) **kaddeishim.** This term usually refers to a prayer recited by a mourner, often called "the mourner's kaddish." The expression *to say kaddish* (translation of Yiddish *zogn kadesh*)
also refers to the mourner's kaddish. The mourner's kaddish is technically
called *kaddish yosom*, literally, 'orphan's kaddish,' because it is recited by
a son at his parent's grave during the funeral, then for the next eleven
months at daily prayer services, and thereafter on every anniversary (**yahrzeit**) of the parent's death. See also **mourning terms.** Despite its name,
the *kaddish yosom* is recited not only by orphans but by other mourners as
well, such as a bereaved father, husband, or brother, and in non-traditional
synagogues by women who have lost a parent. The kaddish is said in the
presence of a minyan, or quorum of ten adult males.

The word *kaddish* comes from Aramaic, in which it means 'holy, sacred' (after the second word in the prayer, *yisgadal veyiskadash*, 'be ex-
alted and made holy'), and is first encountered in the minor tractate *Soferim
10:7*: "We do not say kaddish . . . with fewer than ten (worshipers)." In
Yiddish, a *kadesh* is a son, especially a firstborn son, so called because he
would someday say the mourner's kaddish after his parents.

The kaddish is not, however, primarily a mourner's prayer. It is a majes-
tic hymn of praise to God, and as such it is recited in public prayers in a
full form (*kaddish sholem)* and in half form (*chatzi kaddish*) by the person
leading the prayers. A special rabbinic kaddish (*kaddish derabbanan*) is
recited in the presence of a minyan, usually by mourners; after study of the
Mishnah, Gemara, or Midrash.

Following talmudic study, this **kaddish** is usually preceded by a short
aggadic or midrashic passage. It is not known when precisely the custom
arose for mourners to recite the kaddish, but it may have sprung naturally
from the need of mourners to affirm their faith in God at the time of a close
relative's death, and, according to mystical tradition, reciting the kaddish
serves to elevate the souls of the deceased to a higher plane, thereby helping them attain eternal peace.

kaftan. See under **clothing terms.**

kallah, plural **kallahs.** A Jewish bride. See under **wedding terms.** *Kallah* is
also the title of a minor tractate of the Babylonian Talmud that begins with
the word *kallah* and deals in part with betrothal and marriage. *Kallah* is
also the name given in the Babylonian Talmud (*Berachos 8b; Bava Basra
22a; Bava Kama 113a*) to a large gathering of yeshiva students and rabbis
held twice a year, in the months of Adar and Elul, at the yeshivas of Babylonia during the amoraic and geonic periods. The Talmud does not explain

why this biannual assembly was called *Kallah*.The students at the Kallah were called **benei kallah** and the head of the Kallah was known as **resh kallah**. The Kallah months, known as **yarche kallah,** have been reestablished in recent years for similar large gatherings or assemblies of yeshiva students and rabbis for the purpose of strengthening Torah and Talmud study.

kamea. See under **Hasidic terms.**

kapl, kapote. See under **clothing terms.**

kasher. *To kasher* is 'to make (an unkosher thing) kosher.' Technically this means: (1) to boil pots, dishes, silverware, or other utensils in hot water (*hagalah*) so as to remove all traces of unkosher use; (2) to pass through fire (*libun*) a vessel used normally in fire, such as a barbecue grill, until it glows or turns white (3) to scour an unkosher knife or stab it into hard ground ten times. Most commonly the verb is used to refer to utensils in which chometz or leaven has been cooked or baked and that therefore need to be made kosher for Passover use by being immersed in boiling water or heated in fire. The verb is also used, both in the form *kasher* and the form *kosher*, in the sense of 'to render (meat) kosher for cooking.' This is done by first soaking, salting, and rinsing the meat to remove surface blood, or by grilling (the liver, which is filled with blood) over an open fire until it changes color and forms a crust. (See **kosher.**) The verb *kasher* comes from Eastern Yiddish *kashern*, which is derived from the adjective *kosher* (like other verbs derived from Hebrew adjectives, such as Yiddish *poter*, 'exempt, free,' *patern*, 'to rid, free,' and *oser*, 'forbidden,' *asern*, 'to forbid'). In its Anglicized form, *kasher* is inflected as other English verbs: *kashered, kashers, kashering*. The verb should not be confused with the similarly spelled Hebrew adjective **kasher,** the source of the Yiddish adjective **kosher.**

kasha. See under **food terms.**

kashrus or **kashrut**. The Jewish laws, often called **(Jewish) dietary laws,** dealing with the kinds of food that may or may not be eaten. A major part of these laws concern animals that are designated in the Torah (Leviticus 11, Deuteronomy 14: 3–21) as either clean (*tahor*) or unclean (*tamei*). Animals whose flesh may be eaten include mammals that chew the cud and have wholly cloven hooves, fish that have both scales and fins, and birds that are by tradition considered clean, such as the chicken, pigeon, turtledove, duck, goose, and turkey. All other animals, such as pigs, camels, birds of prey, worms, and insects, may not be eaten. The flesh of only those clean mammals and birds that undergo proper ritual slaughter (**shechitah**) and inspection (**bedikah**) may be eaten. A **nevelah,** or carcass of an animal that dies without proper ritual slaughter, may not be used for food. A **tere-fah,** or animal suffering from various diseases or defects (originally refer-ring to an animal mauled by a wild beast), is equally forbidden. Certain parts of clean animals other than birds may not be eaten after *shechitah* and must be removed. One is the sciatic nerve (*gid hanoshe*), based on Genesis 32:33; the other is the forbidden fat (*chelev*) attached to the organs of animals that were used as sacrifices (Leviticus 7:23–25). The fat and sinews are removed by **porging** (Hebrew *nikkur*, Yiddish *treybern*), a process requiring special training and skill. The blood of mammals and birds may not be eaten (Leviticus 17:10–14) and therefore their meat has to be kashered (see **kasher**). For the same reason, eggs with blood specks are prohibited. A conspicuous feature of kashrus is the separation of meat (**fleishig**) and dairy (**milchig**) food, dishes, and utensils in a kosher house-hold, based on the Biblical verses (Exodus 23:19, 34:26, and Deuteronomy 14:21) prohibiting the cooking of a kid in its mother's milk, from which the rabbis derived the threefold prohibition of cooking, eating, or benefit-ing from a mixture of meat and dairy foods. Foods that are neutral (**pa-reve**), such as fruits, vegetables, and eggs, may be eaten with either meat or dairy foods. From Ashkenazi Hebrew *kashrus* and Sephardi *kashrut*, derived from Hebrew *kasher* 'kosher.'

Kenaanic. The Slavic vernacular of Bohemian and Moravian Jews in the Middle Ages. From Hebrew (*lashon*) *Kenaan*, 'Slavic (language)'; so called in allusion to Genesis 9:25, "May Canaan be a slave to them," since it was believed that the name *Slav* (from Latin *Sclavus)* meant 'slave,' al-though most likely it derived from the Slavic word *slovo*, 'speech, word.' Formerly called **Judeo-Czech.**

kevutzah. See under **Israeli terms.**

khamsa. See **hamsa.**

kibbutz. See under **Israeli terms.**

kibitz. See under **Yiddishisms.**

kiddush. A benediction sanctifying the Sabbath and festivals, recited in the synagogue and at home before the evening dinner and before the midday mealover a cup or glass of wine. By extension, a synagogue reception after the Sabbath morning prayers at which kiddush is made over wine or whiskey is called *a kiddush*. From Hebrew, literally, 'sanctification.' An American innovation is the *kiddush club*, consisting of a group of men who on Sabbath morning, before the Musaf service, leave the sanctuary "to make kiddush." This practice has drawn criticism in some Orthodox circles.

kippah or **kippa,** plural **kippahs,** or (Sephardic) **kippot.** The skullcap worn symbolically by religious male Jews. Modern Orthodox Jews usually wear a colorful **kippah serugah,** or knitted skullcap, often embroidered with the wearer's name. From Hebrew, originally, 'dome, vault'; by extension, 'cap, skullcap.' Compare **yarmulke.** See also *kapl* under **clothing terms.**

kishke. See under **food terms.**

kittel. A long white frock or tunic symbolizing ritual purity, worn by religious Ashkenazi adult males over their clothing on solemn occasions, as at Yom Kippur (and sometimes Rosh Hashanah) services and at the Passover seder. It is worn by the person who leads the prayers on Rosh Hashanah, Yom Kippur, Hoshana Rabbah, and during the Musaf prayer for rain (*Geshem*) on Sukkos and the Musaf prayer for dew (*Tal*) on Passover. It is also often worn by the groom under the bridal canopy and sometimes used as a burial garment in place of the burial shroud or tachrichim. From Yiddish *kitl*, derived from Middle High German *kitel*, a kind of cotton frock, probably ultimately from Arabic *qutn, qutun*, the source of English *cotton*.

klezmer, plural **klezmorim.** A Yiddish-origin word used as a noun and adjective to denote the lively Ashkenazi folk music of Eastern Europe as re-

---

Three different terms are used by English-speaking Ashkenazim for the cup or goblet used in making kiddush. The most common is **kiddush cup,** a partial translation of Yiddish *kidesh-bekher*. Also used is the term **becher** (short for Yiddish *kidesh-bekher*), from German *Becher*, 'goblet, cup.' A third is the Ashkenazi Hebrew term **kos,** 'cup, goblet, glass' (plural **kosos**). The latter is also used in the Hebrew-origin phrases **kos shel beracha,** 'cup of benediction,' referring to the cup of wine over which the after-meal blessings are said, and **kos (shel) eliyahu,** 'Elijah's cup,' the goblet of wine placed on the Passover seder table in honor of the prophet Elijah.

vived and popularized in America, or the Jewish musicians or bands playing such music, chiefly with string and wind instruments. Thus one speaks of playing or listening to *klezmer* or enjoying *klezmer music, a klezmer band, klezmer repertoires*. Modern klezmer groups often build their names on the word *klezmer*, as in *Klezmatic, Klezical,* and *New Klez.* In Yiddish, *klezmer* is a noun meaning a musician or a musical band. In Eastern Europe, klezmorim played at weddings and other festive occasions. The Yiddish word was derived from Hebrew *kley-zemer,* 'musical band,' literally, 'instruments for song.'

kloyz. See under **Hasidic terms.**

kneydl, knish. See under **food terms.**

kohen, plural, **kohanim.** Often capitalized **Kohen.** A **kohen** is a male descendant of the family of Aaron, of the tribe of Levi. Aaron and his descendants were consecrated to the service of God (*Exodus 28–30*) in the Tabernacle (*Mishkan*) in the desert and later in the Holy Temple. The commentator Rashi points out (*Exodus 28:3*) that the term *kehuna* means 'service' and cites Old French *serventrie* as a synonym. Accordingly, the widespread use of the term "priest" as a rendering, synonym, or translation of *kohen* is infelicitous and should be avoided, especially since in common usage "a priest" refers to a Roman Catholic, Eastern Orthodox, or Anglican clergyman. Moreover, the word *priest* derives from the Latin term *presbyter,* meaning literally 'elder' (from *presbys,* 'old man') and is thus etymologically associated with Christian presbyters and the Presbyterian Church. A more appropriate English rendering of *kohen* would be *Aaronite,* which is included in several dictionaries. *Aaronite* closely parallels English *Levite* and *Israelite,* neither of which is vitiated by unsuitable translations. The translation of Hebrew *kohen gadol* as "high priest" is likewise unfortunate; "chief kohen' or "chief Aaronite" would be more appropriate and true to the original. It is also worth remembering that the functions of today's kohanim have very little resemblance to those of ancient times. No kohen today can be considered remotely similar to a priest. A kohen's title is purely hereditary (from father to son) and his only functions are to bestow the *birkas kohanim* or Blessing of the Kohanim (not "Priestly Blessing") on the worshipers during certain synagogue services (see **duchen**), to be the first to be called up to the Torah during its public reading (see **aliyah**), and to officiate at the redemption of the firstborn son of an Israelite (see **pidyon haben**). Among the restrictions imposed on a kohen are the Biblical prohibitions that he may not marry a divorced woman and that he may not come in contact with a corpse (except if the deceased is one of his immediate relatives). It is customary (but not obligatory) to honor a kohen with the recital of a communal *birkas hamazon* ("Grace after Meals"). See also **Levite.**

kolel or **kollel,** plural, **kolels** or **kolelim, kollels** or **kollelim.** A term designating a group of young married yeshiva students or rabbis who devote themselves to higher Talmudic and other Jewish studies and are financially supported by a yeshiva or a community. The term was originally used by Rabbi Israel Salanter (1810–1883) to describe a special yeshiva for married men devoted to the study of musar, or Jewish ethics. The kolel as an institution for advanced Talmudic studies by married young men became established in Israel, the United States, and other countries during the latter half of the 20th century. An earlier, pre-19th century, use of the term referred to any group of Ashkenazi Jews in Eretz Israel who received financial support from funds collected for them in the countries or provinces in Europe where they originated. From Hebrew, literally, 'inclusive, all-embracing, comprehensive.'

kosher. Probably the most widespread and best-known word of Yiddish origin, this adjective came into English from Western Yiddish (Germany, Holland, Switzerland, etc.) in the mid-19th century. Because of its unique meaning, 'fit and proper according to Jewish dietary laws,' the word became quickly known among non-Jews, as did the verb *to kosher*, 'to make (meat) kosher,' borrowed from Western Yiddish *koshern* (compare **kasher**). The Yiddish word was derived from the Hebrew *kasher*, literally, 'fit, proper.' By the late 1800s, the extended sense of the verb, 'reliable, satisfactory, legitimate, correct, honest, fair' (which already existed in Yiddish) entered English slang.

For food to be considered kosher, all the laws of **kashrus** must be applied in its selection, preparation, and storage. ("Kosher-style," a commercial term introduced in the United States by entrepeneurs wishing to circumvent the strictures and expenditures of kashrus, is not kosher.) The **hashgachah** or kosher supervision in a slaughterhouse, food-processing factory, restaurant, catering hall, or the like is the responsibility of a **mashgiach** (plural **mashgichim**), a qualified supervisor or inspector of kashrus. Packaged kosher food must bear an authoritative kosher label called a **hechsher** ('kosher permit or authorization') identifying the rabbi or Orthodox organization under whose hashgacha the food was prepared and packaged. Anything that is unkosher is **treyf.**

kreplech, kugl. See under **food terms.**

kvater. A friend or relative who at a circumcision ceremony is given the honor of taking the infant from his wife (the **kvatern**) or occasionally someone else and handing him to the **mohel.** See **bris.** From Yiddish, literally, 'godfather,' from German *Gevatter.*

– L –

Ladino. A formal written variety of **Judezmo** used to translate Jewish Biblical and liturgical texts. The term is often mistakenly used as the name of Judezmo as a whole. The term Ladino comes from Judezmo *ladíno*, derived through Old (Castilian) Spanish from Vulgar Latin *Ladinum*, variant of Latin *Latinum*, 'Latin.' Compare **ivre-taytsh.**

Lag B′omer. See under **holiday terms.**

lamdan, plural **lamdonim.** A learned man, especially one learned in Talmud. From Hebrew and Yiddish. Related to **limud, lomdos, melamed, talmid, Talmud.**

lamedvovnik. See under **Hasidic terms.**

landsman, plural **landslayt.** A Jewish immigrant hailing from the same country, town, or region in Europe as another or others; a fellow countryman or compatriot. A society or organization of landslayt, especially one formed in the United States at the beginning of the 20th century, is called a **landsmanshaft,** plural **landsmanshaftn.** From Yiddish, cognate with English *landsman* (plural *landsmen*), 'a person living or working on land.'

lashon kodesh or **lashon hakodesh.** Hebrew as the sacred tongue; Biblical or rabbinical Hebrew. Literally, 'holy tongue,' but it can also mean 'language of holiness.' The Yiddish form is *loshn-koydesh.* Compare **Ivrit.**

latke. See under **food terms.**

laybtsudekl (layb′tsudekl). A Yiddish-origin word for the four-cornered tasseled garment worn under the shirt by Orthodox Jewish males that is usually called **tzitzis, arba kanfos,** or **tallis katan.** Literally, the Yiddish word means 'small body-cover,' formed from *layb*, 'body' + *tsudekl*, 'small cover' (diminutive of *tsudek*, 'cover').

lechayim! or **l'chayim!** See under **greetings and salutations** and under **wedding terms.**

lechem mishne. The two **challah** loaves placed together on the Sabbath or holiday table. The lechem mishne symbolizes the double portion of manna gathered in the desert on the sixth day so as to leave over a portion for the Sabbath, when gathering the manna was prohibited. From Hebrew, literally, 'double bread' (Exodus 16:22).

lekech. See under **food terms.**

lemaan Hashem! See under **exclamations and interjections.**

levayah. See under **mourning terms.**

levirate. Also, **levirate marriage.** The marriage of a man to the widow of his deceased brother who has died childless (Deuteronomy 25:5–10). The Hebrew term is **yibbum.** From Latin *levir,* 'husband's brother.'

Levite or **levite.** A member or descendant of the tribe of Levi. Though Aaron, the brother of Moses, was a Levite, he and his descendants were chosen to serve as kohanim (see **kohen**). The Levites (Hebrew *leviim,* singular *levi*) who did not belong to the family of Aaron became assistants to the kohanim in the Temple, serving as administrators, gatekeepers, and notably as singers and musicians. A Levite is second to be called up to the Torah during its public reading (see **aliyah**), and he is charged with washing the hands of a kohen before the *birkat kohanim* (see **duchen**). Like a kohen, a Levite is exempt from redeeming his firstborn son in a **pidyon haben**, but he may not preside over the redemption of an Israelite's firstborn, as a kohen does.

Leviticus. See **Pentateuch.**

limud, plural **limudim.** Jewish subject of study; learning or instruction in Jewish subjects. From Hebrew and Yiddish. Related to **lamdan, lomdos, melamed, talmid, Talmud.**

Litvak. A Yiddish-origin name for a Lithuanian Jew (from *Lite,* Yiddish name of Lithuania), often used humorously or disparagingly. A Litvak is

---

leviathan: a word history

The leviathan was a huge sea animal mentioned in the Bible (*Job 40*) along with another large, powerful beast, the **behemoth**. Both words came into English before 1382 through John Wycliffe's translation of the Bible and used later to mean figuratively anything of enormous size or power. The immediate source of the word was Latin, as found in the Vulgate, Jerome's Latin translation of the Bible. Ultimately they came from Hebrew *livyatan* and *behemot*. The Yiddish form of *livyatan* is ***leviyosen***. The Gemara (*Bava Basra 74b–75a*) describes the leviathan in detail, including Rabbah's statement that in the World to Come God will make a banquet for the righteous from the flesh of the leviathan and a tabernacle for the righteous from the skin of the leviathan. Based on this and various Midrashic sources, a tradition developed that at the *seudah shel leviyatan* ('banquet of leviathan') the righteous will eat the leviathan and the *shor habor* ('wild ox,' identified in the Midrash with the behemoth), and drink the *yayin hameshumor* ('preserved wine,' i.e. wine preserved in grapes from the six days of creation, according to *Berachos 34b*). A Hasidic version, popularized in song, adds that Moses will lecture on the Torah and King David will play the harp at the great banquet. Maimonides, in his Mishnah Torah (*Hilchos Teshuva 8:1–2*), affirms a different Talmudic tradition which holds that only the souls of the righteous will exist in the World to Come and they will not indulge in any physical pleasures, including eating and drinking.

---

conventionally regarded as more skeptical, rational, and intellectual than Jews from Poland and other regions of Europe.

Loez. Any of various Romance dialects or languages spoken by Jews in France (western Loez) and Italy (southern Loez) in early medieval times. Loez, incorporated into dialectal High German, was instrumental in the formation of Yiddish. Rashi, in his commentaries, often gives the Loez equivalents of difficult Hebrew words. From Hebrew *loez*, 'strange (or foreign) language.' See **belaaz.**

lokshn. See under **food terms.**

lomdos. Jewish learning or scholarship, especially in Talmud. From Hebrew and Yiddish. See also **lamdan.**

lox. See under **food terms.**

luach, plural **luchos.** A Jewish calendar. It is also the Modern Hebrew word for a blackboard. The plural, *luchos,* usually refers to the *luchos hoeydus* (Tablets of the Testimony) or *luchos habris* (Tablets of the Covenant), the two stone tablets on which the Ten Commandments were engraved. From Hebrew and Yiddish.

luftmentsh, plural **luftmentshn.** A person who has no profession, trade, occupation, or any visible means of support, and seems to be living "on air." Luftmentshn were common in the shtetls of Eastern Europe, but in the usage of British and American Jews the term has come to be used somewhat disparagingly of any dreamer or visionary. From Yiddish, literally, 'air person.'

– M –

maamad[1], plural **maamados.** Any of twenty-four groups into which all Israelites (i.e., not kohanim or Levites) were divided in times of the Temple. Approximately twice a year selected members of a maamad went for a week to the Temple to be stationed at designated posts and serve as assistants to the kohanim and Levites at the daily sacrifices (*Taanis 27a*). The remaining members of the maamad remained home to fast and recite sacred texts, which came to be known as *maamados.* The practice of reciting daily *maamados* has endured in modern times and the texts have found their way into some prayerbooks and special compilations such as the *Chok Leyisrael,* which includes daily passages from the weekly Torah portion, parts of Tanach, excerpts from the Mishnah and Gemara, etc. From Hebrew *maamad,* 'deputation, representation,' literally, 'standing, station.' Compare **mishmar.**

maamad[2]. The governing council of a western Sephardi congregation or community after the Spanish expulsion. From Judezmo *maamad, mahamad,* derived from Hebrew *maamad;* see **maamad[1.]**

maamados. See **mourning terms.**

maariv. See **ritual terms.**

maaser, plural **maasoros.** One tenth of one's agricultural produce set aside for a sacred or special purpose; a tithe. The laws of maaser are set forth in the Bible (*Leviticus 27:30–31; Numbers 18:21–29*). The first tithe (*maaser rishon*) was given to the Levites, who owned no land; the second (*maaser sheni*) had to be brought to Jerusalem and eaten there or (if converted into money) spent there; the "poor tithe" (*maaser ani*) is actually *maaser sheni* given every third year to the poor. A separate tithe was set aside three times a year from one's herd of animals (*maaser behemah*) and brought to the Temple to be sacrificed and its meat eaten by the owner (*Leviticus 27:32*). Another type of maaser, set aside since time immemorial though not Biblically ordained, is that of a tenth of one's income to be given to charity (*maaser kesafim*, 'tithe of monies'). From Hebrew, literally, 'a tenth,' derived from *eser*, 'ten.' The English word *tithe* means 'tenth' and is a literal translation of Hebrew *maaser*.

Magen David. An ancient symbol made up of two triangles interlacing to form a six-pointed star (hexagram). It is part of the flag of the State of Israel, centered in blue on the white field between the two horizontal blue stripes that symbolize the tallis or prayer shawl. The Hebrew phrase *magen david*, 'shield of David,' is found in the third blessing following the recital of the weekly haftorah (reading from the Prophets after the Torah reading): "Blessed are you, Hashem, Shield of David." It is uncertain how the hexagram became a symbol of the Jewish people and why it came to be called Magen David, since a much older Jewish symbol is the **menorah.** Until the Middle Ages, the Magen David was used by Jews mainly as an ornament. In the Middle Ages, kabbalists used it in amulets as a magical sign. Its first appearance as a Jewish symbol was in the 1300s in Prague, where

---

macabre: a word history

This English word, meaning 'gruesome, horrible,' was borrowed from French in the mid-1800s. The French word derived from *Danse Macabré*, the title of various literary and artistic works of medieval times in which Death is shown leading mankind in a dance to the grave. The phrase *Danse Macabré* (translated in English as 'The Dance of Macchabree' as early as 1460), appears to be a translation of Medieval Latin *Chorea Macchabeorum*, 'The Dance of the Maccabees,' a term alluding to the martyrdom of the heroes of the Maccabeean revolt (175–135 B.C.E.) described in the apocryphal Books of the Maccabees, especially II Maccabees, dealing with the heroic deeds of Judah Maccabee.

Maccabee: the story of a name

Maccabee comes from the name of Judah Maccabee, the hero of the Jewish revolt against the Syrian-Greeks who fell in battle in 161 B.C.E. The origin of this sobriquet has long been a matter of dispute. The popular spelling of the Hebrew name is מכבי (with a *kaph*, כ), but a variant spelling is with a *koph* (ק), leading some scholars to believe that the name derives from Hebrew מקבת, 'hammer,' so that the Hebrew name *yehuda hamakkabee* can be translated as 'Judah the Hammer.' By the time the four apocryphal Books of the Maccabees were written (between 100 and 80 B.C.E.), the family name of *Hasmoneans* had been replaced by the name *Maccabees,* in honor of Judah Maccabee. Hence all the Hasmonean heroes came to be known as the Maccabees.

In 1896, some two thousand years after the Maccabeean revolt, a British Zionist benevolent society named itself the *Order of Ancient Maccabeans,* and in 1914 the Order founded the *Maccabean Land Company* to purchase land in Eretz Israel. While these names imitated those of Masonic groups, an international Jewish sports organization that had been in existence since 1903 named itself in 1921 the *Maccabi World Union,* directly after Judah Maccabee. Ten years later this organization, now a part of the Zionist movement, established the **Maccabiah**, or Jewish Olympic games. The first Maccabiah was held in Tel Aviv in 1932. The Maccabiah is recognized by the International Olympic Committee and is held every four years in Israel.

---

it became an official emblem of the Jewish community. But there is no basis for associating it with the Jewish religion, and its widespread use since the 1800s as a religious symbol (on synagogues, Torah covers, etc.) was apparently a way of imitating the Christian cross with a distinctive sign symbolizing Judaism. Similarly, the name of Israel's first-aid society, *Magen David Adom,* 'Red Shield of David,' was modeled on the Red Cross. During the Holocaust, the Nazis used the Magen David as an identification badge to be worn by all Jews (see ***Judenstern*** under **Holocaust terms**). It is often called the **star of David.**

maggid, plural **maggidim.** The literal meaning of this Hebrew word, 'teller, narrator,' is found in two uses: (1) in the Passover haggadah, as the fifth step of the seder service, signaling the celebrator of the seder to begin narrating the story of the exodus from Egypt, and (2) in the phrase ***maggid***

shiur, literally, 'teller of (the) lesson,' referring to a scholar who gives a regular lecture or lesson (*shiur*) in the Talmud, usually to lay people. But the word is more commonly used in the sense of a traveling preacher or *darshan* (see **derasha**) who in former times delivered popular sermons laced with stories and parables. Among the Hasidic maggidim, the most famous was the Mezritscher Maggid (Dov Ber, c.1710–1772), the successor of the Baal Shem Tov; among the Lithuanian misnagdim (opponents of Hasidism) the best known was the Dubno Maggid (Yaakov Krantz, 1741–1804). In kabbalah, the term *maggid* refers to an angel or spirit that reveals deep secrets to a kabbalist in a dream or while he is engaged in study or writing. The most celebrated kabbalistic maggid was the one described by R. Yosef Caro (1488–1575), the author of the *Shulchan Aruch*, as a heavenly being that communicated with him through most of his adult life and even spoke through him in a voice not his own.

mamaliga. See under **food terms.**

mame-loshn. An informal name for the Yiddish language. To speak *mame-loshn* means to speak Yiddish. Though the term literally means 'mother tongue,' it is not equivalent to English *mother tongue,* 'a person's native language.' See **Yiddish.**

mamzer, plural **mamzerim.** A word commonly mistranslated in English as 'bastard,' which means the child of an unmarried mother. In Jewish law,

---

Mammon: the story of a word

This English word, meaning 'money or riches regarded as evil,' came into English about 1390 from the Septuagint, the Greek translation of the Bible. The Greek word was borrowed from Aramaic *mamon, mamona,* meaning 'money, wealth,' which is a word commonly used in the Talmud in discussions of civil law or monetary matters (*dinei mamonos*). In the Middle Ages the word was often capitalized as *Mammon* to personify the devil of greed, a use popularized in the following passage in Milton's *Paradise Lost* (I. 678): "Mammon led them on, /Mammon, the least erected spirit that fell/ From Heaven, for even in Heaven his looks and thoughts/ Were always downward bent, admiring more/ The riches of Heaven's pavement, trodden gold,/ Than aught divine or holy else enjoyed/ In vision beatific."

the child of such a woman is not a mamzer. Yet many English dictionaries as well as Hebrew-English and Yiddish-English ones misleadingly define *mamzer* as 'bastard; illegitimate child.' In Jewish law, a mamzer (male) or *mamzeres* (female), is a child born of adultery or incest, i.e., from the union of a man with another man's wife, or the union of a man with any female blood relative or with the wife of any of his blood relatives. The English translation of Deuteronomy 23:3 as "A bastard shall not enter into the congregation of the Lord" is misleading; the translator should use the Hebrew word *mamzer* and add in parenthesis "(the offspring of a union forbidden by Jewish law)." This Biblical verse prohibits a mamzer or mamzeres from marrying a legitimate Jew, but it permits marrying another mamzer or mamzeres or a convert. A mamzer is not subject to any other liability, having, for example, the same rights to inheritance as any other heir as well as the right to hold any public office in the Jewish community. The colloquial Hebrew and Yiddish meaning of *mamzer*, 'a devilishly clever or shrewd fellow; an impudent rascal,' is mostly used playfully and does not have the insulting and offensive connotation that English "bastard" has.

maris ayin. See under **halachic terms.**

marranos. The forced Jewish converts to Christianity in medieval Spain and Portugal and their descendants have been called by various names, including the Hebrew ***anusim*** (literally, 'forced ones'), Spanish ***conversos*** ('converted ones'), Portuguese ***Critaos Novos*** ('New Christians'), Majorcan ***chuetas*** (either from *chuya*, 'pork' or from a diminutive of Catalan *Jueu*, 'Jew'), and most recently, ***crypto-Jews*** ('secret Jews'). The most widespread and common name has been ***marranos***, which in English documents is found as early as 1583. Though the name was scornful and derogatory, it was adopted by Jews as a badge of honor and is used even today neutrally, not only as a singular noun, usually capitalized (*Marrano*) but as an adjective ("Marrano poetry," "the Marrano diaspora").

The term *marrano* comes from Spanish, and was apparently a special use of Spanish *marrano*, 'pig, swine,' a word probably formed from Arabic *mahram*, meaning 'something forbidden' and the Spanish suffix *-ano*. Originally the epithet may have been used in reference to the Jewish and Moorish (Muslim) prohibition against eating pork or ham; later, it came to be used as a term of abuse and disparagement, much as the word for swine has long been used in German, English, and other languages as a popular term of disparagement.

Nevertheless, a number of other etymologies have been proposed for *marrano* as applied to forcibly converted Jews and Muslims. Among the best known ones are: Arabic *mura'in*, 'deceiver,' Hebrew *mumar* 'apostate' + Spanish *-ano*, Arabic *barrani*, 'foreigner,' and ecclesiastical Latin *(anathema) maranatha*, an invocation against evil based on I Corinthians 16:22.

That the term was an insulting use of the Spanish word for swine is corroborated by the fact that two other names applied to converted Jews in Spain and in nearby Majorca were similar terms of abuse. The Majorcan *chuetas* was long applied to the crypto-Jews, and though its use was officially banned in 1782, it continued to be used well into the 20th century. The other term of abuse applied to the crypto-Jews was *alboraycos*, a name believed to be derived from *Al-Buraq*, the Arabic name of the fantastic animal that, according to Islamic tradition, carried Muhammad, the founder of Islam, to heaven. This animal was a hybrid with a mare's body and a woman's head. Similarly, many regarded the converted Jews as hybrid creatures, part Jewish and part Christian, and therefore neither Jews nor Christians.

Of the various terms used to designate the so-called marranos, the most neutral and therefore preferred one is *crypto-Jews*. All the others have unfavorable connotations. Despite the widespread acceptance of *marranos*, the stigma of its historically pejorative use, plus the fact that it was applied to converted Muslims as well as Jews, makes it inappropriate if not uncceptable. *New Christians* also includes both converted Jews and converted Muslims and does not distinguish between those converts who abandoned Judaism and those who continued to practice Judaism secretly. And *conversos* emphasizes the conversion of the Jews to Christianity without indicating or implying the forced nature of the conversion or the secret allegiance of the forced converts to their Jewish heritage.

mashgiach. See **kosher.**

mashiach. See **moshiach.**

maskil, plural **maskilim.** Any of the European Jewish intellectuals who belonged to the Haskalah (Jewish Enlightenment) movement of the 18th and 19th centuries. The maskilim emphasized modern scholarship, secular studies, and religious reform. They were bitterly opposed by Orthodox leaders and the term *maskil* retained a disparaging connotation in traditional Jewish circles until the early twentieth century. From Hebrew, literally, 'enlightened, understanding, or wise person,' from the root of *sechel*, 'reason, intellect, understanding, wisdom.' The term *maskil* is found in the introductory verse of thirteen of the Psalms (e.g., Psalms 32, 42, 52), and according to the Gemara (*Pesachim 117a*) the word indicates that the psalm was expounded by a *meturgeman*, an interpreter, who, judging by the use of the term *maskil* to describe him, was an erudite or wise person. It is not certain who first applied the term to an adherent of the Haskalah, but since both *maskil* and *Haskalah* sprang from the same root, *skl*, the likelihood is that both words were introduced at the same time. The adjective is **maskilic.**

Masorah. The body of knowledge concerned with the exact and proper spelling, pronunciation, cantillation, and arrangement of the text of the Torah. In a narrower sense, a *Masorah* means a traditional or accepted text in the Torah. The **Masoretes** were the scholars (preceded by the **Sopherim** or **Scribes**) who developed the Mesorah from the 6th to the 10th centuries C.E. A **Masoretic text** includes vowel signs, diacritical marks, accentuation signs, grammatical notations, and orthographic devices such as crowns and tittles on the letters (*tagin*). From Hebrew, literally, 'a handing down, transmission,' derived from *masar*, 'to hand over, transmit.'

A synonym of *Masorah* is **Masoret,** which also means 'tradition.'

Masorti. The name by which Conservative Jews call themselves in Israel. Examples of usage are: *the Masorti movement, Masorti congregations. That kibbutz is Masorti.* From Hebrew *masorti*, 'traditional,' derived from *masoret*, 'tradition.'

maven or **mavin.** A Yiddish-origin word meaning 'an expert or connoisseur, a person who is knowledgeable in a particular field.' *Maven* or *mavin* is often used with a modifying noun, as in *a wine maven, a food maven*, and *a computer mavin*. The word became popular in general English in the mid-1960s through television commercials for Vita Herring that featured a "herring maven." It was further popularized by the journalist William Safire, who called himself a "language maven" and entitled two of his books *Language Maven Strikes Again* (1990) and *Quoth the Maven* (1993). The word came from Yiddish *meyvn* (plural *meyvinim*). In Yiddish the word does not so much mean 'an expert' as 'a good judge of ' and is normally used without a modifier, as in *a meyvn af doktoyrim*, 'a good judge of doctors.' The Yiddish word derives from Hebrew *mevin*, literally, 'one who understands.'

mayofesnik or **mayofes.** A pair of Yiddish-origin terms used pejoratively to describe a Jew lacking in dignity and pride, especially one who is given to servile flattery of gentiles. The terms are derived from the Ashkenazi Hebrew phrase *ma yofis*, literally, 'how beautiful,' the title and initial phrase of one of the Sabbath songs (*zemiros*) sung on Friday night. The song is based on a verse in the *Song of Songs (7:8)* that begins with the words: *ma yofis uma noamt*, "How beautiful and how pleasant," the phrase suggesting unctuous flattery. According to legend, the Sabbath song *ma yofis* was sung with a special melody by Polish Jews, and the nobles they worked for would often request that the Jews sing *ma yofis* for their entertainment; hence "to sing *ma yofis*" to a gentile came to mean to serve him obsequiously or slavishly.

mazel. The common Jewish word for 'fortune, luck,' from Yiddish *mazl* and Hebrew *mazzal.* The word is often used informally in the sense of 'good luck,' as in such phrases as "You got to have mazel," "It should go with mazel!" "Some people just don't have any mazel." The phrase *mazel tov!* (literally, 'good luck!') uses the word in the formal sense of 'fortune, luck.' (See **congratulatory terms.**) The basic meaning of the word is 'a group of stars, a constellation.' It appears only once in the Bible, in *II Kings 23:5,* in the plural form and in connection with idol worship: "He [King Josiah] also dismissed . . . those who burned offerings to the Baal, to the sun and to the moon and to the constellations [*mazzolos*] and to all the heavenly hosts." The word also appears in a variant form in *Job 38:32*: "Did you ever take out the constellations [*mazzoros*] in their times. . . ?" Through the influence of astrology, the term came to be associated with a person's fate, and hence his good or bad fortune. But the Gemara *(Shabbos 157a,b),* after citing various opinions concerning the influence of the constellations on the fate of individuals, concludes that *eyn mazzal leyisrael*, "Israel is immune from the influence of constellations." And Maimonides, in the *Mishneh Torah* (Laws of Idolatry 11:8, 16), strongly condemns astrological beliefs as falsehoods and superstitions. Today's use of the term *mazel* no longer implies any astrological belief but is simply a formula for wishing someone well.

mazuma. See **mezumen.**

mechitza or **mechitzah.** A dividing wall or partition separating the women from the men in the synagogue during prayers. This division was based on the practice in the Holy Temple (as described in the tractate *Sukkah 51a,b*), where a balcony for women was built over the men's section to prevent frivolity resulting from mixing of the sexes. The Biblical support for the separation of men and women in public worship and the like is a verse in

Zechariah 12:12–14 describing such a separation in the future Messianic Age. Mechitzas were integral parts of synagogues until the 19th century, when liberal Jews in western Europe and later in the United States questioned or opposed their need. As a result, a series of decisions by leading Orthodox authorities established halachic parameters for constructing and maintaining mechitzas. The most influential rulings are those of Rabbi Moshe Feinstein (*Igros Moshe, Orach Chaim 1:39, 3:23–24, 4:30–32*), which maintain that the separation of men and women during public prayers is Biblically ordained, that a properly constructed mechitza serves that purpose, and that a mechitza, to be considered valid, must be at least 66 inches in height or, under extenuating circumstances, 60 inches high between the men's and the women's sections. Temporary mechitzas are often erected among Orthodox Jews at public functions such as weddings and melave malkas. See also **mixed.**

mechuten, plural **mechutonim.** The father-in-law of one's daughter or son. There is no equivalent term in formal English, although informally, the parents of a son-in-law or daughter-in-law are often called *in-laws.* Loosely, the term *mechuten* is applied to any relative by marriage, and, informally, to anyone pretending familiarity. From Yiddish *mekhutn*, derived from Hebrew *mechutan*, from *chatan*, 'bridegroom, son-in-law.' The Yiddish-origin feminine is **mechuteneste.**

megillah. The Biblical Book of Esther, read in the synagogue on Purim. The word is a short form of its Hebrew name, *megillas ester*, 'Scroll of Esther.' From Yiddish *megile* and Hebrew *megillah*, literally, 'scroll,' since the Book of Esther is read from a parchment scroll. Traditionally "the Five Megillahs" are *The Song of Songs* (read on Pesach), *Ruth* (read on Shavuos), *Lamentations* (read on Tisha B'Av), *Ecclesiastes* (read on Sukkos), and *Esther.* Another ancient text called Megillah that is not included in the Bible but described in the Talmud (*Shabbos 13b*) is *Megillas Taanis*, 'Scroll of Fasting,' which enumerates all the joyful events in Jewish history on which mourning and fasting is forbidden. In Yiddish, the word *megile* came to mean popularly a long letter or any long document, i.e., as long as the Scroll of Esther. Especially common in Yiddish is the phrase *a gantse megile*, 'a whole megillah,' meaning anything tiresomely long and complicated. The word *megillah* and the phrase *a whole megillah* became part of American English slang in the 1950s, thereafter undergoing several changes in meaning. In the 1970s, *the whole megillah* came to mean 'the whole thing, everything,' as in "We took in all the shows, the whole megillah." In the 1990s, the slang word took on the additional meaning of something very great or sensational, usually in the phrase *big megillah*, as in "If the World Series is the big megillah of baseball, the Olympics is the biggest megillah of sports."

melamed, plural **melamdim.** A teacher in a **cheder,** or traditional elementary religious school for boys. From Yiddish, derived from Hebrew *melammed,* related to **lamdan** and **limud.**

melave malka. A festive meal celebrating the conclusion of the Sabbath. From Hebrew *melavve malka,* literally, 'escorting the queen (Sabbath).' The custom is based on the Talmudic statement (*Shabbos 119b*) of R. Chanina that one should always set his table on the conclusion of the Sabbath even to consume as much as an olive, a custom observed more lavishly by R. Abbahu, for whom a calf was prepared at the conclusion of the Sabbath. The meal is also called *seudoso dedovid malko* (Aramaic for 'King David's feast'), so called from the festive dinner held by King David every Staturday night to celebrate his living another week, since it was ordained from heaven that he should die on a Sabbath (*Shabbos 30a*). The custom of having or attending a melave malka is established chiefly among Hasidim, especially as an occasion to gather informally with their rebbes. Other Orthodox Jews observe it only occasionally, and mainly as a community or social gathering to honor someone, as a fundraising event, or to celebrate an anniversary or similar event.

meldados. A Judezmo term for the reading or study of sacred texts. From **meldar,** 'to read (a sacred text)'; probably from Vulgar Latin *melodar,* from *melodus* 'religious song.'

mellah. A Jewish quarter or ghetto in a city or town in North Africa. The first mellah was established in Fez, Morocco, about 1348. Another mellah was established in Marrakesh in 1557, and others were formed in the 19th century. The origin of the word is uncertain; it may come from a dialect of Berber or Arabic.

Menachem Av. A traditional name of the month of **Av,** from Hebrew, literally, 'Comforter of Av,' in allusion to the consolation sought during the month in which both Temples were destroyed.

menahel. See under **Israeli terms.**

menorah. The seven-branched candelabrum in the Tabernacle (*Exodus 25:31–40*) and in the Temple (*II Chronicles 13:11*). In common usage, the term is often applied to the eight-branched candelabrum used on Chanukah, but a preferred term is *Chanukah menorah* or **Chanukiyah.** Since the seven-branched menorah was one of the sacred vessels used in the Tabernacle or Mishkan, replicating it is prohibited by law (*Shulchan Aruch Yoreh Deah 141:8*). It is, however, frequently represented in Jewish art and artifacts, especially as a symbol of Judaism. Compare **Magen David.** The Hebrew word means literally 'candleholder' and derives from Hebrew *ner*, 'candle, lamp.'

mensch. A Yiddish-origin word used in English in the sense of 'a decent, humane person, a good human being,' as in *I couldn't repay the loan, but he was a real mensch about it and let me off the hook.* The Yiddish word *mentsh* means 'a human being, person,' but in certain phrases it implies decency and humaneness (as in *zayn a mentsh*, 'to behave properly, act decently,' *vern a mentsh*, 'become a mature person'), and phrases like these influenced the English usage. The English spelling was adopted from German *Mensch*, whose meaning is identical with that of Yiddish *mentsh*; both words came from the same Germanic root as English *man*, which originally also meant 'a human being, person' and only in the Middle English period did it take on the meaning of a male adult person. **Mensch** has no plural in English. The Yiddish plural, **mentshn**, means 'human beings, people.'

meshuga, meshugas, meshugener. See under **Yiddishisms.**

meshulach, plural **meshulochim.** A collector of funds for a yeshiva, kolel, or other religious institution. Meshulochim have existed since the time of the Babylonian Exile. In Europe, a meshulach was often an official appointed by a Jewish community to collect funds for needy institutions. A meshulach should not be confused with a **shaliach,** who is an emissary, agent, or representative charged with a mission. Both Hebrew words derive from the root *shalach*, 'to send.'

meshummad, plural **meshummadim.** A Jew who has converted to another religion; a Jewish convert or apostate. From Hebrew, derived from *shemad*, 'conversion, apostasy.' The Yiddish form is **meshumed** (plural **meshumodim**). Compare **mumar.**

mesivta. A Jewish Aramaic word corresponding to the Hebrew-origin **yeshiva.** Both words mean literally 'sitting, session, seat.' The term *mesivta* in the sense of a Jewish college or academy, or its sessions, occurs in the

Gemara *(Gittin 6a, Bava Kama 117a,* and other places). *Resh mesivta* (often abbreviated as *ram*) is the Aramaic equivalent of a *rosh yeshiva,* literally, 'head of a yeshiva.' Both terms designate any member of the faculty of a yeshiva. In current usage, a *mesivta* usually means a yeshiva high school.

Messiah. See **Moshiach.**

meturgeman. An interpreter or translator who in ancient times rendered the Torah reading at services in the vernacular, such as Aramaic or Greek, verse by verse. From Jewish Aramaic, derived from *tirgem,* 'to explain, interpret, translate.' See **Targum.**

metzora. The Biblical term for a person afflicted with a **tzoraas,** any of various skin diseases contracted as punishment for personal vices, especially talebearing and slander *(Leviticus 13–14).* The widespread translation of this term as 'leper' and *tzoraas* as 'leprosy' is inappropriate and misleading, if for no other reason than the fact that leprosy is a bacterial disease successfully treated medically, whereas the Biblical affliction is a spiritual one that renders a person impure until he undergoes a purification process and is declared pure by a kohen. These two are some of the Hebrew terms in the Bible (other terms are **kohen** and **zav**) that are untranslatable in any language and should therefore be left without translation. It is quite possible to define or explain the Hebrew terms without attempting to replace them with other, unsuitable, terms from a different language.

mezumen. A Yiddish-origin word for ready money, cash, derived from Hebrew *mezumman,* 'ready, prepared.' In Ashkenazi usage, the term is also used to designate a group of three or more adult males who join together to recite the after-meal blessings, often in the phrase *to bentsh mezumen* (see **bentsh).** The Hebrew-origin term for such a combination of three or more is a **zimmun.** In the sense of ready money or cash, the Yiddish word came into colloquial English around 1900 in the form **mazuma,** a word still used in American slang and to some extent in British slang. Variant forms of the slang word have included *mazoom, mazoola, and mazoo,* but *mazuma* is the commonest form and is also used sometimes in the sense of 'a dollar,' as in *He borrowed from me ten mazumas.*

mezuzah or **mezuza.** The plural is **mezuzahs** or **mezuzas** or *(Ashkenazi)* **mezuzos,** *(Sephardi)* **mezuzot.** A parchment scroll on which a scribe has written in Hebrew the passages from Deuteronomy 6:4–9 *(Shema)* and

11:13–21(*Vehayah*) and that is usually placed in a small metal or wooden case and attached to the upper right-hand doorpost of every room in the house where people live, eat, or sleep. No mezuzah is affixed to a bathroom. The practice of wearing a miniature replica of a mezuzah on a chain as a good-luck charm or amulet began during World War II and is still popular, but has no basis in Jewish custom or law. See also **bendel** and **chai.** From Hebrew, literally, 'doorpost.'

Midrash. The body of rabbinic literature that interprets Biblical passages to explain and elaborate on teachings of the Oral Law. The Midrash comprises both aggadic and halachic teachings. *A midrash* (plural *midrashim*) is any part or passage of the Midrash, especially an aggadic part (see **aggadah**). Literally, Hebrew *midrash* means 'study, investigation,' and derives from the verb *darash,* 'to seek, investigate'; also, 'to interpret, explain, lecture.' The adjective is **midrashic.** The Yiddish form of the word is **medresh.** A *beis midrash* (Yiddish *besmedresh*) is a house of Torah learning and discourse. See also **derasha.**

mikveh or **mikve.** This is the Yiddish- and Hebrew-origin word for a communal pool or bath used for ritual immersion, as by brides before marriage, women after menstruation or childbirth, converts, or any ritually impure person or vessel requiring purification. In formal English the mikveh is often called a *ritual bath, ritual pool,* or *ritualarium* (a term coined in the 1930s on the model of *aquarium*). A very common spelling is *mikva* or *mikvah,* formed on the pattern of other Hebrew-origin words ending in –*a(h),* such as *Chanuka(h), mitzva(h), aliya(h).* Though there is a related Hebrew word *mikvah,* meaning any body of water, pool, or reservoir, the standard Hebrew word for a ritual bath is *mikveh,* as it is in Yiddish. The Mishnaic tractate that deals with this subject (*Mikvaos 1:7, 2:2, ff.*) invariably uses the form *mikveh,* which derives from the Biblical use (*Leviticus 11:36*) and which reflects the pronunciation of the word in Hebrew. The recommended English spelling of this word is therefore *mikveh* (or the variant *mikve*).

milah. The act of circumcision, or cutting of the foreskin of a male child on the eighth day after birth (*Genesis 17:10–15*). The ceremony or ritual of circumcision is called *bris milah,* usually shortened to *bris.* (See **bris** or **brit.**) Technically, the *milah* is only the first step in the ritual. The next step is removal of the foreskin and uncovering the glans (*peria*). The third and final step is the stanching of blood by oral suction (*metsitsa*). From Hebrew, derived from the verb *mal, mul,* 'to circumcise.' See **mohel.**

milchig. (of food) made of milk or dairy products; (of utensils) used only for milk or dairy products. From Yiddish *milkhik*, literally, 'of milk,' from *milkh*, 'milk.' Compare **fleishig** and **pareve**. See **kashrus**.

min, plural **minim**. A term used in the Talmud and Midrash for a Jewish heretic or sectarian. The *birkas haminim* ("blessing against the heretics") is the twelth in the shemone-esrei (amidah) and was originally inserted by the tanna and Nasi Rabban Gamliel of Yavneh (80–110 C.E.) to counteract the influence of Jewish sectarians such as the Sadducees and the Jewish Christians of that time. Its present wording, *velamalshinim*, 'And for the slanderers,' was a substitution for *velaminim*, 'And for the heretics,' to avoid the threat of Christian censorship. From Hebrew, of uncertain origin; possibly a transferred or euphemistic use of Hebrew *min*, 'kind, sort, species.' Compare **apikores**.

minchah. See under **ritual terms**.

minhag, plural **minhagim**. A Jewish religious custom or practice, typically one that is not halachically required but has through long usage taken on the force of law in a community. The broadest difference in minhagim is between the Ashkenazi and Sephardi communities, especially as exemplified in their different versions of the prayers (see **nusach).** Two examples of minhagim, both observed on Shavuos, are decorating the synagogue with plants and eating at least one dairy meal. From Hebrew, derived from the verb *nahag*, 'to be accustomed, be in use,' literally, 'to lead, conduct.' The Yiddish reflex of the Hebrew is *min(h)eg*, plural *minhogim.*

minyan, plural **minyanim**. The minimum of ten male adult Jews required to form a congregation and hence to perform any ritual designated as holy, such as public prayers, the reading of the Torah scroll, or the recital of the kaddish at a burial. It also means any group of ten or more Jews that meets this requirement, as in the phrases *to daven with a minyan, to attend the daily minyan in shul, to bentsh with a minyan*. From Hebrew, literally, 'number,' derived from the verb *mana*, 'to count, reckon.' The Yiddish reflex of the Hebrew is *minyen*, plural *minyonim.*

mishmar, plural **mishmaros**. Any of twenty-four groups of kohanim or Levites who were on watch in the Temple approximately twice a year. Each mishmar was assisted by a group of Israelites called a **maamad**[1]. Another meaning of *mishmar* developed in yeshivas of the Diaspora (originally in Europe), where the word came to mean a regimen of learning Talmud late into the night once a week, usually Thursdays. From Hebrew, literally, 'watch, guard,' derived from the verb *shamar*, 'to guard, watch.'

Mishnah or **Mishna.** The body of oral laws expounded by the tannaim and forming the basis of the Talmud. It was compiled by R. Yehuda HaNasi in the 200s C.E., is written in Rabbinic (*"Mishnaic"*) Hebrew, and consists of six orders (see **Shas**) divided into 63 tractates. A chapter or section of the Mishnah or of a Mishnaic tractate is called *a mishnah* (plural *mishnayos*), and in common usage "to study mishnayos" (from Yiddish *lernen mishnayes*) means to study the Mishnah or a particular tractate of the Mishnah. From Hebrew, literally, 'study, teaching,' derived from the verb *shana*, to 'study, teach.' Compare **Gemara.**

Misnaged or **Mitnaged,** plural **Misnagdim** or **Mitnagdim.** The name given by Hasidim to their opponents within Orthodoxy, chiefly the traditionalists of Lithuania who accused Hasidim of heretical practices in the mid-1700s and, led by the Vilna Gaon, placed them under a ban of excommunication. The struggle between the Hasidim and the Misnagdim did not abate until the late 1800s, when both factions had to confront the threat of modernism brought on by the Haskalah (Jewish Enlightenment) movement. Since the differences between Hasidic and traditional Orthodox practices are no longer questioned, the term *Misnaged* has become a neutral term applied to any religious Jew who is not a Hasid. Thus, to be **Misnagdic** (or **Mitnagdic**) is to follow the customs or rites of non-Hasidic Ashkenazim. From Yiddish and Hebrew, literally, 'opponent,' derived from the Hebrew verb *nagad*, 'to be against, oppose.' Also spelled **Misnagid** or **Mitnagid.**

mitzvah or **mitzva,** plural **mitzvos** or **mitzvot.** Any religious precept or commandment, especially any of the *taryag mitzvos*, or 613 commandments of the Torah enumerated by the Sages (e.g., *Makkos 23b-24a*). Broadly, the word is used to mean a meritorious or benevolent act, a good deed, as in *A kind person does many mitzvos.* From Hebrew, literally, 'commandment,' derived from the root *tsav*, 'command, order.'

mixed. This adjective is specialized in Jewish usage in the following ways: (1) in the phrase *mixed marriage*, which is a marriage occurring between a Jew and a non-Jew, i.e., an instance of intermarriage. Humorously, the phrase is applied to the marriage of a Jewish couple from markedly different backgrounds (e.g., Hasidic and non-Hasidic, Lithuanian and Polish, observant and non-observant). (2) in the phrases *mixed seating, mixed bathing* or *swimming*, and *mixed dancing*, meaning that there is a public mixing of the sexes, with men and women sitting together, as at synagogue services or at a wedding; or bathing or swimming together in a pool or at the beach; or dancing together socially as couples. (3) in the phrase *mixed kinds* or *species*, referring to different kinds of seeds or trees planted or grafted together, different species of animals yoked together, and fabrics containing wool and linen mixed together, all of which are prohibited as *kilayim* or *shaatnez* (*Leviticus 19:19, Deuteronomy 22:10–11*).

mizrach. The eastern wall within a Jewish home or a synagogue, which Jews face while reciting the prescribed prayers, especially the principal prayer of *shemone-esrei.* In most synagogues, the *aron kodesh* or holy ark containing the Torah scrolls is situated at the eastern wall, the east representing the direction of Jerusalem, where the Temple stood. A *mizrach* is also the name of a picture or painting placed on the east wall of a home or of a synagogue or chapel to mark the direction of prayer. This type of picture or painting often bears biblical or kabbalistic symbols or a legend in Hebrew from the Psalms, such as "From the rising of the sun to its setting, the Lord's Name be praised" (*Psalms 113:3*). From Hebrew, literally, 'east.'

mohel, plural **mohels** or **mohalim.** The individual who performs a circumcision or **bris milah** by cutting and removing an infant's foreskin according to the prescribed ritual. See **milah.** From Hebrew, derived from the same verb as *milah.*

Moshiach or **Mashiach.** The name, title, or designation of a descendant of King David (*Moshiach ben Dovid*), who, according to the Sages (e.g., *Sukkah 52a*) will appear someday to redeem the Jewish people from exile and rule over them as king. Since his appearance will be preceded by another Moshiach descended from Joseph (*Moshiach ben Yosef*), who will die in the victorious war against Gog and Magog, the Midrash uses the plural **Meshichim** for the two Moshiachs. The standard English name **Messiah** is used by Jews in formal contexts, especially in writing, though colloquially *Moshiach* or *Mashiach* is the preferred name, particularly since a phrase like *the Messiah* is used by Christians to refer to Jesus. (Jesus's designation as "the Christ" is synonymous with "the Messiah," since *Christ* derives from Greek *Christos*, which was the Septuagint's translation of Hebrew *mashiach*, 'the anointed.') The form *Messiah* was introduced into English in the Geneva Bible (an English Bible published in 1560 in Geneva), as an alteration of the earlier, Greek-origin *Messias* in order to make the word resemble the Hebrew *mashiach.* The Hebrew word means literally 'the anointed (one),' derived from the verb *mashach*, 'to anoint,' since Jewish kings were anointed (*I Samuel 15:17, I Kings 1:39*).

motz(o)e. See **erev**.

mourning terms. Among the Jewish terms dealing with death and mourning, the best-known ones are **kaddish, shivah,** and **yahrzeit,** which require more than a simple definition and are therefore found separately in this book as main entries. In terms of usage, the ones listed below require little explanation beyond a gloss or definition. Unless otherwise indicated, all the terms come from Hebrew or Yiddish.

aron, plural *aronos.* A coffin or casket, traditionally a plain pine box. Literally, 'ark.'

avel, plural *avelim.* A person who formally mourns the death of a close relative; a mourner. See *avelus.*

avelus or *avelut.* Also spelled *aveilus* or *aveilut.* The period or process of formal mourning, especially the period of eleven months at which kaddish is recited after the death of parents and of thirty days after the death of other close relatives.

bes olam or *bes almin.* A Jewish cemetery or graveyard. Literally, 'house of eternity.'

chevra kadisha. A voluntary society whose members prepare the dead for burial. Literally, 'holy fellowship.'

El moleh rachamim. 'God, full of compassion,' opening words of a prayer for the dead.

goses or *gosses.* A person who is dying. Jewish law forbids touching or moving a goses lest the action hastens the moribund person's death.

hashkavah or *hashkava.* A prayer for the repose of deceased relatives, recited by Sephardim at a funeral or in the synagogue. Literally, 'lying down.'

hazkarah or *hazkara.* A memorial service or prayer for the dead. In Yiddish, *haskore.*

hazkoras neshomos. Same as *yizkor.* Literally, 'memorial prayer for souls (of the dead).'

hesped. A eulogy for the dead; a funeral oration.

kaddish. See the main entry.

keriah or *keria.* The formal rending of one's clothes as a sign of mourning upon the death of one's father, mother, brother, sister, daughter, son, husband, or wife. For parents, the clothing is torn on the left side, over the heart; for other relatives, it is torn on the right side. According to the Rabbis (*Moed Katan 26a*), *keriah* is also performed on the death of one's teacher of Torah, on hearing evil news or God's name blasphemed, when a scroll of the Torah has been burned, and at the sight of the remains of the Holy Temple.

kever, plural *kevorim.* A Jewish grave or tomb.

kever avos. The grave of parent. "To go on *kever avos*" is to visit one's parents' graves.

kevurah or *kevura.* The act or ceremony of burying the dead; burial or interment.

kittel. See the main entry.

levayah or *levaya.* A funeral. Literally, 'accompaniment (of the dead), escort.'

maamados. Halts made every four cubits or several times during the funeral procession at the graveside to recite passages from the Psalms. Plural of *maamad*, 'standing, halting.'

matzevah or *matzeva*, plural *matzevos.* An engraved stone monument erected on the site of a grave as a memorial to the deceased. See *unveiling.*

nichum avelim. The custom of comforting mourners during the first seven days of mourning (*shivah*). Literally, 'consolation of mourners.' The traditional verb phrase among Ashkenazim is *to be menachem avel*, 'to console mourners during the shiva' (translated from Yiddish *menakhem-ovl zayn*). In colloquial Jewish English, the custom of nichum avelim is expressed in the phrase *to make* (or *pay*) *a shivah call.*

nifter or *niftar*, plural *niftorim* or *niftarim.* One who has died; the deceased person.

ohel. A large tomb; a mausoleum. From Hebrew, literally 'tent.'

onen, plural *onenim.* A mourner on the day of death or before the burial. An onen is exempt from all religious duties until after the funeral.

petirah or *petira.* Death; demise. Literally, 'departure.'

rechitza. Sephardic term for the *taharah.* Literally 'washing.'

sargenes. A Sephardi term for burial shrouds. Of Loez origin (compare Old French *sarge*, 'a kind of ridged cloth,' the source of English *serge*). Compare *tachrichim.*

seudas havraah. A meal prepared by friends for mourners returning from a funeral, traditionally a simple meal of round cakes and peeled hard-boiled eggs. Literally, 'meal of recovery.'

sheloshim. The first thirty days of mourning, after which certain restrictions are eased. Literally, 'thirty.'

shemirah or *shemira.* A vigil kept over the deceased before burial, usually by a member of a chevra kadisha. Literally, 'watch, guard, vigil.'

shivah or *shiva.* See the main entry.

shomer, plural *shomrim.* A person who keeps *shemirah* or vigil over the deceased before burial. Literally, 'watchman, guard.' The feminine form is *shomeres,* plural *shomros.*

shurah or *shura.* A row formed by ten or more men facing each other, through which the mourners pass immediately after the burial. Literally, 'row.'

tachrichim. The shrouds in which a deceased person is buried, consisting of a white linen garment or a *kittel* sewed together with long stitches. Plural of Hebrew *tachrich,* 'robe, cloak.' Compare *sargenes.*

taharah or *tahara.* The ritual washing of the deceased's body before dressing it in shrouds, usually performed by members of a chevra kadisha. Literally, 'purification.'

tzidduk hadin. A prayer consisting of a selection of Biblical passages of consolation and acceptance of the Divine decree, recited at graveside before burial. Literally, 'justification of the Divine decree.'

unveiling. A custom among modern Ashkenazi Jews, especially in the United States and Canada, of having a mourner pull off a veil from a tombstone on the day of its dedication as part of the dedication ceremony. The dedication ceremony is also called an *unveiling.*

viddui. A formal confession made before death, the full prescribed form including an admission of guilt for wrongdoing and a prayer for atonement. Literally, 'confession.'

yahrzeit. See the main entry.

yizkor. A memorial prayer or service for the dead, recited by Ashkenazim on the last days of the festivals of Sukkos, Pesach, and Shavuos, and on Yom Kippur. Literally, 'may He remember,' the first words of the prayer. Also called *hazkoras neshomos.* Compare *hashkavah.*

muktzeh or **muktze.** The rabbinical prohibition against moving or handling on the Sabbath or holidays any object whose normal use involves weekday work or activity. The major categories of muktzeh include objects such as money, tools, and merchandise; objects not prepared for use on the Sabbath or holiday, such as pieces of rock or stone; dirty or repulsive objects that are usually avoided; newly formed or created objects, such as an egg laid on the Sabbath or holiday (a category called *nolad,* 'born'); and any object that serves as a base or support for a forbidden object. From Hebrew *muktzeh,* literally, 'set apart or excluded' (from Sabbath or holiday use). The term is used chiefly as an adjective, as in *Pens and pencils are muktzeh on Shabbos.*

mumar, plural **mumarim.** A Jew who has changed his religion but is not as complete an apostate as a **meshummad.** There are several categories of mumarim: one who rejects the entire Torah; one who rejects one precept only, as by publicly desecrating the Sabbath; one who breaks the law out of spite or rebelliousness; one who breaks the law to satisfy his appetite, as by choosing to eat non-kosher food; and one who becomes an idolater. The Talmud discusses at length the various types of mumarim (see *Eruvin 69a,b; Chulin 5a; Avodah Zarah 26b*). From Hebrew, derived from the verb *hemir,* 'to change.'

musaf. See under **ritual terms.**

musar or **mussar.** Jewish religious ethics as a subject of study and instruction; the study or teaching of the ethical and moral behavior required of a Jew. The term appears in the Bible (e.g., *Jeremiah 2:30, Proverbs 1:2–3,8*) in the sense of 'discipline, chastisement, reproof, rebuke,' a meaning still extant in such phrases as *to give musar* and (in Yiddish) *zogn muser,* both meaning 'to lecture (someone), scold.' Though ethical teachings are found in the Mishnah, notably in tractate *Avos* ("Ethics of the Fathers"), it was with the appearance of pietistic and moralistic books (Yiddish *muser-sforim*) during the Middle Ages that the term *musar* took on the meaning of "religious instruction in ethics and morality." Among the early classics of *musar* are *Chovos HaLevovos* ("Duties of the Heart"), by the 11th-century scholar Rabenu Bachya, *Shaarei Teshuvah* ("Gates of Repentance") by Jonah ben Abraham Gerondi (1200–1263), and the introductory *Shemono Perokim* ("Eight Chapters") of Maimonides to his commentary on *Avos.* Later influential works of Jewish ethics include the *Shenei Luchos Habris* ("Two Tablets of the Covenant") by the kabbalist Isaiah Horowitz (c. 1565–1630), known as the *Sheloh* (from the first letters of his work's title), and the *Mesilas Yeshorim* ("Path of the Just") by the Italian kabbalist and poet Moshe Chayim Luzzatto (1707–1746).

A modern *musar* movement was started in the mid-1800s by Rabbi Israel Salanter (1810–1883), who introduced into the yeshivas of Lithuania the practice of studying ethical works as part of the daily curriculum and of applying principles of ethics and morality to the students' everyday activities. In yeshivas such as Slobodka, Mir, Navahardok, and Telz (and after World War II in the successors of such yeshivas in the United States and Israel), the weekly *muser shmues* ("musar talk") by a *mashgiach ruchoni,* a spiritual supervisor or mentor, became a fixture of yeshiva life. A commonly used and neutral Yiddish name for adherents of the musar movement is *musernik.* Of the two schools of the movement, the moderate

Slobodka school became dominant, while the more psychology-oriented Navahardok school, which intruded deeply into the personal lives of students, remained a footnote (although an influential one) in the movement's history.

music and dance terms. Most of the terms in this group are of Ashkenazi origin and derive from Yiddish. The following is a selection of the commonest ones.

> **badchen,** plural **badchonim** or (Anglicized) **badchens, badchan.** An entertainer or master of ceremonies, especially at a wedding, who usually sings sentimental or moralistic rhymes improvised for the occasion and often leads in the dancing and singing. From Yiddish, derived from Hebrew *badchan,* 'jester, merrymaker,' from *badach,* 'merrymaking, jocular.' See *gramen* below.

> **broygez tantz.** A wedding dance (now almost obsolete) in which the groom dances with his father and father-in-law. Literally, 'angry dance'; so called from the supposed hostility between the groom's and the bride's father.

> **chalil,** plural, **chalilim** or (Anglicized) **chalils.** An Israeli flute or recorder. From Hebrew.

> **chazzan** or **chazan.** See the main entry.

> **flash tantz.** A wedding dance in which one or more men dance with a bottle balanced on the head. From Yiddish, literally, 'bottle dance.'

> **freylechs.** A cheerful tune. Also, a lively folk dance. From Yiddish *freylekhs,* derived from the adjective *freylekh* 'merry, cheerful.'

> **gramen.** Rhymes, often improvised and rendered with a catchy tune and a refrain, sung by a **badchen** or other type of entertainer at a festive occasion, as on Purim or at a wedding, and dealing usually with the occasion and its participants. From Yiddish, plural of *gram,* 'rhyme.'

> **hora.** An Israeli round dance of Romanian origin. From Hebrew, ultimately from Turkish.

> **kapelye.** A Jewish band or orchestra. From Yiddish, from German *Kapelle,* 'orchestra, choir,' from Italian *cappella,* 'choir, chapel,' derived from the same Medieval Latin word as English *chapel.*

> **kazatzke.** A lively dance of Cossack origin. From Yiddish, literally, 'Cossack's.'

> **klezmer.** See the main entry.

> **marshelik.** Another name for a **badchen.** From Yiddish, literally, 'jester,' of Slavic origin.

> **meshorer**, plural **meshorerim.** A cantor's assistant; member of a choir.

From Yiddish, derived from Hebrew, 'singer, poet,' ultimately from *shir*, 'song, poem.'

mitzvah tantz. A wedding dance in which men take turns dancing with the bride, each holding a handkerchief or napkin whose opposite end is held by the bride. From Yiddish, literally, 'mitzvah dance.'

niggun, plural *niggunim* or (Anglicized) *nigguns.* A melody or tune, especially a Hasidic one, sung without words. From Yiddish *nign* and Hebrew *niggun*, 'tune.'

sher. A kind of square dance with partners. From Yiddish, perhaps a transferred meaning of *sher*, 'pair of scissors,' from German *Schere.*

musmach. See **semicha.**

– N –

naches. This Yiddish-origin word, meaning 'pleasure, delight, satisfaction,' is used specifically in reference to children and grandchildren, and is found in such verb phrases as *have naches, get naches, give naches*, and *shep naches* (from Yiddish *shepn nakhes*, 'draw or derive naches'). The term is commonly used by well-wishers, as at a circumcision, bar mitzvah, or wedding (*Mazel Tov! May you have much naches from him!*). When used by parents or grandparents, it is often in a negative context (*I wish we could have more naches from him. She's not giving us all the naches we hoped for.*) As these examples show, the word implies an expectation of reward or recompense for the effort of having brought into the world and raised children or (by extension) grandchildren. Thus, even a positive statement is often couched in negative terms, as in *He was a terrible student in high school, but now, in colllege, thank God, he's finally giving us naches.* In a more general sense, *naches* can be obtained not only from offspring but also from other things on which one has spent time, money, and effort, such as a business venture or an investment. The phrase *yidishe naches*, meaning 'Jewish naches' and suggesting a higher, spiritual level of naches instead of the merely materialistic satisfaction implied in *naches* alone, is also often used in reference to children, especially among religious Ashkenazim. From Yiddish *nakhes*, derived from Hebrew *nachas*, literally, 'quiet, calm, tranquility.'

Nagid, plural **Negidim.** The title of the official head of the Egyptian Jewish community until the 16th century. Maimonides' son, Abraham, and his grandchildren bore the title of Negidim. A Nagid had various powers, as to impose taxes and punish wrongdoers. The office of the Nagid was abolished by the Turks. The title Nagid was also used in certain other Jewish communities, notably Moorish Spain. The scholar, statesman, and poet Samuel Hanagid (993–1055) was appointed Nagid by the caliph of Granada, Spain.

From Hebrew *nagid*, literally, 'governor, commander, leader.' The Yiddish form of the word, *noged*, means 'a very wealthy man.'

Nasi, plural **Nesiim.** A high-ranking title given in the Bible (*Numbers 7:2–78*) to the heads or leaders of the twelve tribes of Israel. The title is often translated as 'prince,' 'leader,' or 'chief.' Historically the term had various applications. According to the Mishnah (*Chagiga 2:2*), the Great Sanhedrin in the latter part of the Second Temple period was led by a Nasi, who presided over the court; he and the *av bet din* were called the *zugos*, or 'pairs.' After the destruction of the Temple, the Nasi became the official head of the Jewish community under the Romans, corresponding to the Exilarch in Babylonia. In the Diaspora, the title was often applied to the president of a Jewish community, and in the State of Israel, it became the title of the President. The Hebrew word means literally 'elevated one' and derives from *nasa*, 'to raise, lift.'

Nazir (plural **Nezirim**), **Nazirite,** or **Nazarite.** A man or woman (Hebrew *nazirah*) who has made a vow to abstain from wine and grapes, from cutting his or her hair, and from making contact with a corpse, including that of a close relative (*Numbers 6:2–21*). After completing the period of *nezirus* (*Naziriteship* or *Naziritehood*), which is usually thirty days (but could be lifelong), the nazir brings an appropriate sacrifice to the Temple.

The most famous Nazir was Samson (*Judges 13–16*). The Talmudic tractate *Nazir* deals with the laws pertaining to a Nazir or Nezirim. The form *Nazarite* should not be confused with *Nazarene*, a native of Nazareth (Jesus was called *the Nazarene*). From Hebrew, derived from the verb *nazar*, 'to abstain from, separate oneself from, withdraw.'

nebbish. See under **Yiddishisms.**

neder, plural **nedorim** or **nedarim.** A solemn vow or promise to do something or to abstain from doing something. The source is Biblical (*Numbers 30:2–17*) and the laws dealing with vows and their annulment are discussed in the Talmudic tractate *Nedarim.* The common expression *beli neder*, 'God willing,' means literally 'without (making) a vow.' The ceremony of *hatoras nedorim*, 'release from vows,' is performed prior to Rosh

Names: Jewish naming practices

1. *Double given names.* Among Ashkenazim, double given names of males consist usually of a sacred (Biblical) name and a corresponding vernacular name (*kinnui*). The two names may be equivalent in meaning, as *Tzvi Hirsh* (Hebrew and Yiddish, 'deer'), *Dov Ber* (Hebrew and Yiddish, 'bear'), *Asher Zelig* (Hebrew and German, 'happy'), *Boruch Bendit* (Hebrew and Loez, 'blessed'); or the vernacular name may derive from the sacred name, as *Yitzchok Isaac, Shlomo Zalmen, Shmuel Zanvil, Yisroel Iser*; or they may be traditionally related, as *Yehudah Aryeh* or *Yehudah Leyb* ('lion,' based on Genesis 49:9), *Naftali Hertz* ('deer,' based on Genesis 49:21), *Binyomin Zev* ('wolf,' based on Genesis 49:27); or they may be phonetically similar, as *Menachem Mendel, Abraham Abba, Noson Note*. Double given names are rarer among females and are open to any combination; for example, *Shifra Beyla* (Hebrew and Loez, 'beauty'), *Chaya Golda* (Hebrew and Yiddish, = Vivian Aurelia), *Zlata Charna* (Yiddish, from Salvic = Aurelia Catherina).

2. *Naming customs.* Among Ashkenazim, a newborn child may be named only after a deceased parent, grandparent, rabbi, etc., never after a living one. Among Sephardim, naming children after living grandparents is to honor them and an omen for the children's longevity. Among Yemenite Jews, it is customary to name a son after his living father, especially in a family where a child has died.

3. *Israeli given names.* Since the establishment of the State of Israel, it has become common to name children with nontraditional Hebrew names. Some examples of coined names are *Ahuva, Amichai, Batel, Benaya, Elad, Eliraz, Hadara, Hadas, Levona, Matan, Mayan, Meytal, Oz, Revaya, Saar, Tohar.*

4. *Acronyms.* The titles and names of many rabbis and Torah scholars have been often shortened by fusing their initial letters into pronounceable words. For example: *Radak* (R. David Kimchi), *Ralbag* (R. Levi ben Gershon), *Ritva* (R. Yom Tov ben Avraham), *Rosh* (Rabbenu Asher—R. Asher ben Yechiel), *Gra* (Gaon R. Eliyahu—the Vilna Gaon), *Maharal* (Morenu Harav Yehudah Loew), *Maharshal* (Morenu Harav Shlomo Luria). (See also **notarikon.)** Common usage favors prefixing an acronymic name with the article *the*, e.g., *the Rambam, the Rosh, the Maharal*. The traditional exception is the acronymic name of *Rashi* (R. Shelomo Yitzchaki), which is never preceded by *the*. Less commonly, though increasingly, the model of Rashi is followed and the article is dropped before the acronym, as in *Both Rambam and Raavad say . . . According to Rosh . . . Maharal holds*, etc.

5. *Book Names.* A uniquely Jewish practice is to call the authors of important halachic or ethical works by the names of their books. Thus, the famous halachist known as the *Chasam Sofer* is actually the name of his best-known work; his real name was R. Moshe Sofer (1762–1839). Other examples are the *Chazon Ish* (actual name, R. Avraham Yeshaya Karelitz, 1878–1953), the *Chofetz Chaim* (R. Yisrael Meir HaCohen, 1838–1933), the *Magen Avraham* (R. Avraham Gombiner, 1634–1682), the *Gur Aryeh* (R. Yehudah Lowe, 1526–1609, also known as the *Maharal*), the *Beis Yosef* (R. Yosef Caro, 1488–1575), and the *Tur* (R. Yaakov ben Asher, 1270–1340). Sometimes the authors are called by the *abbreviated* names of their books, as the *Bach* (abbreviation of *Bayis Chodosh*, by R. Yoel Sirkes, 1561–1640), the *Taz* (abbreviation of *Turey Zohov*, by R. David Halevi, 1586–1667), and the *Sheloh* (abbreviation of *Shenei Luchos Habris*, by R. Isaiah Horowitz, c.1565–1630).

Hashana (see **ritual terms**). Yom Kippur services open with *Kol Nidre,* 'all vows,' a public proclamation annulling all vows made to God during the preceding year. The Yiddish-origin verb *shnoder* (Yiddish *shnodern*), meaning 'to pledge a donation to the synagogue, to charity, etc.' comes from the Hebrew word *shenodar* in the phrase *baavur shenodar,* 'because he pledges' (an amount of money); this phrase is in the *misheberach* blessing for those who are called up to the Torah, *shenodar* coming from the verb *nodar,* 'to make a neder.'

Neolog or **Neologist.** The name of any of the Reform or liberal Jews in Hungary and Transylvania, especially before the end of World War II. The Neologs wanted Orthodox Jews to modernize along the lines of the Reform movement in Germany, as by replacing Hebrew and Yiddish with Hungarian in Jewish congregations. The ideology of the Neologs is called **Neology** or **Neologism.** From Hungarian *Neolog,* literally, 'new speech,' from *neo-* 'new' + *-log* 'speech' (from Greek *logos*).

Neo-Orthodoxy. The modern form of Orthodoxy introduced in Germany by R. Samson Raphael Hirsch (1808–1888) and Azriel Hildesheimer (1820–1899) to combat the Reform movement's successful assault on traditional Judaism in the first half of the 19th century. The **Neo-Orthodox** rabbis and leaders maintained the supremacy of the Torah while relating its teachings to the prevailing culture, as by allowing the study of science and other useful secular subjects. See also **derech eretz.**

ner tamid. See under **synagogue terms.**

Neviim. The Prophets (books of the Bible), usually divided into *Neviim Rishonim* (the "Early Prophets"), which include Joshua, Judges, and Samuel I and II, and *Neviim Acharonim* (the "Later Prophets"), which include Isaiah, Jeremiah, Ezekiel, and the twelve Minor Prophets (Hosea, Joel, Amos, Obadiah, Jonah, Micah, Nahum, Habakkuk, Zephaniah, Haggai, Zechariah, Malachi). See **Tanach.**

New Christian. Any of a group of crypto-Jews living in northern Portugal whose ancestors were forcibly converted during the Inquisition, and though outwardly Catholic, continued to secretly practice certain Jewish observances. The halachic status of New Christians and other crypto-Jews was for centuries a subject of debate among Jewish scholars. Translation of Portuguese *Critaos Novos.* See also **marranos.**

New Moon. A formal English name for Rosh Chodesh, the beginning of a new month in the Jewish calendar. It is so called because on that day the crescent of a new moon first appears in the sky. See **Rosh Chodesh** under **holiday terms.**

nichum avelim. See under **mourning terms.**

niddah. This is the common Jewish term for: (1) a woman in her period of menstruation; and (2) the period of menstruation. The closest English word for the former is *menstruant,* and for the latter, *menses,* but these terms are rarely used in the religious community where the laws of *niddah* are observed. These laws are concerned with the Biblical prohibition (*Leviticus 15:19–24)* of marital relations between a husband and wife during her menstrual flow. Their separation is for a minimum of five days, followed by seven days without menstrual flow before ritual immersion in the **mikveh.** The Talmudic tractate *Niddah* deals with this and allied subjects. From Hebrew, apparently derived from the same source as **niddui.**

niddui. A rabbinical ban imposed on a person, usually to enforce obedience to an order or decree issued by a *bet din* or Jewish court. See **herem.** From Hebrew, derived from the verb *niddah,* 'to cast out, banish, expel.'

niggun. See under **Hasidic terms, music and dance terms.**

-nik. A popular noun-forming suffix of Yiddish (originally Slavic) origin, usually attached to another noun or an adjective, and used (1) to designate, usually in a disparaging manner, a person who does or is (something specified), as in *allrightnik*, 'a newly rich, smug upstart,' *no-goodnik*, 'a good-for-nothing,' *holdupnik*, 'a robber'; (2) to designate a person connected with some activity or group, as in *aliyahnik*, 'one who makes aliyah,' *Chabadnik*, 'an adherent of Chabad,' *musarnik*,' a devotee of musar or the musar movement' (from Yiddish *musernik*), and *baal-tshuvenik*, 'a penitent Jew; a returnee to Judaism.'

Nine Days. The nine days leading up to the fast day of Tisha B'Av (see **fast days**); the final nine days of the **Three Weeks**. These are days of partial mourning in which religious Jews, especially Ashkenazim, abstain from meat and wine (except on the Sabbath) and from other pleasures, such as swimming. Translation of Yiddish *nayn teg.*

Ninth of Av. Another name for **Tisha B'Av.**

nitl or **nitel.** This is the traditional Ashkenazic term for Christmas eve. The word comes from Yiddish, but it exists also in Hebrew. It was borrowed

---

Nimrod: The story of a name

Nimrod makes its first appearance in Genesis 10:8–10 as the name of the son of Cush and great-grandson of Noah. He is described as a powerful man who was "a mighty hunter before the Lord." The Midrash derives his name from the Hebrew word *marad*, 'to rebel,' explaining that he incited the people of Assyria to rebel against God by building the Tower of Babel for idol worship. He is also described as a tyrant and world ruler who made Abraham's father Terach his minister and had Abraham thrown into a fiery furnace when he balked at worshiping idols. In Hebrew, a *nimrod* is a hunter, a usage found also in English since the 1700s. Earlier, in the 1500s, *nimrod* was also used in English as a synonym for tyrant. A 20th century usage that has puzzled students of English is the use of **nimrod** in American slang in the sense of a dimwitted or stupid fellow. The usage is first recorded in 1932, but apparently was popularized in the 1940s in several children's cartoons in which the character Bugs Bunny taunts the silly hunter Elmer Fudd, who is pursuing him, by calling Fudd a *nimrod*. The cartoons suggest a link between *nimrod*, 'hunter,' and *nimrod*, 'stupid person,' but the appearance of the latter meaning in the 1930s (some ten years before the cartoons) makes the link questionable.

from Late Latin *(dies) natalis*, literally, 'nativity (day),' or from Medieval Latin *natale (domini)*, literally, 'birth of (our lord).' Among observant Jews, the term has retained a very specific connotation, namely, that the study of Torah is suspended on that evening. Instead of study, it became customary in the Middle Ages to engage in cardplaying or some other frivolous activity. Various reasons have been given for the suspension of Torah study. One popular reason connects that night with mourning, and mourners are deprived from the joy of study during the *shivah* or mourning period. A kabbalistic reason based on permutations of the name *yeshu* (Jesus) associates Christmas with the invasion of dogs in homes where Torah was studied on this holiday. The most widely accepted reason is that in the Middle Ages Jews were often attacked and beaten in the houses of study during the Christmas eve celebrations. To prevent a possible carnage, Jewish leaders of those days decreed that scholars and students refrain from studying publicly that night and confine themselves to study in their homes. Since most Jews lacked either the books or the necessary knowledge to engage in solitary study, the custom of not studying at all on Christmas eve became widespread.

Popular etymologies have derived the word *nit(e)l* from various similar-sounding Hebrew words, such as *natal*, 'to take, lift, kill, etc.' But there is no doubt that the word is of Latin origin.

Noachide or **Noachite.** Any descendant of Noach (Noah) who is, therefore, subject to the **Noachide** or **Noachite laws**, the seven commandments given to Noach (Hebrew, *sheva mitzvos benei noach*) that are binding on all human beings (*Sanhedrin 56a*). One of the seven laws is to establish courts of law or a legal system (*dinim*); the six other laws are prohibitions against blasphemy (*birkas haShem*), idol worship (*avodah zorah*), incest and adultery (*gilui arayos*), murder (*shefichas domim*), robbery (*gezel*), and eating flesh cut or torn from a living animal (*eyver min hachai*). While the Noachide laws are universal and apply to Jews and non-Jews alike, Jews are distinguished from Noachides and in legal usage the term *ben noach* (Noachide) refers only to a non-Jew, i.e., one who is subject but to seven of all the commandments in the Torah. Compare **gentile, goy.**

nosh. See under **Yiddishisms.**

notarikon. A notarikon is either: (1) an abbreviation or acronym using the initial letter or letters of a Hebrew word or phrase, as in "The notarikon H″YD stands for *HaShem yinkom domo*, 'may God avenge his blood'"; or (2) a system of aggadic or kabbalistic interpretation using such abbreviations or acronyms, as in "The word *pardes* ('orchard, paradise') stands in notarikon for *peshat, remez, derush, sod* ('plain sense, allusion, homily, secret')." The plural of notarikon, especially for sense (1) is the Hebrew form *notarikonim* or the Anglicized form *notarikons.* The Mishnah (*Shabbos 12:5*) states that if one writes on the Sabbath one letter as a notarikon, the sages exempt him from liability. The notarikon is one of thirty-two hermeneutic rules used in the aggadic interpretation of Biblical passages. In the Talmud, acronyms are used as *simanim* ('signs') for mnemonic purposes (e.g., *yaknehaz,* denoting the order *yayin, kiddush, ner, havdalah, zeman* for the kiddush blessings recited when a Festival occurs on Saturday night) or as shortenings (e.g., *Resh Lakish,* for *Rav Shimon ben Lakish*).

In medieval times Hebrew acronyms came to be widely used, especially for the names of oft-quoted rabbinic scholars and sages, e.g., *Rashi (Rav Shelomo Yitzchaki), Rambam (Rav Moshe ben Maimon),* and *chazal* (for *cha*chomeynu *z*ichronom *l*ivrochoh, 'our sages of blessed memory'). This usage expanded in application in modern times to form:

1. the titles of sacred and scholarly books, e.g., *tanach* (for *torah, neviim. kesuvim,* "Torah, Prophets, and Writings"), s*has* (for *shisha sidrei,* 'Six Orders' of the Mishnah and Talmud), and s*emag* (for *Sefer Mitzvos Gadol,* by Moses of Coucy);
2. certain surnames, e.g., *Katz* (for *kohen tzedek,* designating a descendant of kohanim), *Bak* (for *bal kore,* 'Torah reader'), and *Shatz (*for *sheliach tzibbur,* 'congregational messenger' or cantor);
3. certain honorifics, e.g., *admor* (for *adonenu, morenu, verabenu,* 'our master, teacher, and rabbi,' applied to Hasidic rabbis), and *zatzal* (for *zecher tzadik livrocho,* 'the memory of the righteous is blessed,' after Proverbs 10:7, appended to the name of a deceased rabbi or scholar);
4. the names of many groups and organizations, such as *Bilu* (for b*eis yaakov lechu venelchu,* 'House of Jacob, come and let us walk,' after Isaiah 2:5), *Nili* (for n*etzach yisrael lo yeshaker,* 'the Eternal One of Israel will not lie,' after I Samuel 15:29), *Chabad* (for c*hochmah, b*inah, d*aas,* 'wisdom, understanding, knowledge,' a Hasidic concept), *Tzahal* (for *Tzeva Haganah Leyisrael,* 'Israel Defense Forces'), and *Yesha* (for *Ye-hudah, Shomron, Aza,* 'Judea, Samaria, Gaza').

The word *notarikon* was borrowed from Greek, where it meant a system of shorthand writing used in ancient courts of justice. The Greek word derived ultimately from Latin *notarius,* 'shorthand writer, clerk,' from *nota,* 'shorthand character, letter, note.' *Notarikon* should not be confused with **gematria**, the more popular method of aggadic interpreation, which consists mainly of explaining Hebrew words and phrases according to the numerical value of the letters. See also **abbreviations and acronyms.**

nudnik. See under **Yiddishisms.**

Numbers. See **Pentateuch.**

nusach, plural **nusachim** or (from Yiddish) **nuschoes** or (Anglicized) **nusachs.** The version of Jewish prayers traditionally used by a community (in full, **nusach hatefillah,** 'prayer version'), especially as arranged in the prayerbooks of the community. The most common liturgical versions are *nusach Ashkenaz,* the version used by most Ashkenazim; *nusach Sepharad,* the version used by most Sephardim; and *nusach ha-Ari,* the revised Sephardic version introduced by the kabbalist R. Isaac Luria (known as the *Ari,* 'Lion') in the 1500s and adopted by Hasidim. These terms are also used sometimes to refer to the rites and rituals specific to these groups, as in the way they put on tefillin (phylacteries) or on which occasions they recite the *hallel* prayers; used in this way, *nusach* overlaps with the preferred term **minhag.** More properly, the term *nusach* is used to designate different musical styles, modes, and melodies in the public rendition of the prayers and the public reading of the Torah or the haftorah. Originally, the term referred to variant forms or readings in a text or texts. From Hebrew, literally, 'text, copy, formula.'

–O–

olam haba. A term found in the Talmud, Midrash, and Zohar in two, sometimes overlapping, senses: (1) The next world, i.e., the world to come after death, the afterworld or afterlife, consisting of *gan eden,* Eden or paradise, inhabited by the souls of the righteous, and *gehenem,* gehenna, the place where the souls of the wicked are damned to eternal suffering. The olam haba is usually contrasted with the **olam hazeh,** this world, the world of the living, the corporeal or physical world. (2) A future age or era of redemption and universal peace following the advent of Messiah (see **Moshiach),** known as the Messianic age. From Hebrew *olam haba,* literally, 'coming world,' *olam hazeh,* 'this world.' The Yiddish forms are *oylem habe* (oy'lem ha'be) and *oylem haze* (oy'lem ha'ze).

Old Testament, New Testament. These two terms are of Christian origin. The Jews who use them are usually unaware of their provenance and implications, like those who use the Christian abbreviation *A.D.* (See **B.C.E.** and **C.E.**) The two terms derive from the Christian belief that God made two covenants (the word "testament" is from Latin *testamentum*, meaning a contract or covenant), the first with the Children of Israel as a chosen people, and the second with the Christians as followers of Jesus. The name "New Testament" or "New Covenant" (a phrase derived from Jeremiah 31:30) was therefore applied by Christian scholars to the Christian scriptures, while "Old Testament" or "Old Covenant" was the name given to the Jewish scriptures. Terms like "the Torah," "the Tanach," or, on the formal English side, "the Bible," "the Scriptures," are acceptable substitutes for "Old Testament." And in place of "New Testament," one may speak of "the Christian scriptures" or "the Christian Bible" without offending anyone's sensibilities.

oleh, feminine **olah,** plural **olim.** 1. An immigrant to Israel. 2. One who is called up to the Torah. From Hebrew, literally, 'one who ascends.' See **aliyah.**

omed. Yiddish form of **amud.**

omer. The 49-day period between the second day of Pesach and the holiday of Shavuos (see **holiday terms**), each day of which is individually counted with a special blesssing. The "counting of the omer" (*sefiras haomer*) is a Biblical commandment (*Leviticus 23:15*). Originally, the *omer* was: (1) a sheaf of barley cut during the barley harvest; (2) a specific measure of ground barley that was brought to the Temple for a meal-offering before the produce of the harvest could be eaten; and (3) the meal-offering itself, which was brought to the kohen on the second day of Pesach (*Leviticus 23:9–11*). The customary name of the 49-day period is **sefira.** From Hebrew, literally, 'sheaf of barley.' See **Lag B'omer** under **holiday terms.**

oneg shabbat or **oneg shabbos.** Often shortened to **oneg.** A party, reception, or other social gathering held on the Sabbath, at which snacks are served and participants sing *zemiros* (Sabbath songs), *niggunim* (Hasidic melodies), or other Jewish songs and listen to or deliver Torah discourses. In the Gemara (*Shabbos 118a*), the term *oneg shabbat* refers to the pleasures or enjoyment of the Sabbath, especially the delicacies served at the Sabbath table. The current use is a modern innovation. From Hebrew, literally, 'Sabbath delight,' from the passage in Isaiah 58:13, *and you shall call the Sabbath a delight.*

opsherenish, plural **opsherenishn.** This Yiddish-origin word means literally 'a shearing (of hair)' or 'a haircut.' It derives from the verb *opshern*, 'to shear or cut (the hair).' In Ashkenazi usage, *opsherenish* is the name given to the custom of cutting a boy's hair for the first time when he has reached his third year, a custom traditionally accompanied by a festive celebration.

The custom of opsherenish is not mentioned by any of the early or latter rabbinical decisors. Its first mention is in the writings of the kabbalist R. Chayim Vital (1542–1620), who in his *Sha'ar ha-Kavonos (87:)* describes the haircutting ceremony as a well-known one even at the time of his teacher, R. Isaac Luria (the Ari). As Vital describes it, his teacher's custom was to go every Lag B'omer to the *hillula* or festivity at the graves of R. Simeon ben Yochai and his son Eleazar at Meron, a village in Upper Galilee, and, he writes, "one year . . . my teacher, of blessed memory, took his young son there together with his entire family and cut his hair there according to the well-known custom and they made it a day of feasting and celebration."

Though Vital did not specify the boy's age, the custom of cutting the first growth of hair on the third birthday or thereafter was adopted by the kabbalists and became widespread among Sephardic and Hasidic Jews. The boy's age was tied to the Biblical law of **orlah**, which prohibits the pruning of the fruit of young trees during their first three years: just as it is forbidden to cut off the fruit until three years have passed, so the boy's hair is not shorn until he has reached his third year. In Israel, the custom is called **chalaka,** from an Arabic word for 'haircutting' or 'shaving,' and is observed either on Lag B'omer or on Chol Hamoed of Pesach.

The importance attached by Hasidim to this custom is due to its indirect connection to the Biblical commandment (*Leviticus 19:27*) prohibiting the removal of the *peos* (Yiddish *peyes*), or earlocks (See **peyes**). In the act of cutting the hair, the earlocks are left uncut, and thereby a Torah commandment is fulfilled. The performance of this commandment justifies the festive celebration that follows the opsherenish. Some Conservative communities have recently extended the first-haircut custom to girls who have reached the age of three. Hasidim and other Orthodox Jews, however, criticize this innovation, since they hold that the primary purpose of the custom is to cut a boy's hair in order to leave the sidelocks uncut, a practice that does not apply to girls.

Though the general custom is to observe the opsherenish at the age of three, some do it as early as the age of two and some wait until the boy reaches five. As to where and when the haircutting takes place, most choose to have it at home and on the child's third birthday (or a day later).

Others prefer to have it on a festival, especially on Chol Hamoed (the weekday part) of Pesach or Sukkos, while many of those who live in Israel wait until Lag B'omer and journey to Meron on that day to perform the custom in the manner of R. Isaac Luria and his followers.

The standard word and transliteration in English is *opsherenish*, not the misguided "upshern," which combines the English prefix *up-* with the Yiddish verb *opshern*.

Oral Law. Translation of Hebrew *torah she-be-al peh* (literally, 'Torah that is oral'), meaning those parts of the Torah that were transmitted by Moses orally to supplement the **Written Law** and eventually incorporated in the Mishnah and Gemara. The teachings of the Sages in the Talmud constitute the Oral Law. See also **Torah.**

Oriental Jew. Any of the indigenous Jews of the Middle East and North Africa, especially those who lived under Muslim rule and emigrated to Israel after 1948. Oriental Jews (Hebrew *benei hamizrach*, 'children of the Orient') had lived in Babylonia since the 8th century B.C.E. and constitute the oldest division of Diaspora Jews, older than the Ashkenazi and Sephardi division. The Oriental Jewish community (Hebrew *edot hamizrach*, 'communities of the Orient') was strongly influenced by Muslim culture since the rise of Islam in the 7th century C.E.

orlah. The fruit of a tree during the first three years of its growth, when its consumption or use is Biblically prohibited (*Leviticus 19:23–24*). The prohibition itself is also called *orlah*. In the fourth year after its planting, the fruit (called *neta revai*, 'fourth-year planting') is brought to Jerusalem to be eaten there, or is redeemed for money which is then brought to Jerusalem to be spent there on food and drink. *Orlah* is also the name of a Mishnaic tractate that deals with the laws of orlah and other prohibited agrarian produce. From Hebrew, literally, 'uncircumcised,' meaning 'unpruned, untrimmed.'

Orthodox. An adjective applied since the early 19th century to Jews who adhere strictly to rabbinical law and tradition. The term first appeared in the name of the Eastern *Orthodox* Church, which differed doctrinally from the mainstream Christian Church and used the name *Orthodox* to indicate that it espoused the right or true doctrine, the word *orthodox* meaning literally 'having the right doctrine.' *Orthodox* was borrowed from Greek *orthodoxos*, formed from *orthos*, 'straight, right, correct' and *doxa*, 'opinion, doctrine.' In the beginning of the 19th century, members of the new Reform movement in Germany began to apply the adjective *orthodox* and the noun *Orthodoxie* to strictly religious Jews and their practices in the somewhat derogatory sense of 'rigidly doctrinal, adhering unwaveringly to dogma.' Partly because of the success of the Reformers and partly because of the lack of a united leadership among their opponents, the term *Orthodox* soon became universally adopted as the distinctive name of traditional Jews. The term came into English in the late 1800s, after which the beliefs and practices of strictly religious Jews fell under the rubric of **Orthodox Judaism** or **Orthodoxy**. The latter came to be widely regarded as a "branch" or "denomination" of Judaism, on a par with the **Reform** and **Conservative** branches or denominations and paralleling long-established divisions within Christianity. Opposition in the traditional community to the term Orthodox led to the use of such new qualifying terms as *Torah-true, authentic, traditional, rabbinic*, and *normative* in place of *Orthodox*. The latter, however, is now the standard term and unlikely to be replaced in general usage by any other. The term *Orthodox* has itself become qualified in such varieties as *Modern Orthodox* and *ultra-Orthodox*. See also **Neo-Orthodoxy**.

– P –

parashah. See **sidrah**.

pareve or **parve**. A Yiddish-origin term for any food or utensil that is neither **milchig** nor **fleishig** and can therefore be eaten or used with either dairy or meat products and utensils. Pareve products typically include eggs, fish, vegetables, fruits, nuts, coffee, tea, various nondairy snacks, and any synthetic or chemically produced foodstuff or ingredient. The Hebrew equivalent is *stami*, literally, 'indefinite, neutral,' though *pareve* (borrowed from Yiddish) is commonly used by Hebrew speakers. The term comes from Eastern Yiddish. (Speakers of Western Yiddish use the term *minikh*.) Diverse theories have been advanced concerning the origin of Yiddish *pareve, parve, parev*, but the one that seems to be most acceptable is that the word is of West Slavic (Czech or Polish) origin, probably Czech *párový*, an adjective meaning 'of a pair, dual,' derived from the noun *pár*, 'pair,' from Latin *par*. The Slavic word served to fill the empty slot in Yiddish for a word designating a twofold use, with either dairy or meat dishes.

Pentateuch. This is the standard English name for the Five Books of Moses (Hebrew **chamishah chumshei torah**, or **chumash** for short). The term

---

paradise: a word history

The English word *paradise*, meaning the blissful abode of the righteous in heaven, comes ultimately from the same source as the Hebrew word *pardes*, 'orchard, fruit garden.' *Paradise* and its cognates (e.g., French *paradis*, German *Paradies*, Spanish *paraíso*) were borrowed from Greek *paradeisos*, whose origin was the Avestan (ancient Iranian) word *pairiadeza*, meaning an enclosed garden, park, or orchard. In the Septuagint (Greek translation of the Hebrew Bible), Greek *paradeisos* was used to translate the Hebrew *gan eden*, 'Garden of Eden,' which in the Midrash and kabbalah came to be associated with the abode of the righteous in heaven (see **olam haba**). The Hebrew word *pardes* (found in *Song of Songs 4:13, Ecclesiastes 2:5*, and *Nehemiah 2:8*), was independently borrowed from Avestan *pairiadeza*, hence its meaning, 'orchard, fruit garden.' In the Talmud (*Chagiga 14b*) and kabbalistic literature, *pardes* assumed the figurative meaning of 'secret or mystical teachings.' In the Middle Ages, the word was reinterpreted as an acronym (see **notarikon**) for the four methods of Biblical interpretation (*peshat, remez, derush, sod*, 'literal meaning, allusion, homily, secret').

Some sources also record the use of Hebrew *pardes* (apparently through the infuence of Greek *paradeisos*) in the sense of 'paradise, Eden.'

---

comes from Greek *Pentáteuchos*, literally, 'five books,' formed from *pénte*, 'five' and *teuchos*, 'book, work.' The English names of the Five Books also derive from Greek, but through the medium of Latin, as follows:

	Hebrew name	Greek name	Latin name	English name
1.	*Bereshis*	*Génesis*	*Genesis*	*Genesis*
2.	*Shemos*	*Éxodos*	*Exodus*	*Exodus*
3.	*Vayikra*	*Leuitikós*	*Leviticus*	*Leviticus*
4.	*Bamidbar*	*Arithmoí*	*Numeri*	*Numbers*
5.	*Devarim*	*Deuteronó-mion*	*Deuterono-mium*	*Deuteronomy*

The Hebrew names come from the first significant word in each of the Five Books: (1) *Bereshis*, 'In the beginning'; (2) *Shemos*, 'Names'; (3) *Vayikra*, 'And He called'; (4) *Bamidbar*, 'In the wilderness'; (5) *Devarim*, 'Words.'

In the Mishnah (*Megillah 3:5, Yoma 7:1*), other names are given for the third and fourth book: *Toras Kohanim* ('Torah of the Kohanim') for Leviticus; *Chumash Hapekudim* ('Book of Numbers') for Numbers. In the Gemara (*Megillah 31b*), the fifth book is called *Mishneh Torah* ('Repetition of the Torah'), derived from the phrase *mishneh hatorah hazos* ('copy of this Torah') in Deuteronomy 17:18. In contrast to the Hebrew names, the Greek names, which appear in the Septuagint (Greek translation of the Bible), are descriptive of the content of each book: *Génesis* means 'origin, birth, creation,' since the first Book of Moses deals with the creation of the world; *Éxodos* means 'a going out, departure' and it deals with the departure of the Israelites from Egypt; *Leuitikós* means 'of the Levites, Levitical,' which is the chief subject of the third book; *Arithmoí* means 'numbers,' because one of the main themes in the fourth book is the census taken of the Israelites in the desert in which every individual was separately counted; *Deuteronómion*, literally, 'second law' (from *deúteros*, 'second' + *nómos*, 'law'), is the fifth book's title because it reviews or repeats parts of the first four books, such as the Decalogue. It has been proposed that the Greek *Deuteronómion* is a translation of the Hebrew phrase *mishneh hatorah hazos* ('copy of this Torah') in Deuteronomy 17:18, which would accord with the Talmudic name of *Mishneh Torah*. However, this would run counter to the thematic way in which the other Books are named in the Septuagint.

Pentecost. This name for the holiday of Shavuos (see under **holiday terms**) has been in English since the Middle Ages, first appearing about 1382 in John Wycliffe's translation of the Bible. However, the preferred English name of Shavuos is (*the Feast of*) *Weeks*, which is a translation of Hebrew *shavuos*, since the holiday occurs seven *weeks* after Passover. Unlike the names *Passover, Tabernacles, Day of Atonement, Feast of Lights*, and other English names of Jewish holidays, the name *Pentecost* is seldom used among Jews. This avoidance is due to the word's association with Christianity, traceable to the Christian Bible, in which chapter two of the Book of Acts describes the disciples of Jesus "speaking in tongues" on Shavuos, which is rendered in Greek as *pentecostet* (*hemera*), 'fiftieth (day),' from its occurrence fifty days after Passover. Moreover, the Christian use of the name *Pentecost* has been reinforced since the early 1900s by the rise of the Protestant *Pentecostal* churches, which preach *Pentecostalism*, or the supernatural experience of falling into a trance in which one sees visions and begins "speaking in tongues." These practices are so far removed from the celebration of Shavuos that Jews are justified in dropping the name *Pentecost* from their holiday vocabulary.

Perushim. A group of influential teachers and rabbis who succeeded Ezra and the Scribes (*Sopherim*) and were active during the Second Temple period in interpreting and transmitting the Written and Oral Law. The Perushim opposed the *Tzeddukim* (Sadducees), who rejected the Oral Law and the doctrine of Free Will, and as the religious leaders of their day their teachings led to the development of the Mishnah. From Hebrew, literally, 'separatists,' derived from *parush*, 'separated, reclusive, abstaining,' from the verb *parash*, 'to separate, abstain,' probably so called from their unwillingness to compromise with their opponents in matters of Jewish law. See **Pharisees.**

peyes. The sidecurls or sidelocks worn by certain Orthodox Jews, as Hasidim and Yemenites, in strict observance of the commandment prohibiting males from removing the hair from the corners of the head (*Leviticus 19:27*). See **opsherenish.** Peyes are usually called *earlocks* in English, because they hang away from the hairline in front of the ears, as distinguished from sideburns. Though sideburns comply with the prohibition in Leviticus 19:27, they are not called **peyes.** From Yiddish *peyes*, plural of *peye*, 'earlock,' derived from Hebrew *peah*, literally, 'edge, corner.' The Hebrew form **peah** (plural **peos**) denotes both an earlock and the corner of a field, which according to Biblical law (*Leviticus 19:9–10*) is to be left to the poor to glean.

Pharisees. The English name of the **Perushim.** The singular form *Pharisee* was derived from Latin *Pharisaeus* and Greek *Pharisaios*, which came from Aramaic *perishayya*, a plural of *perish*, 'separated,' corresponding to Hebrew *parush*, 'separated, abstaining.' The name Pharisee has long been used pejoratively in the Christian and secular world because of the hostile references to the Perushim in the Christian Bible. Thus the word *pharisee* (in lower-case) has meant since the 1500s a sanctimonious, hypocritical, and self-righteous person, the adjective *pharisaic* 'sanctimonious, hypocritical, self-righteous,' and the derivative *pharisaism* 'sanctimonious behavior, character, or practice.' Despite the negative connotations of these words, Jewish Bible commentators, historians, and writers often choose to refer to the Perushim as *Pharisees* and to their practices as *Pharisaism*, relying on a tenuous spelling device (capital letters versus lower-case ones) to keep the meanings distinct. To avoid the implied pejorativeness in the term Pharisees, it is advisable to use the Hebrew name *Perushim*. See **Sanhedrin** for a similar usage.

pidyon haben. See under **ritual terms.**

pikuach nefesh. See under **halachic terms.**

pilpul. A term used in the study and exposition of the Talmud, denoting sharp argumentation and subtly logical reasoning to prove a point or thesis. It is also used pejoratively to mean hairsplitting or excessively complex or convoluted argumentation bordering on sophistry or casuistry. The positive meaning is reflected in the Mishnaic statement (*Pirkei Avos 6:6*) that one of forty-eight qualities by which the Torah is acquired is *bepilpul hatalmidim,* 'in the sharp argumentation of students.' The negative meaning evolved during the Middle Ages, and can be found, for example, in the classic 15th-century work *Orchos Tzaddikim* ('The Ways of the Righteous,' of unknown authorship), which opposes the use of pilpul at the expense of traditional learning and flatly states that "in this generation the Torah is being forgotten because those who study cling to pilpul (*hechzik bepilpulim*) . . . and because of the difficulty of study, concentration, and pilpul (*haiyun vehapilpul*) many abandon the study of the Talmud." The negative view of the term *pilpul* is dominant in many yeshivas today, though the **pilpulistic** method of study, involving sharpwitted analysis and argument, has not been entirely abandoned. From Hebrew *pilpul* (Yiddish *pilpl*), derived from *pilpel,* 'to argue sharply,' from *pilpel,* 'pepper.'

pinkas, plural **pinkasim.** The book of records of a Jewish community, guild, or council, containing day-to-day information about communal or local activities, events, ordinances, and the like. Much historical information about Jewish life since the Middle Ages has been obtained from pinkasim, as those kept by the Council of Four Provinces (*Vaad Arba Artzos*) of Poland and Lithuania. The term *pinkas* is found in the Mishnah (e.g., *Shevuos 7:5*) in the sense of a notebook or ledger for keeping accounts. It was an altered form borrowed from Greek *pinak-, pinax* 'writing board or tablet.'

piyyut, plural **piyyutim.** Any of the numerous Hebrew hymns and poems inserted into the mandatory synagogue prayers, especially those of the Sabbath and holidays, from the early centuries of the Common Era until the 18th century. There are various types of piyyutim, but the best known are the *yotzros,* those inserted before and after the *Shema* ("Hear O Israel") prayer during the holiday morning (*Shacharis*) service. Nevertheless, in common usage all holiday piyyutim are usually—and erroneously—referred to as *yotzros.* Composers of piyyutim are called **paytanim** (singular, **paytan**). The most prolific and original paytan was R.

Eleazar haKallir, who lived in Tiberias sometime in the 700s C.E. R. Yosef Caro in the *Shulchan Aruch* (*Orach Chaim 68*) regards the insertion of piyyutim before the *Shema* as an interruption, but the Ashkenazi decisor *Ramo* (R. Moshe Isserles) permits their insertion. From Hebrew *piyyut*, derived from the verb *piyyet* 'to compose poems,' borrowed from Greek *poiētēs*, 'poet, creator' (the source of English *poet*).

plombe. A metal tag attached to poultry to certify that it is kosher. From Eastern Yiddish, 'leaden seal, metal seal, dental filling, metal tag,' borrowed from French *plomb*, 'sounding lead, plumb,' from Latin *plumbum*, 'lead.'

porge. A verb meaning 'to make (meat from a ritually slaughtered animal) kosher by removing the forbidden fat, veins, and sinews, especially from its hindquarters. A Yiddish-origin synonym of *porge* is the verb **treyber** (from Yiddish *treybern*, derived from a Slavic source). Yiddish also has a Hebrew-derived synonym, *zayn menaker*, 'to do *nikkur*' (Hebrew for *porging*). The laws of porging derive from Genesis 32:33, prohibiting the eating of the *gid hanoshe*, the 'displaced sinew or tendon' identified as the inner sinew or sciatic nerve of the animal's thigh, and from Leviticus 7:23–25, prohibiting the fat (*chelev*) attached to the organs of animals used as sacrifices. The Sages in the Talmud (*Chullin 91*) also prohibit the outer sinew or peroneal nerve, along with the fat covering the sciatic nerve and sorrounding veins and nerves. Special knowledge and skill is required to porge meat according to the strict requirement of Jewish law, hence a qualified **porger** (or **treyber**) is in great demand. Though the term *porger* (implying *porge*) is first recorded in English in 1773, the word has a long and complex history that ultimately leads back to Latin *purgare*, 'to purge, purify,' from *purus*, 'pure.' See **kashrus.**

posek, plural **poskim** or **posekim.** A scholar or rabbi who pronounces authoritative decisions on matter of halachah or Jewish law; (in formal English) a *decisor.* A posek is one who *paskens* (from Yiddish *paskn*) or gives a *pesak* (from Hebrew *pesak* and Yiddish *psak*, 'decision, judgment, verdict') on a halachic question. The plural *poskim* or *posekim* is used primarily to designate the post-Gaonic scholars who collected, arranged, and systematically codified the halachahs, notably R. Isaac Alfasi (*Rif*, 1013–1103), R. Moses ben Maimon (*Rambam*, 1135–1204), and R. Jacob ben Asher (*Baal Haturim* or *Tur*, c.1270–1343), and their successors, R. Yosef Caro (1488–1575, author of the *Shulchan Aruch*) and R. Moshe Isserles (*Ramo*, c.1525–1572). The *poskim* are distinguished from the *meforshim* or commentators, such as Rashi and the Tosafists, who analyzed and expounded halachic matters without attempting to rule on them or codify them. From Hebrew, literally, 'one who divides or disconnects,' from *pasak*, 'to stop, discontinue.'

prayer shawl. A common English term for a **tallis,** recorded since the 1920s. An earlier term, *praying shawl*, is found in Israel Zangwill's *Children of the Ghetto* (1892).

Prophets. See **Neviim.**

prosbul. See **shemitah.**

proselyte. See **ger.**

pshetl. See **derasha.**

Purim. See under **holiday terms.** See also **adloyada.**

– R –

R. Abbreviation of the title **Rabbi** or **Rav.**

Rabban, plural **Rabbanan.** An Aramaic-origin title for a rabbi or teacher; see **rabbi.**

Rabbanit, plural **rabbaniyot.** A rabbi's wife or widow. From Hebrew, feminine of **Rabban.** Compare **rebbetzin.**

rabbi or **Rabbi.** When written in lower-case, *rabbi* denotes any Jewish cleric ordained by another rabbi or by a religious institution, as in *a prominent rabbi, a seminar for rabbis, an assistant rabbi.* The capitalized form *Rabbi* (abbreviated *R.*) is a title and form of address for: (1) the official religious leader of a congregation or synagogue; (2) a rabbinically ordained scholar or teacher; (3) anyone who has received rabbinical or seminary ordination. Examples of usage: *Rabbi Fine is not a professional or practicing rabbi but works in the field of education. Being a pulpit rabbi, Rabbi Gold is usually addressed by his congregants as "Rabbi."* The capitalized plural form *Rabbis* usually designates the tannaim and amoraim of the Talmudic period and is synonymous with *Sages.* The term *rabbi* has been in English since the 1300s and was a borrowing from Latin and Greek, which took it from Hebrew *rabbī* (pronounced as in *abbey*), meaning 'my master, my teacher' (derived from *rav*, 'master, teacher'), a title conferred on scholars and sages who received proper *semicha* (the ancient judicial ordination) in Eretz Israel, as opposed to the Babylonian sages, who did not receive *semicha* but were given the honorific title of **Rav**. The forms **rabbinate** and **rabbinical** derive from obsolete English *rabbin*, 'rabbi' (used in the 1500s), which was borrowed from French. The French *rabbin* and the German *Rabbiner*, both meaning 'rabbi,' were apparently formed from a fusion of the Aramaic words *rabbīn* (plural of *rav*, 'master, teacher') and *rabbān*, a title of scholars and teachers, literally, 'chief, leader' (derived from *rav*, 'master, teacher'). The title **Reverend**, used especially formerly by some synagogue functionaries (as chazzanim, mohels, and shammosim), is of Latin origin (from *reveriri* 'to revere') and unrelated to *rabbi, rav, rebbe*, etc.

rav or **Rav**, plural **rabbanim** or **rabbonim.** The term *rav* and the title or form of address *Rav* are used to designate Orthodox rabbis, especially to distinguish them from those who bear the title Rabbi but have not received *heter horaah*, or rabbinical ordination (often loosely called *semicha*) from an Orthodox rabbi or yeshiva. Originally, the title *Rav* was used in Babylonia as an honorific for scholars who were qualified to receive *semicha* (the ancient judicial ordination) but were not eligible for it outside Eretz Israel. From Talmudic Hebrew and Aramaic, literally, 'master, teacher,' derived from Biblical Hebrew *rav*, 'great, much, superior, important.' Derivative terms are **Rabbenu**, 'Our Master,' as in *Moshe Rabbenu, Rabbenu Tam, Rabbenu Hakadosh* (title of R. Yehudah Hanasi); *rabbanut* or (Ashkenazi) *rabbanus*, 'rabbinate.' A *rav hamachshir*, literally, 'kashering rabbi,' is a *mashgiach* or kashrus supervisor. A rav is addressed as *harav* or *Harav*; a synagogue or community rav is often called the *mara deatra* or (Ashkenazi) *mora deasra*, literally, 'master of the country or locality,' from Aramaic. The variant forms of **rov** or **Rov** are from Yiddish.

Reb. A formal Ashkenazi title corresponding to the English *Sir* and prefixed to the first name of the person addressed, as in *Reb Moshe, Reb Aharon, Reb Dovid*. Some dictionaries inappropriately translate the word as "Mr." From Yiddish, derived from Hebrew *rav*, 'master'; see **rav.**

rebbe[1], plural **rebbes.** A Hasidic master or spiritual leader; a *tzaddik* or *Grand Rabbi*. From Yiddish *rebe*, 'rabbi, teacher,' literally, 'master,' derived from Hebrew *rabbī*; see **rabbi.** See under **Hasidic terms.**

rebbe[2] or **rebbi,** plural **rebbes** or **rebbis** or **rebbeim.** A rabbi or religious teacher, as at a yeshiva, often used as a form of address. From Yiddish *rebe*; see **rebbe**[1].

rebbetzin, plural **rebbetzins.** A rabbi's wife or widow. From Yiddish *rebetsin*, feminine of *rebe* 'rabbi'; see **rebbe**[1]. When used as a title, it is capitalized. Compare **Rabbanit.**

Reconstructionism. A movement in American Judaism launched in the 1920s by Rabbi Mordecai M. Kaplan (1881–1983) in an article entitled "A Program for the Reconstruction of Judaism," which appeared in the *Menorah Journal* of August 1920. His program was intended to revitalize Conservative Judaism, which he regarded as lagging behind modern thought, but eventually he and his followers broke away from the Conservative ideology to form a new liberal sect or denomination. Reconstructionism views Judaism as an evolving civilization in which religion is a part of Jewish history and culture rather than its prime mover. Adherents of Reconstructionism are called *Reconstructionists* and their beliefs and practices are described as *Reconstructionist* as in the *Reconstructionist movement, Reconstructionist Judaism,* the *Reconstructionist Haggadah.* These terms are not exclusively Jewish: *Reconstructionism* and *Reconstructionist* are also used by an ultraconservative Christian group that opposes public education and the separation of Church and State.

Reform. An adjective denoting a form of Judaism that originated in Germany in the early 1800s for the purpose of "reforming" traditional religious practices to bring it into conformity with the Emancipation and modern enlightenment. At first the term *Reform* was not popular, since it suggested a similarity to the radical transformation of the Christian Church by the German Protestant *Reformation* under Martin Luther. The Berlin *Reformgemeinde* ("Reform Congregation"), formed in 1845, was regarded by modernizers as extremist and instead of *Reform* many preferred the political designations "Liberal" or "Progressive" (terms still used in the Reform movement). In Great Britain and the United States, however, the *Reformers* broke away entirely from what they called *Orthodox* Judaism and introduced the radical changes of the German *Reformgemeinde*, such as mixed seating in the sanctuary, bareheaded worship in the English language, use of the organ, and celebration of the Sabbath on Sunday. Since World War II, the ideology of the Reform movement has undergone many changes, including acceptance of Zionism, the use of Hebrew language and liturgy, and the observance of various traditional practices. In recent years, it has adopted some of the traditional vocabulary of Orthodoxy, terms like *beit midrash, mitzvot, kollel, klal yisroel.* Nevertheless, Reform Judaism continues to maintain an ultraliberal position on such crucial issues as intermarriage, conversion, Sabbath observance, and dietary laws. Compare **Conservative, Orthodox.**

resh galuta or (*Ashkenazi*) **resh galusa.** Title of the highest-ranking Jewish civil ruler during the Babylonian Exile, from the 6th century B.C.E. to the 10th century C.E. The title was hereditary, its bearer a royal descendant of the House of David. The resh galuta served the Persian rulers of Babylon, who granted him princely powers, such as the power to appoint judges and levy taxes. From Aramaic, literally, 'head of the Exile.' The Hebrew title was **rosh hagolah.** The English name used by scholars is **Exilarch.**

responsa. A formal or scholarly term for the written replies given by a qualified rabbinical authority (a *decisor* or *posek*) to questions of Jewish law. The singular is **responsum.** The traditional Hebrew and Yiddish term for responsa is *sheilos uteshuvos* (Yiddish *shayles (un) tshuves*), literally, 'questions and answers.' *Responsa* is a translation of Hebrew *teshuvos*, literally, 'answers.'

Reverend. See **rabbi.**

rishon, plural **rishonim.** A *rishon* (from Hebrew, literally, 'first one') refers to any of the early rabbinical expounders or codifiers of Jewish law, from the 10th century C.E. to the 15th century, as distinguished from the *acharonim* or later rabbinical authorities. (See **acharon.**) The period of the rishonim began at the end of the Geonic era and ended when Rabbi Yosef Caro completed his great code of law, the *Shulchan Aruch.* The important Torah commentator Rashi was a rishon, as was the great codifier Rambam (Maimonides). The rishonim also included early kabbalists, poets, and statesmen, such as Ramban (Nachmanides), Shlomo Ibn Gabirol, Abraham Ibn Ezra, Samuel Hanagid, and many important Talmudists, among them Abraham Ibn Daud (Ravad), Shlomo Ibn Aderet (Rashba), Rabbenu Nissim (Ran), and Asher ben Yechiel (Rosh).

ritualarium. A modern formal term for a **mikveh,** coined in the United States on the model of such words as *aquarium* and *oceanarium.* The first use of the term was in the name *Boro Park Ritualarium,* a mikveh built in the 1930s. An earlier formal coinage was *ritual bath*, which may have been translated from the formal German term *Ritualbad.*

ritual terms. Jewish rituals are usually designated by their Hebrew-origin names, though occasionally a term of Yiddish, Judezmo, and even English origin is used to name a customary rite or ritual. A number of ritual terms appear as main entries in this book, among them such terms as **bris**, **kaddish**, **kiddush**, and **mikveh**. Other ritual terms can be found in the sections on **holiday terms**, **mourning terms**, **synagogue terms**, and **wedding terms**. Listed below are common rites and rituals that require little commentary and are therefore not separately entered or covered under the aforementioned sections. Unless indicated otherwise, all the terms come from Hebrew.

bedikah or *bedika.* See under **halachic terms.**

hatoras nedorim. A ceremony performed usually on the morning before Rosh Hashanah, in which three unrelated adult male Jews form a *bet din* or court of law and by reciting a prescribed formula release each other from certain vows and oaths they may have made in the course of the year. Literally, 'annulment of vows.' See also **neder.**

havdalah (*Ashkenazi* havdo'le; *Sephardi* havdala'). A ceremony performed at the conclusion of the Sabbath or a festival, consisting of a blessing over a cup of wine, a blessing over *besamim* (aromatic spices), and a blessing over the light of a plaited candle. Literally, 'separation' (of the holy from the nonholy or profane).

Kabbalas Shabbos or *Kabbalat Shabbat.* The part of the Friday night prayers preceding the *maariv*, consisting of six psalms (Psalms 95–99 and Psalm 29), followed by the *Lechah Dodi*, a song greeting the queen Sabbath, and the Sabbath Psalms 92 and 93. Literally, 'reception of the Sabbath.'

kiddush levanah. A ceremony in which a new moon is sanctified at the conclusion of the Sabbath by a *minyan* under a clear sky. The ritual, consisting of reciting a prescribed blessing and various psalms while sighting the moon, may be performed until the middle of the month if the moon cannot be seen earlier. Literally, 'sanctification of the moon.'

maariv. The third and last of the three daily prayers, to be recited after dark; the evening prayer or service. A less common Hebrew name is *arvit.* The other two daily prayers are *shacharis* and *minchah*, but whereas the latter are mandatory, since they correspond to the daily offerings in the Temple, the maariv is ruled optional in the Talmud (*Berachos 27b*). Nevertheless, its daily recital is established by ancient custom. Literally, 'evening prayer,' derived from *erev*, 'evening.'

melave malka. See the main entry.

minchah or *mincha.* The second of the three daily prayers, to be recited in the afternoon until sunset. The early afternoon recital (from about 12.30) is called *minchah gedolah* ('great minchah'); the late recital (close to sunset) is called *minchah ketanah* ('small minchah'). Literally, 'gift, offering,' so called from its corresponding to the daily afternoon offering in the Temple.

musaf. An additional prayer or service recited after shacharis on the Sabbath and holidays. It corresponds to the additional communal offerings brought on the Sabbath and holidays in the Temple. Literally, 'addition, supplement,' from *yasaf,* 'to add.'

negl-vaser. The ritual of washing the hands on rising from sleep in the morning. From Yiddish, literally, 'nail-water,' so called from the belief that the fingernails harbor impurities.

neilah. The concluding prayer or service of Yom Kippur, recited from sunset until nightfall. Literally, 'closing,' from *naal,* 'to close,' in reference either to the closing of the Temple gates at nightfall or the closing of heaven's gates after the day's prayers.

neilas hachag. A festive synagogue celebration at the end of Pesach, Shavuos, and Sukkos.

nesias kapayim. The ritual of *duchening* in which the kohanim raise their hands to bless the congregation. Literally, 'lifting of the palms (of the hands).' See **duchen.**

pidyon haben. The ceremony in which the father of a month-old male child who is his mother's firstborn redeems the child by giving a kohen five silver shekels or its equivalent in dollars in exchange for his son. The ceremony, derived from the Biblical commandment to redeem a firstborn son (Exodus 13: 1–16), takes place on the 31st day after the child's birth. If the boy's father is a kohen or a Levite, or if his mother is the daughter of a kohen or a Levite, redemption is unnecessary and no pidyon haben takes place. Literally, 'redemption of the son.'

seder, plural *seders* or *sedorim.* The ritual celebration of the Exodus from Egypt, taking place on the first two nights of Passover (in Israel, only the first night) and consisting mainly of the recital of the *haggadah.* Literally, 'order (of service).' See also *Pesach* under **holiday terms.**

sefirah or *sefira.* 1. The 49-day period of *sefiras haomer* between Pesach and Shavuos, during which no weddings are held. See also **omer.** 2. The formal count of the 49 days during this period. 3. See under **kabbalistic terms.** Literally, 'count, number.'

selichos. 1. The penitential prayers recited on fast days, in the month preceding Rosh Hashanah, and during the **Ten Days of Penitence** between Rosh Hashanah and Yom Kippur. 2. *Selichos.* A book containing penitential prayers. Plural of *selichah,* 'pardon, forgiveness.'

seudah shlishis or *seudah shlishit.* Hebrew name of *shalosh seudos.* Literally, 'third meal.'

shacharis. The first of the three daily prayers, recited in the morning; the morning prayer or service. The other two prayers are *minchah* and *maariv.* Literally, 'dawn prayer,' from *shachar,* 'dawn.'

shalach manos or *mishloach manos.* Gifts of food and drink sent to, or exchanged between, friends, relatives, and neighbors on Purim, as instructed in the Book of Esther (*Megillas Ester 9:22*). Literally, '(for) sending gifts,' the words used in *Megillas Ester.* The Yiddish form is *shlakhmones.* See also **Purim** under **holiday terms.**

shalom bat. A reception in honor of a newborn female, held usually in her parents' home on the first Sabbath after her birth. It is a contemporary innovation modeled on the ritual of sholem zochor. The name, meaning approximately 'peace to the daughter,' is also modeled on **sholem zochor.** Compare **simchat bat, zebed habat.**

shalosh seudos. The third Sabbath meal, eaten late in the afternoon and accompanied by special Sabbath songs inspired by kabbalistic thought. The Yiddish form of the term is *shaleshudes.* The Hebrew name is *seudah shlishis* (or *shlishit*), plural *seudos, shlishis* (or *shlishit*). The obligation to eat three meals on the Sabbath is derived in the Talmud (*Shabbos 117b*) from the Biblical verse (*Exodus 16:25*) commanding preparation for the Sabbath; in this verse the word *hayom* ('today') is used three times, implying preparation for three meals. Literally, 'three meals,' derived from various references to "three meals" in the Talmud, such as the statement attributed to Bar Kappara (*Shabbos 118a*): "He who observes three meals on the Sabbath is saved from three evils: the travails of Messiah, the retribution of gehenna, and the wars of Gog and Magog."

shechitah or *shechita.* The ritual slaughter of animals and birds by a qualified *shochet,* often called *shochet ubodek* if he is also authorized to perform **bedikah,** or the inspection of an animal's internal organs, especially the lungs, to determine whether the animal is clear of any disease that would render it **treyf** or unfit for consumption. Literally, 'slaughter,' from *shachat,* 'to slaughter.' See also **kashrus.**

sholem zochor or (*Sephardi*) *shalom zachar.* A reception in honor of a newborn male, held usually in his parents' home on the first Friday night after his birth. In the Talmud (*Bava Kamma 80a*) such a reception or feast is called *shavua haben*, 'week of the son.' The present name, meaning roughly 'peace to the male,' is first recorded in the Middle Ages and said to be based on the Talmudic saying, "As soon as a male (*zachar*) comes into the world, peace (*shalom*) comes into the world" (*Niddah 31b*).

simchat bat. 1. A festive gathering or reception to celebrate the birth of a daughter, held usually at the parents' home. It is a contemporary innovation intended to parallel the celebration attendant to an infant boy's circumcision. A simchat bat is held at any time during the infant's first year. Literally, 'festivity of a daughter.' 2. Another name for **shalom bat.**

siyyum or **siyum,** plural **siy(y)umim** or (*Anglicized*) **siy(y)ums.** A ritual held to mark the completion of the study of a tractate of the Gemara or the Mishnah or of the entire Talmud. Participants in the **daf yomi** cycle of Talmud study usually hold a siyyum at the conclusion of every tractate, and a large public siyyum is held at the end of the cycle. The siyyum consists of explaining the passage that concludes the tractate, followed by the recital of the **hadran** (an Aramaic prayer for repeating or returning to the tractate), and a special rabbinical **kaddish,** after which the participants partake in a festive religious meal. The term *siyyum* is also applied to a Torah-dedication ceremony (*siyyum ha-Torah*) held at the completion of the writing of a *sefer Torah* or Torah scroll. At this ceremony, individual donors and others are given the honor of completing the writing of the last lines of the scroll. Literally, 'conclusion, completion.'

taanis or **taanit.** A fast or fast day, especially a *taanis tzibbur*, one observed by the entire community or Jewish people, such as **taanis ester** (the Fast of Esther) before Purim. The **taanis bechorim** (the Fast of the Firstborn) on the eve of Nisan is usually broken by having a **siyyum** (*siyyum bechorim*). See **fast, fasting,** and **fast days.**

tachanun. The propitiatory prayers or supplications recited immediately after the *shemone-esrei* every morning and afternoon (except on Sabbath and the holidays, during the month of Nisan, in the presence of a bridegroom, or where a circumcision is to be held). The central part of the tachanun is the **nefilas apayim,** the act of putting down one's face on the arm in a supplicatory posture while reciting a passage from Samuel II, 24:14. Literally, 'supplication.'

tashlich. The custom of going to a river, seashore, or other body of running water on the afternoon of the first day of Rosh Hashanah (or the second day, if the first day falls on the Sabbath) and there recite certain penitential verses, especially from Micah 7:18–20, which includes the verse "And You will cast into the depths of the sea all their sins." The custom is first described by the Maharil (R. Jacob ben Moses Moellin, *c.*1360–1427). The practice of shaking out the pockets of one's clothes during the tashlich ceremony is believed to symbolize the transferring of one's sins to the fish in the water. The Maharil, however, warned against carrying food to the water to feed the fish as a desecration of the holiday. Literally, 'You will cast.'

tefillas haderech. A special prayer said on setting out on a long trip, whether by car, bus, ship, or plane, to protect oneself from the dangers of travel. It is usually recited when one is about a mile beyond the city or town of departure. The text of the prayer in the Talmud (*Berachos 29b*) is in the first person singular, but the Ashkenazi custom is to recite it in the first person plural in accordance with Abbaye's view (*Berachos 29b-30a*) that one should associate oneself with others in prayer. Variations have been made on the original prayer for air and sea travel and for members of the Israel Defense Forces. Literally, 'prayer for the road.'

tevilah. 1. Ritual immersion in a *mikveh* for purposes of ritual purification. 2. Immersion of new metal utensils, dinnerware, or glassware, or used ones purchased from a non-Jew, before they are put to use. Literally, 'dipping, immersion,' from *taval*, 'to dip, immerse.'

yotzer. See **yotzros.**

zebed habat. A Sephardic ceremony for welcoming or naming of an infant girl. From Hebrew, literally 'gift of a daughter.'

zemiros or *zemirot.* 1. Sabbath songs or hymns, sung at the table Friday night, Sabbath morning, at shalosh seudos, at the conclusion of Sabbath, or at a melave malka. A variety of tunes are used for the standard songs, with many of them transmitted for generations within a family. 2. In Sephardi usage, the preliminary morning prayers, called *Pesukei Dezimrah* ('verses of singing') by Ashkenazim. Plural of *zemirah*, 'singing, song,' from *zamer*, 'to sing.'

rosh yeshiva. The term has two meanings: 1. The head or dean of an academy or seminary for advanced Talmudic studies. In this sense, the term is usually preceded by the article *the,* as in *Rabbi Kotler is the Rosh Yeshiva of Beth Medrash Govoha.* 2. A teacher or member of the faculty of such an academy or seminary, as in *The yeshiva faculty includes both young and older rosh yeshivas.* The term has two plurals: *roshei (ha)yeshiva* (from Hebrew) and *rosh yeshivas* (from Yiddish *rosheshives*). Literally, 'head of yeshiva.'

rov. See **rav** or **Rav.**

– S –

Sabbatean, Sabbateanism, Shabbatean, Shabbateanism. These terms derive from and relate to the false Messiah *Shabbetai Zevi* (1626–1676), and to the Messianic movement he engendered. The terms have no connection with the words Sabbath or Shabbat, nor with the term **Sabbatarian,** which refers to a person who is a strict observer of the Sabbath, or the derivative **Sabbatarianism,** meaning strict observance of the Sabbath as a day of rest. A more accurate spelling for derivatives of the name *Shabbetai* would be *Sabbetean, Sabbeteanism, Shabbetean, Shabbeteanism.*

Sabbath. The formal English word for Saturday, the seventh day of the week, as the Jewish holy day of rest. The word is recorded since the late Old English period (about 950). Unless used attributively (as in *Sabbath songs*), the noun is always preceded by an article, as *the Sabbath* or *a Sabbath*. In non-Jewish usage, the term usually refers to Sunday, which is the main day of Christian worship. The word came into English from Latin *sabbatum* and Greek *sábbaton*, borrowed from Hebrew *shabbat;* see **Shabbat.** The adjective is **sabbatical** (as in *sabbatical rest*) and denotes the seventh day of the week or a seventh year.

sabbatical year. The formal English name of **shemitah,** every seventh year in the fifty-year cycle culminating in the *yovel* or Jubilee. The term has been in English since the 1600s. The same term, also called *sabbatical leave,* denotes a one-year leave of absence granted to professors every seventh year of service. These terms were adopted in American colleges in the 1880s in allusion to the Biblical law (*Exodus 21: 2–6*) requiring the release of a Hebrew bondservant in the seventh year.

sages. The tannaim and amoraim of the Talmudic period. Translation of Hebrew *chachamim.* See **chacham.**

sandek. The man honored to hold on his lap an infant child about to be circumcised. This honor is given to a grandfather, a rabbi, and the like. The infant is usually placed on a pillow that is laid on the sandek's lap. See

bris; milah. From Yiddish, derived from Hebrew *sandak*, earlier (in the Midrash) *sindikos*, *sindiknos*, probably an alteration of Greek *synteknos*, 'godfather,' from *synteknoun*, 'to raise a child together,' formed from *syn-*, 'together' + *teknon*, 'child.' Compare **kvater.**

Sanhedrin. The highest Jewish legislative and judicial body in the Second Temple period, also called the **Great Sanhedrin** (*Sanhedrin Gedolah*), consisting of 71 judges who met in the Temple's Chamber of Hewn Stone (*lishkas hagozis*) and were presided over by a **Nasi.** The lower courts, comprised of 23 judges, were known as *sanhedrin ketanah* ('small sanhedrin') and functioned as district or regional courts. The Talmudic tractate *Sanhedrin* deals with the various courts and their procedures, the examination of witnesses, the modes of execution in capital cases, and related judicial matters. In Jewish history, the Sanhedrin has always been held up as one of the glories of Israel, and an attempt was made to revive the institution in Napoleonic France in 1807 (the "French Sanhedrin"). In the Christian and secular world, however, the term *sanhedrin* has long been used pejoratively (in phrases like "a sanhedrin of hypocrites") because, according to the Christian Bible (Matthew 26:59), the Sanhedrin conducted the preliminary trial of Jesus and condemned him to death. (See **Pharisees** for a similar usage.) From Mishnaic Hebrew, borrowed from Greek *synédrion*, 'council,' (literally) 'a sitting together,' formed from *syn-*, 'together' + *hédra*, 'seat.'

sefer, plural seforim. A Jewish book or tome, especially a religious one, such as a *siddur* (prayerbook), *Tanach* (Bible), or a copy of the *Shulchan aruch* (Code of Law). A sefer is usually written in Hebrew. The term is sometimes used to refer to a *sefer Torah,* a scroll of the Torah, as in *Take out a sefer from the aron kodesh.* The plural of *sefer Torah* is either *sifrei Torah* (from Hebrew) or *sefer Torahs* (from Yiddish *seyfer toyres*). From Hebrew, 'book,' literally, 'scripture.' Originally, Hebrew *sefer* meant a document or scroll written by a *sofer* or scribe; with the advent of printed books it came to have the meaning 'book.'

selichos. See under **ritual terms.**

semicha or **semichah.** Rabbinical ordination, usually in the form of an official diploma signed by a qualified rabbi or rabbis, authorizing the recipient to render halachic decisions. A recipient of semicha is called a *musmach* (plural *musmachim*). This semicha is essentially a *heter horaah*, a permit or license to practice as a rabbi, and is not meant to be an extension of the historical semicha conferred in Eretz Israel from Biblical times until about four hundred years after the destruction of the Second Temple. The attempt by R. Jacob Berav of Safed in 1538 to restore the ancient semicha and thereby reestablish the Sanhedrin (whose members had been *musmachim*) met with controversy and eventual failure. See also **rabbi; rav.** From Hebrew, literally, 'laying on (of hands),' derived from the verse in Deuteronomy 34:9, "Joshua son of Nun was filled with the spirit of wisdom, for Moses had laid his hands (*somach es yodov*) upon him."

Sephardi or **Sefardi.** A Jew whose customs and traditions originated in the Iberian Peninsula (Spain and Portugal) and spread after 1492 to other Mediterranean countries and the Balkans, as distinguished from an **Ashkenazi,** a Jew whose customs and traditions originated in Germany. The name is also used as an adjective, along with **Sephardic** or **Sefardic,** as in *Sephardi* (or *Sephardic*) *Jews, the Sephardi* (or *Sephardic*) *Hebrew pronunciation.* The plural form is **Sephardim** or **Sefardim.** See also *nusach Sepharad* (under **nusach**).

shaatnez, shatnez. A mixture of wool and linen. Wearing a garment that contains shaatnez is Biblically prohibited (*Leviticus 19:19; Deuteronomy 22:11*). An exception to the prohibition was the *avnet* (girdle or sash) made with shaatnez that was worn by the kohanim in the Temple. Shaatnez is the

---

Sephardi derives from *Sepharad*, a geographical name first found in the Bible (*Obadiah 1:20*), in the phrase "and the exile of Jerusalem that is in Sepharad." The Targum Jonathan identifies Sepharad with *Aspamya*, 'Hispania' (Spain), which led to the custom of referring to Spanish-Portuguese Jews as *Sephardim* (the variant spelling *Sefardim* was borrowed from Spanish). Until relatively recently, the name *Sephardi* referred only to Spanish and Portuguese Jews and their descendants. During the 20th century, however, chiefly after the establishment of the State of Israel, the name was popularly expanded to include *all* non-Ashkenazi Jews, including those of Middle Eastern and North African origin. The terms *Oriental Jew* and *Oriental Jewry* are often used to distinguish Jews of Middle Eastern and North African origin from both Ashkenazi and Sephardi Jews. But the distinction does not seem to be holding in popular usage, which prefers the dual division of Ashkenazim and Sephardim, using the latter as an umbrella term for all non-Ashkenazim.

most widely known form of prohibited *kilayim* (mixed species), and in many cities special laboratories exist at which clothing is checked for shaatnez and the mixture is removed. According to the Talmud (*Niddah 61b*), the term *shaatnez* is a blend of the words *shua, tavui, nuz,* 'fulled, spun, woven,' which were the three ways the mixture occurred in clothing.

Shabbat, plural **Shabbatot.** The Sephardi Hebrew name of the Sabbath. The corresponding Ashkenazi Hebrew name is **Shabbos.** The word derives from the Hebrew verb *shavat,* 'to rest, cease from work.'

shabbaton. A social gathering for the Sabbath or weekend, as by a group of teenage or college students, usually including discussions and study sessions, as in *a pre-collegiate shabbaton.* From Hebrew, literally, 'Sabbath rest.'

shabbat shalom! See under **greetings and salutations.**

Shabbos, plural **Shabbosim.** The Ashkenazi Hebrew name of the Sabbath. From Yiddish *shabes,* plural *shabosim.* It often occurs in phrases such as the following:

    Shabbos clock. An automatic timer set before the Sabbath or a holiday to turn on or off lights or appliances (such as an air conditioner) at preset times. Shabbos clocks are common in Orthodox homes. Translation of Yiddish *shabes zeyger.*

    Shabbos goy. A non-Jew who by prearrangement performs chores for a Jew on the Sabbath or holidays, such as turning up the heat in cold weather. Plural, *Shabbos goyim.* From Yiddish, literally, 'Sabbath gentile.' The feminine is *Shabbos goya.*

    Shabbos house. A house or apartment in the vicinity of a synagogue, bought or rented by an Orthodox Jew solely for the purpose of spending the Sabbath there, since his regular home is too far away for walking to a synagogue.

    Shabbos key. A house key in the form of a tie clip or decorative pin for wearing on the Sabbath, since carrying it in the hand or pocket is prohibited on the Sabbath in a community lacking an **eruv.**

shacharis. See under **ritual terms.**

Shaddai. One of God's sacred names, found repeatedly in the Bible (e.g., *Genesis 17:1*), often in the form *El Shaddai* (pronounced *Kel Shakkai*), and explained by the commentator Rashi as deriving from Hebrew *She-*

dai, 'Who is sufficient' (in His mercy and in granting one's needs). The Midrash explains the name as deriving from God's saying "Enough!" at the Creation to keep the world within bounds. It is customary to write in Hebrew the name *Shaddai* on the back of a mezuzah scroll and to show it through an opening in the case.

shaliach, plural **shelichim** or **sheluchim.** An agent, messenger, emissary, or delegate, as in *a Hadassah shaliach, a shaliach of the Jewish Agency, Chabad shelichim* (or *sheluchim*). A shaliach's charge or mission is his **shelichus** (sheli'khus). The feminie **shelucha** is also used. From Hebrew (and Yiddish), from the verb *shalach*, 'to send.' See also **meshulach.**

shalom bat. See under **ritual terms.**

shammes or **shammash,** plural **shaammosim** or **shammashim.** 1. The caretaker or beadle of a synagogue. 2. A rav's or rebbe's personal assistant. 3. The extra candle used to light the candles of a Chanukah menorah. 4. The longest strand of each tassel of the tzitzis, wound around the other strands. From Yiddish *shames* (plural *shamosim*) and Hebrew *shammash* (plural *shammashim*), literally, 'servant, waiter,' derived from the Hebrew verb *shimmesh*, 'to serve, attend, wait on.'

shamta. See **herem.**

Shas. A popular synonym for the **Talmud.** It is an acronym made up of the initial letters of **Sh**isha **S**idrei, Hebrew for "Six Orders" (of the Mishnah). The Hebrew acronym ש״ס first appeared in the late 1500s in the Basel edition of the Talmud to replace the word *Talmud*, which was objected to by the Swiss censors.

shatnez. See **shaatnez.**

Shechinah or **Shekhinah.** A rabbinic and kabbalistic name of God that emphasizes the Divine Presence dwelling or resting within a place (such as a sanctuary), within a human being (such as a righteous person), or within a people (such as Israel). Even in the World to Come the righteous sit with crowns on their heads and bask in the splendor of the Shechinah (*Berachos 17a*). In the kabbalah, the Sechinah is in the tenth sefirah of *Malchus* ('Kingdom') and represents a female element or aspect of the Godhead. From Hebrew, derived from the verb *shachan*, 'to dwell, inhabit,' especially in Exodus 25:8, "They shall make me a sanctuary, so that I may dwell (*veshachanti*) in their midst."

shechitah. See under **ritual terms.**

sheitel. See under **clothing terms.**

Shem Havayah. A Hebrew term for the Tetragrammaton, or unpronounceable four-letter name of God. Formed from *Shem*, 'Name,' and *Havayah*, 'Being, Existence' (from *havah*, 'to be, exist'). The term was chosen because the word *havayah* consists of the four letters (הויה) that occur also (in different order) in the Tetragrammaton. See also **Hashem.**

shemitah or **shemita.** Every seventh year in the fifty-year *yovel* cycle, properly called **sheviit,** during which the soil in Eretz Israel is to be left fallow. The Bible (*Leviticus 25:1–7*) prohibits plowing, planting, and harvesting during shemitah, and the Rabbis included in the prohibition any activity that improves the land or promotes the growth of produce. Also during shemitah all debts have to be relinquished (*Deuteronomy 15:1–11*), a law modified by the issuance of a *prosbul,* a legal document by which a private loan may be collected by a law court after the shemitah. In formal English, the year of shemitah is called **sabbatical year.** From Hebrew *shemittah,* literally, 'fallow year,' from *shamat,* 'to let fall, release, let lie fallow.'

shemone-esrei or **shemone-esre.** Also capitalized: **Shemone-esrei, Shemone-esre.** The name of the principal prayer of the Jewish liturgy, also called *amidah* and in the Talmud referred to as *tefillah* ('prayer'). The name *shemone-esrei* (Hebrew, literally, 'eighteen') developed from the fact that originally it consisted of eighteen paragraphs, each concluding with a blessing in praise of one of God's attributes. After the destruction of the Second Temple, Rabban Gamliel II, the head of the Sanhedrin in Yavneh, incorporated into the prayer a nineteenth blessing, the *birkat haminim* ('blessing against heretics') in reaction to the spread of heretical sects among Jews. Nevertheless, the traditional name has not been changed, probably because it is based on the Talmud (*Berachos 28b*), which associates the number eighteen with the eighteen times God is mentioned in Psalm 29 and the eighteen times God is mentioned in the *Shema* ("Hear O Israel") prayer. Many prefer to use the term *amidah* because it is applicable to both the weekday and the shorter Sabbath and holiday prayer. For the Sabbath and holiday prayers, *amidah* may be the more appropriate term; but for the weekday prayers, the traditional name *shemone-esrei* is entirely adequate.

sheviit. The seventh and last year in each of the seven-year cycles culminating in the jubilee or fiftieth year (**yovel**); the year of **shemitah**. From Hebrew, literally, 'seventh.'

sheygetz. A Yiddish-origin colloquial term for: 1. A non-Jewish boy. 2. An impudent youth or man. 3. An irreligious or nonobservant Jew. The term is often regarded as disparaging. The plural is **shkotzim**. Compare **shiksa**. From Yiddish *sheygets*, derived from Hebrew *shekets*, 'abhorrent creature,' from *shikets*, 'to abhor, detest.'

sheytl. See under **clothing terms**.

shidduch or **shiduch.** See under **wedding terms**.

shield of David. See **Magen David**.

shiksa. A Yiddish-origin colloquial term for: 1. A non-Jewish girl. 2. a housemaid. 3. an irreligious or nonobservant Jewish girl. The term is often regarded as disparaging. In American English slang, it is applied to a Jewish stereotype of a gentile girl being extraordinarily beautiful, as in the phrase *a shiksa goddess*. From Yiddish *shikse*, derived from Hebrew *shik-tsah*, feminine of *shekets;* see **sheygetz**.

shiur, plural **shiurim.** 1. A lesson, lecture, or discourse on the Torah, Mishnah, or Gemara. See *maggid shiur* under **maggid**. 2. A measure, size, or rate, as in *The minimum shiur of a mikveh is forty seah, or 151 gallons of water.* From Hebrew, derived from *shaar*, 'to calculate, measure.'

shivah or **shiva.** The first seven days of mourning following the death of a close relative, during which the mourner may not leave the house of mourning, engage in work or business, bathe, shave, or cut the hair, wear leather shoes or new clothes, sit on regular chairs, or have sexual relations. From Hebrew, literally, 'seven.' The verb phrase *sit shivah* (or *shiva*) is a part-translation of Yiddish *zitsn shive* and means to observe the shivah period; the phrase derives from the fact that mourners, when sitting down, must not use regular chairs but use instead footstools or (as Sephardim do) sit on the floor. The noun phrase *shivah call* (or *shiva call*), usually in the phrase *pay a shivah/shiva call*, is an innovation modeled on the English phrase *pay a condolence call*; the corresponding Yiddish-origin phrase used by many Ashkenazim is *be menachem-ovel* (Yiddish *zayn menakhem-ovl*, 'comfort the mourner'). See also **mourning terms.**

shlemiel, shlimazl. See under **Yiddishisms.**

shlita or **shelita.** An acronym for the Hebrew phrase *sheyichye leorech yomim tovim, omeyn,* 'May he live long and well, Amen,' said or written after the name of a rabbi or religious leader, especially a prominent one, as in *Horav Feinstein, shlita* or *Reb Dovid, shlita.* See also **abbreviations and acronyms; notarikon.**

shnoder. A Yiddish-origin verb meaning 'to pledge a donation,' as in *I shnodered fifty dollars at yizkor.* See more under **neder.** See also **beli neder.**

shochet, plural **shochtim.** A man certified or authorized by a rabbi or Jewish court to slaughter animals in the manner prescribed by Jewish law; a ritual slaughterer. From Hebrew, from *shachat,* 'to slaughter.' See *shechitah* under **ritual terms.** See also **kashrus.**

shokel. To move rhythmically back and forth or side to side during prayer or Torah study, either habitually and unconsciously or deliberately to express emotion or fervor. Men tend to shokel more than women, and shokeling is more common among the Orthodox, and most vigorous and entrenched among Hasidim. From Yiddish *shoklen,* literally, 'to shake, rock, sway,' a frequentative form derived from Middle Low German *schacken,* 'to shake,' from the same Germanic source as English *shake.*

sholem zochor. See under **ritual terms.**

shtadlan. A Jew serving as a representative or advocate of Jews and their interests before gentile authorities. Formerly and especially in Europe, a shtadlan (plural **shtadlonim)** was often attached to a court as a *Hofjude* or "court Jew," through whom petitions of a community were presented to a royal court or ruler. The office or practice of a shtadlan was known as **shtadlanus,** literally, 'intercession, mediation.' The shtadlan as an official functionary declined in importance in the 19th century, though the concept of an influential Jewish representative or spokesman before non-Jews, often called a shtadlan, lives on. From Hebrew, literally, 'intercessor, mediator,' derived from the verb *hishtadel,* 'to endeavor, strive, induce, persuade,' from the root *shidel.*

shlemiel: the story of a word

This term for a clumsy, bungling person, a simpleton, came from Western Yiddish and first appeared in English in Israel Zangwill's novel *Children of the Ghetto* (1892). Its first appearance in an American English text was in a 1919 issue of the *San Francisco Hebrew*, an Anglo-Jewish periodical.

The origin of the Yiddish word is somewhat obscure. According to Mitford Mathews' *A Dictionary of Americanisms* (1951), the word apparently came from "[Adelbert von] Chamisso's well-known story, *Peter Schlemihl*, of the unfortunate wretch who sold his shadow to the devil." This is very unlikely, however, since the Yiddish word is far older than Chamisso's story, which appeared in 1814. More probably, Chamisso (1781–1838), a German poet, took the name of his hero from the Western Yiddish word.

Two authoritative English dictionaries, *Webster's Third* (1961) and the *Oxford English Dictionary* (*Supplement vol. III*, 1982) suggest that the Yiddish word's ultimate origin is the Biblical *Shelumiel* ben Zurishaddai (*Numbers 1:6*), "said by the Talmud to have met with an unhappy end" (*OED Supplement*). The OED's reference to the Talmud is apparently based on Nathan Susskind's article, "Origin of Shlemiel" (*Comments on Etymology 9, 1980*). According to this account, the transformation of the name of Shelumiel ben Zurishaddai, the chief of the tribe of Simeon, to the designation of a classic bungler is rooted in the identification of Shelumiel in the Talmud (*Sanhedrin 82b*) with Zimri ben Salu, the Simeonite prince who was killed by Phinehas while fornicating with a Midianite woman (*Numbers 25:6–15*).

Zimri's predicament, which is embellished in the Talmud and Midrash, was taken as a morbidly humorous instance of a supremely luckless fellow; but since a direct reference to Zimri might stir lascivious thoughts, pious scholars took to using the name of Shelumiel, the chief prince of the Simeonites, as a veiled reference to the Simeonite prince Zimri. Implied in this "private joke of pious scholars," as Susskind puts it, is the additional irony of Shelumiel's lucklessness in having become—quite innocently—a substitute for the lecherous Zimri.

This explanation of the origin of *shlemiel*, while plausible, is essentially an ingenious hypothesis. The precise origin of the Yiddish word remains uncertain.

Many explanations have been given for the practice of *shokeling*. The best-known one is stated by the 16th century Ashkenazi codifier R. Moshe Isserles (the *Ramo*) in the *Shulchan Aruch* (*Orach Chaim 48:1*): "And those who are meticulous are accustomed to sway during the reading of the Torah in illustration of the shaking that accompanied the giving of the Torah, and similarly during prayer on account of [Psalms 35:10] 'All my limbs shall say, Hashem, who is like unto You?'" In a mystical vein, the Zohar, citing the verse 'A man's soul is the lamp of the Lord' (*Proverbs 20:27*), compares the swaying motion in prayer to the flickering of the light of the Holy Lamp. The philosopher Yehudah Halevi (1075–1141), writing in *The Kuzari*, attributed the swaying to the excitement and fervor generated by study and prayer, but proposed further that the practice grew out of the necessity of moving to and fro when ten or more people would read from a single book, as was not uncommon before the invention of printing.

shtetl, plural **shtetls** or (from Yiddish) **shtetlech** (shtet'lekh). A town or village with many Jewish inhabitants, commonly found in Eastern Europe before World War II. A typical shtetl was economically stagnant but distinguished by a tight-knit Jewish community whose primary language was Yiddish and whose spiritual life centered on the synagogue, cheder, mikveh, and other religious institutions. From Yiddish, literally, 'small town,' from Middle High German *stetel*, diminutive of *stat* (Yiddish *shtot*), 'town, city, place,' related to English *stead*.

shtibl. See under **Hasidic terms.**

shtrayml or **shtreimel.** See under **clothing terms.**

shul. The most widespread Jewish term for a synagogue or Jewish house of worship, used chiefly by Ashkenazim. The term also means a Jewish congregation, as in *The whole shul was at the meeting*, or the act of praying in the synagogue, as in *He attends shul regularly*, or the physical plant or building of a synagogue, as in *The shul needs repairs*. From Yiddish, derived from Middle High German *schuol(e)*, literally, 'school,' from Latin *schola*, the source also of English *school*. During the Middle Ages, the Jews in Germany took to referring to the synagogue as *di schul(e)*, 'the school,' partly because a synagogue functioned traditionally as a school or house of study, but also because calling it a house of worship might have antagonized the Christian authorities. The term *shul* came into English at the turn of the 20th century with the mass immigration of East European Jews to America and England, quickly replacing such formal terms as *synagogue, congregation,* and *temple,* and spawning such compounds as *shulgoer, shulgoing, shul members, shul bulletin, shul meeting.* See also *kloyz* and *shtibl* under **Hasidic terms;** *beis medresh* and *bet (ha)knesset* under **synagogue terms.**

sidrah or **sidra,** plural **sidrahs, sidras,** or **sidros.** The Ashkenazi term for the section of the Pentateuch read each week in the synagogue. From Hebrew, literally, 'ordered arrangement, sequence.' The verb phrase *be mavir sidrah,* 'go over the sidrah' comes from Yiddish *zayn mayver sedre* and refers to the custom of reviewing the week's sidrah by reading two Hebrew verses and one Aramaic verse at a time. The corresponding Sephardi term is **parashah,** plural **parashiyot,** literally, 'section, chapter,' which many Ashkenazim adopted as *parshah,* especially in the phrases *parshas hashavua,* 'section of the week' and *arba parshiyos,* 'four sections' (which are read on the four Sabbaths before Passover). The formal English term for a sidrah is *the weekly portion.*

simchah or **simcha.** A joyful religious occasion or celebration, such as a circumcision, a bar mitzvah or bat mitzvah, or a wedding. The celebrant or host is called a **baal-simchah.** From Yiddish *simkhe* and Hebrew *simchah,* literally, 'joy, rejoicing, gladness.'

Simchas Torah. See under **holiday terms.**

simchat bat. See under **ritual terms.**

siyyum. See under **ritual terms.**

sopher or **sofer,** plural **sopherim** or **soferim.** An expert in the writing or copying of sacred Hebrew texts with a feather quill and parchment; a scribe. A sopher writes scrolls of the Torah (Pentateuch), megillah (Book of Esther), tefillin, mezuzahs, kesubos (marriage certificates), and gittin (bills of divorce). A **sopher setam** is a sopher who specializes in writing scrolls of the Torah, tefillin, and mezuzahs (*setam* is an acronym for *sefer torah, tefillin, mezuzahs*). From Hebrew, 'scribe,' related to *sefer,* 'scripture, book.' The **Sopherim** were the scholars of the pre-Tannaitic period, beginning with Ezra (known as *hasofer,* 'the scribe') in the 5th century

B.C.E. and ending with Shimon Hatzaddik (Simeon the Just) who lived about 300–200 B.C.E. They were precursors of the Masoretes.

Spinnholz. An old name for a **forshpil.** From German, literally, 'distaff' (an old symbol of feminine domesticity), alteration by folk etymology of Latin *sponsalia*, 'espousals, betrothal ceremony,' derived from *spondere*, 'to pledge.'

spodek. See under **clothing terms.**

Star of David. See **Magen David.**

sukkah. See *Sukkos* under **holiday terms.**

synagogue. A Jewish house of worship. The term came into English in the 1100s from Late Latin *synagoga*, which took it from Greek *synagoge*, 'place of assembly,' a part translation of Hebrew *bet haknesset*, 'house of assembly.' The Greek word derived from *synagein*, 'to bring together, assemble' (formed from *syn-*, 'together' + *agein*, 'lead, bring'). Compare **esnoga.** See also **shul, temple.**

synagogue terms. A number of terms associated with the synagogue appear as main entries; for example, **aliyah, amidah, bimah, chazzan, daven, gabbai, mechitza, minyan, mizrach.** Other terms, especially those requiring only a simple definition, are listed below in alphabetical order. Unless otherwise stated, all the terms are from Hebrew.

    aron hakodesh. The chest, case, or closet in which the scrolls of the

---

The phrase "a Jewish synagogue" is as redundant as a "Jewish rabbi." Both are by definition Jewish. Nor is a synagogue the Jewish equivalent of a church. Unlike the latter, a synagogue is not required for formal prayer or observance, since most Jewish rituals can take place in the home or elsewhere. The synagogue serves primarily as a place where Jews can congregate for public prayer and public reading of the Torah, often also providing space for study and social activities. It is a combination of *bet haknesset* ("house of assembly") and *bet midrash* ("house of study").

Torah are kept in the synagogue; the *holy ark*. Often shortened to *aron*. Literally, 'sacred chest.' See also **heichal**.

baal-tefillah or *baal-tefilla*. The person who leads the prayers; the chazzan or cantor. Literally, 'master of prayer.' He may be the *baal-shacharis* (morning service) or the *baal-musaf* (additional service on Sabbaths and holidays).

beis midrash or (*Sephardi*) *bet midrash*. A synagogue or house of study; also, the chapel of a synagogue, usually a room within the synagogue building used for study and daily services. Literally, 'house of study.' Plural *batei midrash* or (double plural) *batei midrashim*. The Yiddish form is *besmedresh*, plural *bote-medroshim*.

bet knesset or (*Ashkenazi*) *beis knesses*. A synagogue. Literally, 'house of assembly.' Plural, *batei knesset* or (double plural) *batei kenessiyot* or (*Ashkenazi*) *batei kenessiyos*. The Yiddish form is *beys-hakneses*, plural *bote-knesiyes*.

chazoras hashatz. The repetition of the *shemone-esrei* or *amidah* by the *chazzan* or *sheliach tzibbur*. Literally, repetition by the *shatz* (= *sheliach tzibbur*).

chiyuv, plural *chiyuvim*. One having the duty to recite the mourner's kaddish and therefore entitled to lead as *sheliach tzibbur*, especially in the weekday services, or entitled to an *aliyah*. Literally, 'duty, obligation.'

chumash, plural *chumashim*. A volume or set of books containing the Torah or Five Books of Moses (*chamishah chumshei torah*), used especially in the synagogue to follow the public reading from the Torah scroll (*keriyas hatorah*).

eternal light or *eternal lamp*. Formal English term for the *ner tamid*.

etz chayim. Either of the two wooden staves, with rounded handles on top and bottom, on which a Torah scroll is rolled. Literally, 'tree of life,' in allusion to the verse, "It [the Torah] is a tree of life to those who grasp it" (*Proverbs 3:18*). Plural, *atzei chayim* or (*Anglicized*) *etz chayims*.

ezras nashim. The women's section of an Orthodox synagogue, either in the form of a balcony or as a separate section divided from the men's section by a **mechitza**. Literally, 'women's court,' from the name of the separate court assigned to women in the Holy Temple.

gartel. The girdle or sash wound around the Torah scroll during *gelilah* to keep it from unrolling. From Yiddish *gartl*, 'belt, girdle.' See *gartel* under **clothing terms**.

gelilah. Among Ashkenazim, the act of rolling up the Torah scroll and closing it up with a girdle or sash while it is held upright by the person who has done the *hagbahah.* Literally, 'rolling up.'

hafsakah. Same as *hefsek.*

haftorah or *haftora.* A portion from the Prophets read on Sabbaths, holidays, and fast days immediately after the Torah reading. The haftorah is read from a printed text by the *maftir.* Literally, 'conclusion.'

hagbahah. The act of raising the Torah scroll for display to the congregants. Among Sephardim this is done before the Torah reading. Among Ashkenazim it is done after the reading, and the person who lifts the Torah scroll sits down to permit another to do the *gelilah.* Literally, 'raising, lifting.'

hashkamah or *hashkama.* An early synagogue service on Sabbath morning, preceding the main service and usually less elaborate and of shorter duration. Literally, 'early rising, reveille.'

hefsek. An interruption in the continuity or order of a prayer or prayers. Literally, 'stop, interruption.' Also called *hafsakah.* See also *mafsik.*

holy ark. Formal English term for the *aron hakodesh.*

kerias hatorah. The public reading from the Torah scroll on Sabbaths, holidays, fast days, and on weekdays on Monday and Thursday. Literally, 'reading of the Torah.'

kibbud, plural *kibbudim.* An honor given to a congregant, such as an aliyah. Loosely, it also means after-prayer refreshments. Literally, 'honor, respect.'

machzor, plural *machzorim* or *(Anglicized) machzors.* A holiday prayerbook, as distinguished from a daily and Sabbath prayerbook or *siddur.* Literally, 'cycle,' because the early machzorim contained the prayers of the entire year arranged according to the yearly cycle of holidays.

mafsik. To be *mafsik* is to interrupt a prayer or service, as by talking where talking is forbidden. Such an interruption constitutes a *hefsek* or *hafsakah.* Literally, 'stopping, interrupting'; the verb phrase is a part translation of Yiddish *mafsik zayn.*

maftir. 1. The last aliyah on Sabbaths, holidays, and fast days, assigned to the person who reads the *haftorah.* 2. The person who reads the haftorah. 3. The haftorah itself. Literally, 'concluding.'

mantle. Among Ashkenazim, the sheath covering a Torah scroll. It is open at the bottom and closed on top except for two openings for the staves (*atzei chayim*) to pass through. Also called *mentele.* From Yiddish *mantl,* literally, 'mantle, cloak' (diminutive, *mentele*).

misheberach (mi-she-be'rach). A blessing made (as by a gabbai) for a person who has received an aliyah, or for a sick person, or to name a newborn girl. In colloquial and humorous usage, *to give someone a misheberach* means to curse or berate him. Literally, 'He who blessed,' from the blessing's introductory phrase.

mispallelim. The people who pray in a synagogue; the congregants. Plural of *mispallel,* 'one who prays,' from *hispallel,* 'to pray.'

ner tamid. A perpetually burning lamp hanging from the ceiling in front of the holy ark. It symbolizes the continuous light of the menorah in the Tabernacle (*Exodus 27:20; Leviticus 34:2*) and later in the Temple. Literally, 'perpetual light.' Also called **eternal light** or **eternal lamp.**

parashah, plural **parashiyos.** 1. Any of the four passages of the Torah relating to tefillin that are inserted into the tefillin cases. 2. Sephardic term for **sidrah.** Literally, 'section, chapter.'

parnas, plural **parnasim.** The president of a congregation; also, any of the officials or trustees of a congregation. Literally, 'supporter, provider.' The Yiddish form is **parnes,** plural **parneysim.**

paroches. The curtain hanging over the holy ark in Ashkenazi synagogues, symbolizing the partition in front of the Holy of Holies in the Tabernacle (*Exodus 26:31*) and later in the Temple. Literally, 'partition.'

pesichah or **pesicha.** The honor of opening the holy ark before the Torah scrolls are removed or during the recital of various piyyutim, as during the high holy days. Literally, 'opening.'

rimmon, plural **rimmonim.** Either of the crowning ornaments or finials often mounted on the staves of a Torah scroll. Literally, 'pomegranate,' so called because pomegranate-shaped tassels were used for decoration (*Exodus 28:34*).

sheliach tzibbur. The person who leads the prayer service in the synagogue. Literally, 'deputy of the congregation.' Compare **baal-tefillah.**

shulchan. The table, somewhat slanted, which stands on the **bimah** for use in reading the Torah scroll in the synagogue. It also serves often as the stand from which a chazzan or sheliach tzibbur leads the prayers. Literally, 'table.'

siddur. The daily and Sabbath prayerbook, usually including the blessings over food and for other occasions, the Sabbath songs (*zemiros*), the after-meal blessings (*birkas hamazon*), the marriage, circumcision, and other special services, and parts of the holiday services. Literally, 'arrangement, order,' shortened from *siddur tefillah,* 'arrangement or order of prayer.' Compare **machzor.**

yad. A pointer used by the reader of the Torah scroll to point at the text, since touching the parchment with the finger is forbidden. The yad is made of wood, silver, or gold, and its business end is usually a sculpted hand with a pointing finger. Literally, 'hand.'

– T –

tachanun. See under **ritual terms.**

tahina or **tehina.** See under **food terms.**

takkanah. See under **halachic terms.**

tallis or (*Sephardi*) **tallit.** The four-cornered garment with fringes (**tzitzis**) that worshipers wear on their backs during morning prayers. A common English name for it is **prayer shawl.** The Ashkenazi plural is **talleisim** (from Yiddish); the Sephardi plural is **tallitot.** Sometimes the tallis is called *tallis gadol* ('large tallis') to distinguish it from a **tallis katan.** From Hebrew, literally, 'cloak, cover, garment,' from Aramaic *talal*, 'to cover.'

tallis katan or **tallit katan.** A smaller version of the large tallis, worn by Orthodox Jewish males, usually under their outer clothes. It is also called **arba kanfos, tzitzis,** and **laybtsudekl.** From Hebrew, literally, 'small tallis.'

talmid, plural **talmidim.** 1. A pupil or student at a cheder or yeshiva. 2. The disciple of a **rav** or **rebbe²**. From Hebrew, from the verb *lamad*, 'to learn, study.' See also **lamdan, melamed, Talmud.**

talmid chacham, plural (double) **talmidei chachamim.** A Jew who is learned or proficient in Tanach and Talmud; a learned or scholarly Jew. A talmid chacham is often contrasted with an **am-haaretz.** From Hebrew, literally, 'disciple of a sage.' The (double) plural means literally 'disciples of sages.'

Talmud. The body of Jewish law and tradition comprising the **Mishnah** and the **Gemara,** compiled from about 30 B.C.E. to about 500 C.E. More specifically, the term designates the Gemara (which incorporates the Mishnah), and even more specifically, the Gemara of the *Talmud Bavli*, the Babylonian Talmud, as distinguished from the *Talmud Yerushalmi*, the Talmud compiled in Eretz Israel. Thus, *to study Talmud* usually means the same as *to study Gemara*, which is also the more common usage (in Yiddish, *lernen gemore* or *lernen a blatt gemore*). The Talmud Bavli consists of 39 tractates (*masechtos*), the Yerushalmi of 37 tractates. A popular synonym of the Talmud is **Shas.** From Hebrew, literally, 'learning, study,' related to *lamad*, 'to learn, study.' Common derivatives are **Talmudic** or **talmudic,** and **Talmudist.** See also **amora, tanna; lamdan; daf.**

Talmud Torah. See **cheder.**

Tanach or **Tanakh.** A popular acronym for the Hebrew Bible or Scriptures, formed from the names of its three sections, *T(orah)*, *N(eviim)*, *K(esuvim)*, 'Pentateuch, Prophets, Writings.' The Tanach is traditionally made up of 24 books, counting the 12 minor Prophets (*Terei Asar*) as one book: Torah (5 Books), Neviim (8 Books), Kesuvim (11 Books, counting Ezra and Nehemiah as one book). See **Torah.**

tanna, plural **tannaim.** Often capitalized: **Tanna, Tannaim.** Any of the Talmudic sages of Eretz Israel whose teachings form the Mishnah. The period of the tannaim extended from the first through the second century B.C. Their teachings also include *beraysos* ('external mishnayos'), which were not incorporated in the Mishnah proper but are often cited in the Gemara. The adjective is **tannaitic,** as in *the tannaitic period.* From Aramaic, 'teacher, scholar.' Compare **amora.**

Targum, plural **Targumim.** Any of various Aramaic translations of the Hebrew Scriptures, especially the translations of Onkelos (*Targum Onkelos*) and Yonasan ben Uziel (*Targum Yonasan*). The language of these Targums is **Jewish Aramaic,** which was the vernacular of most Jews of Babylonia and Eretz Israel for over a thousand years, until the beginning of the Diaspora. *Targum* is also the name of a modern form of Jewish Aramaic used among the Jews of Kurdistan and Azerbaijan. From Aramaic *targum*, literally, 'translation,' from *tirgem*, 'to translate.' In ancient times a **meturgeman** translated the Hebrew Scriptures into Aramaic during the reading of the Torah in the synagogue. See also **Aramaic; Jewish languages.**

Targumic. A former name of **Jewish Aramaic.**

targum-loshen. Yiddish-origin name of **Jewish Aramaic.** From Yiddish *targum-loshn*, literally, 'Targum-language.'

tashlich. See under **ritual terms.**

techinah, plural **techinos.** Any of various printed collections of supplications and prayers in Yiddish, written especially for women, beginning in the early 1600s. From Yiddish *tkhine*, derived from Hebrew *techinnah*, 'supplication.'

tefillah or **tefilla,** plural **tefillos.** 1. Broadly, *tefillah* refers to any of the prescribed prayers recited daily, on the Sabbath, or on the holidays, as in *the tefillah of minchah, the tefillos of Rosh Hashanah.* A *baal-tefillah* is one who leads the prayers in the synagogue; a *beis tefillah* is a house of prayer or synagogue. In the Talmud, *tefillah* refers specifically to the *shemone-esrei* or *amidah.* From Hebrew, literally, 'prayer.' See also the related form *mispallelim* under **synagogue terms.** 2. The singular of **tefillin,** as in *the tefillah of the hand.*

tefillin, singular **tefillah.** This is the traditional name of the pair of black leather boxes containing Biblical passages that are worn by males over thirteen during weekday morning prayer. The boxes are called *batim* ('houses,' singular *bayis*), and each box contains four passages from the Torah (*parashiyos*) written on parchment. The passages, from Deuteronomy 6:4–9 (*Shema*), Deuteronomy 11:13–21 (*Vehoyoh im shamoa*), Exodus 13:1–10 (*Kadesh*), and Exodus 13:11–16 (*Vehoyoh ki yeviacho*), are written on a single parchment for insertion in the *tefillah shel yad* (worn on the arm), and on four separate parchments for insertion in four compartments in the *tefillah shel rosh* (worn on the head). The long black leather straps attached to the tefillin are called *retzuos,* singular *retzuah.* Although *tefillin* is plural, it is often loosely used as a singular, as in *the tefillin shel yad* or *the tefillin of the hand,* instead of the more accurate *the tefillah shel yad* or *the tefillah of the hand.* The ultimate origin of Hebrew *tefillin* is uncertain. Its immediate source was Aramaic, which may have derived it from *palal,* 'to plead, pray,' a word related to the Hebrew *tefillah,* 'prayer.' This derivation is supported by the fact that the singular form *tefillah* is identical with the Hebrew word for prayer. Nevertheless, other derivations have been proposed (such as the Hebrew root *palah,* 'to distinguish') on the grounds that in ancient times tefillin were worn all day long, not only during prayer. The term *phylacteries* (singular *phylactery*), which has been established since the Middle Ages as the English word for *tefillin,* derives from Greek *phylakterion,* a word that is not actually a translation of the Hebrew *tefillin* but rather a biased interpretation of their use. The Greek word means a safeguard or amulet, and it first appears in the Christian Bible (Matthew 23:5) in a hostile remark about the Pharisees, who were seen as exaggerating their piety by wearing "amulets" conspicuously. See **Pharisees.**

temple. Until the middle of the 19th century, Jews used the word *Temple* only in reference to the *beis hamikdash* or Holy Temple in Jerusalem, either the First Temple (*bayis rishon*) built by Solomon (I Kings 6:1) and destroyed by Nebuchadnezzar in 586 B.C.E., or the Second Temple (*bayis sheni*), built by Zerubbabel (Ezra 5:2) and destroyed by Titus in 70 C.E. All Orthodox and many Conservative Jews continue to use the word only in this sense. But beginning with the establishment of the first Reform synagogue in Hamburg, Germany, in 1818–1819, Reform Jews applied the German word *Tempel* and later English *Temple* to their houses of worship, and this practice has endured. It appears in the names of most Reform synagogues and some Conservative ones, such as *Temple Beth El*, *Temple Beth Israel*, *Temple Emanuel*, *Temple Israel*, *Temple Sholom*, and *Temple Sinai*.

The phrase *going to temple* is the Reform equivalent of the Orthodox *going to shul.*

tenaim. See under **wedding terms.**

Ten Days of Penitence. The ten days between Rosh Hashanah and Yom Kippur that are devoted to repentance of sins and during which penitential prayers are recited. Translation of Hebrew *aseres yemei teshuvah.* See also *selichos* under **ritual terms;** *yomim neroim* under **holiday terms.**

terefah. See **kashrus.** Compare **tryef, treyfa.**

teshuvah or **teshuva** (*Ashkenazi* tshu′ve; *Sephardi* teshuva′). 1. Repentance. See **baal-teshuvah.** 2. plural **teshuvos.** An answer or reply; responsum. Used especially in the term *sheilos uteshuvos,* 'rabbinical replies to questions of Jewish law,' literally, 'questions and answers.' See **responsa.**

Tetragrammaton. A scholarly term for the sacred and unpronounceable Hebrew four-letter name of God (יהוה), usually translated in English as 'the Lord' and transliterated as YHVH. The term came into English before the 1400s as a borrowing from Greek *tetragrámmaton,* literally, '(word) of four letters.' See also **Adonai, Hashem, Jehovah, Shem Havayah.**

tevah. In Sephardi usage, the raised platform in the synagogue on which the table or desk for reading the Torah stands. From Hebrew, literally, 'box, case.' Compare **almemar, bimah.**

Three Weeks. The three weeks between *shiva asar betamuz* (17th of Tamuz), when the walls of Jerusalem were breached, and *Tisha B'Av* (9th of Av), when the Temple was destroyed. See **fast days.** The Three Weeks are a period of semi-mourning in which religious Jews do not hold weddings or other celebrations, avoid listening to music, and do not take haircuts. The period is called *dray vokhn* ('three weeks') in Yiddish and *beyn hamtzorim* ('between the straits') in Hebrew. See also **Nine Days.**

tichel. See under **clothing terms.**

tikkun, plural **tikkunim.** 1. See under **Hasidic terms.** 2. See under **kabbalistic terms.** 3. Any of various special (originally kabbalistic) services, such as *tikkun chatzos*, midnight prayers commemorating the destruction of the Temple, *tikkun leyl hoshana rabbah*, and *tikkun leyl shavuos*, passages from the Scriptures, Talmud, Midrash, and Zohar recited respectively on the night of Hoshana Rabbah and the first night of Shavuos. 4. A volume containing the Hebrew text of the Chumash (Pentateuch) without vowels or accents, exactly as it appears in the Torah scroll, to help the *baal-kore* or reader prepare for the public reading of the Torah. Short for *tikkun hakore*, 'reader's tikkun.' From Hebrew, literally, 'reparation, reformation, restoration.'

Tisha B'Av. A day of fasting and mourning for the destruction of the First and Second Temples, occurring on the 9th of Av. See **Av.** It is a major fast day that begins at sundown of the previous night and lasts 24 hours, during which one may not eat and drink, bathe, wear leather shoes, and have marital relations. It is also customary not to sit on regular chairs and to sit on the floor, especially during the reading on the Book of Lamentations (*Eichah*) and the recital of *kinos*, dirges recalling the tragic events that befell the Jewish people throughout history. From Hebrew *tisha b'av*, literally, 'ninth of Av.' See also **fast days.**

Torah. 1. The Five Books of Moses; the **Pentateuch.** 2. The Hebrew Scriptures or Bible; the **Tanach.** 3. The entire body of Jewish learning and tradition, including the **Written Law, Oral Law,** and the codes and commentaries based on both. From Hebrew, literally 'teaching, instruction.'

Tosafos or (*Sephardi*) **Tosafot.** Commentaries on the Babylonian Talmud printed on the outer column of the page opposite Rashi's commentaries. The Tosafos, written in Rashi's script, were composed by **rishonim,** many of them Rashi's students and descendants, in France and Germany between the 12th and 14th centuries. The **Tosafists,** as they are known, included

The narrow translation of the word Torah as 'Law,' especially in the phrases *Oral Law* (for Hebrew *torah she-be-al peh*) and *Written Law* (for Hebrew *torah she-be kesav*) derives from the Septuagint (the Greek translation of the Bible), where *torah* was translated as *nomos*, 'law.' In some uses the translation is valid, as in the verse in Leviticus 6:2: *zos toras haolah*, 'this is the law of the *olah* (elevation offering).' But in other contexts Scripture uses the word in the broader sense of 'teaching,' as in Deuteronomy 4:44: *Vezos hatorah asher som moshe lifnei benei yisrael*, 'This is the teaching that Moses placed before the Children of Israel.'

hundreds of scholars, among them Rashi's grandsons, Rabbenu Tam (1100–71) and the Rashbam (Samuel ben Meir, c.1085–1174), and the Meharam of Rothenberg (c.1220–93). From Hebrew, literally, 'additions.' The term is not to be confused with the **Tosefta** (from Aramaic, 'addition'), which is a collection of tannaitic teachings paralleling those of the Mishnah.

trendl. See **dreidel.**

treyf or **treif.** (of food) not **kosher**; forbidden by the laws of **kashrus.** From Yiddish *treyf*, derived from Hebrew *terefah*, 'nonkosher animal or food,' (originally) 'animal torn by a beast or afflicted with disease,' from *taraf*, 'to tear to pieces.' The extended sense, 'illegitimate, unacceptable, dishonest,' entered English slang from Yiddish.

treyfa. Food that is not kosher. From Yiddish *treyfe*, derived from Hebrew *terefah*. See **treyf** or **treif.**

trop. Any of the traditional chants or cantillations used in reading the Torah, haftorah, and the Books of Esther, Ruth, Ecclesiastes (*Koheles*), Lamentations (*Eichah*), and Song of Songs (*Shir Hashirim*) in the synagogue. From Yiddish, derived from Middle High German *tropes*, 'melodic embellishments in Gregorian music,' ultimately from Greek *tropé*, 'a turning.'

tzaddik, plural **tzaddikim.** 1. A pious or righteous man. The feminine is **tzadekes** or (from Yiddish) **tzedeykes.** 2. See under **Hasidic terms.** From

Yiddish *tsadek* and Hebrew *tzaddik,* 'righteous, just (man),' from *tzedek,* 'justice, righteousness.'

tzedakah. The Biblical meaning of *tzedakah* is 'justice, righteousness, fairness.' The word's common meaning of 'almsgiving, charity, philanthropy' originated in the Talmud and Midrash as a part of righteous conduct. A ***baal-tzedakah*** is a charitable or philanthropic person. A ***tzedakah-box*** is a box into which money intended for a good cause (not necessarily for the poor) is deposited through a slot; a Yiddish-origin word for it is ***pushke.*** From Hebrew, a variant of *tzedek,* 'justice.'

Tzeddukim. See **Perushim.**

tzitzis. 1. The four special fringes attached to a **tallis** or a **tallis katan,** originally intended to be attached to any four-cornered garment (*Numbers 15:38*). 2. A garment with tzitzis attached to each corner, worn in the daytime by Orthodox men and boys, usually under their clothes. Also called **arba kanfos,** literally, 'four corners,' **tallis katan,** literally, 'small tallis,' and **laybtsudekl.** From Hebrew, literally, 'fringe, tassel.'

tzom gedaliah. See **fast days.**

tzoraas. See **metzora.**

– U–V –

ultra-Orthodox. A term applied to Orthodox Jews who are extremely observant in their practice of Jewish laws and traditions. It is used chiefly to designate Jews who are connected with traditional yeshivas or their practices, such as wearing black hats and exposing the ritual fringes (tzitzis) outside their shirts. Among the Orthodox, such Jews are called **frum** or **haredi**. They are sometimes lumped together with Hasidic Jews and sometimes distinguished from them.

unterfirer. See under **wedding terms.**

unveiling. The dedication of a matzevah or stone monument over a grave. It is so called from the modern Ashkenazi custom of having a mourner remove a veil from the monument during the dedication. The Hebrew name for the dedication ceremony is *hakomas matzevah,* 'erection of a gravestone,' whose Yiddish equivalent is *shteln a matseyve.* The custom is based on Genesis 35:20: "Jacob set up a monument over her grave; it is the monument of Rachel's grave to this day." It is customary to engrave on the matzevah, below the name, dates, and dedication, the abbreviation ה"צנת (TNTZVH), which stand for *tehei nafsho(h) tzeruroh bitzror hachayim,* 'May his (her) soul be bound up in the bond of life,' a prayer based on Samuel I, 25:29. See also **mourning terms.**

vaad, plural **vaadim.** A committee or council, such as a *Vaad Hakashrus,* a committee supervising the production and sale of kosher food, *Vaad Hatzalah,* the committee organized to rescue Jews from the Nazis in World War II, and *Vaad Leumi,* the national council in charge of health and education in Eretz Israel from 1920 to 1948. From Hebrew, derived from the verb *vied,* 'to invite, convene, assemble.'

vachnacht. A traditional vigil held among Ashkenazim in the house of a newborn male child on the night before his circumcision to ward off evil spirits, especially the female demon Lilith (*Isaiah 34:14*). From Yiddish *vakhnakht,* literally, 'vigil night,' from German *Wachnacht.* Compare **holekrash.** See also *sholem zochor* under **ritual terms.**

vasikin or **vatikin.** A group of pious Jews devoted to the meticulous observance of the laws, noted especially for their custom of rising early every morning to recite the *shemone-esrei* prayer punctually at sunrise (*Berachos 9b*). Such groups have been found in many communities since Talmudic times. The phrase *to get up* or *rise vasikin* (a translation of Yiddish *oyfshteyn vasikin*) means to rise early as the vasikin do to pray at sunrise. From Hebrew, plural of *vasik* or *vatik,* 'conscientious, earnest, dependable,' as in *talmid vasik,* 'conscientious student.'

Veadar. See **Adar.**

viddui. See under **mourning terms.**

vitz. See under **Yiddishisms.**

vort. This Yiddish-origin term, meaning literally 'word,' has acquired a specialized meaning among Orthodox Jews. A *vort* is a social gathering to celebrate a couple's engagement. The gathering is informal, like a housewarming. Its purpose is to make the engagement public but in an informal manner, rather than by having a formal or official ceremony, such as the writing of tenaim, or conditions of betrothal. (See *tenaim* under **wedding terms.**) The origin of the usage is the secondary Yiddish meaning of *vort*, which is 'a promise, a pledge,' since the engaged couple have "given their word" or promised themselves to each other. The usage is reinforced by the custom of the groom or a rabbi or teacher delivering a *vort*, or short discourse, in honor of the occasion. The Yiddish plural of *vort* is *verter*, but the Anglicized form *vorts* is commonly used in referring to several engagement parties. Many rabbis object to the *vort* as an excessive and expensive indulgence. Compare **lechayim** under **wedding terms.**

– W –

wedding terms. Jewish usage abounds in special terms dealing with the formal rites of marriage. A number of common terms associated with courtship and marriage, such as **aufruf, bashert, forshpil, mechuten,** and **vort,** are found listed separately in the book as main entries. Others are given below.

aufruf. See the main entry.

badchen, plural *badchonim* or (*Anglicized*) *badchens.* An entertainer or master of ceremonies at a traditional wedding who sings moralistic and often witty rhymes in Yiddish and Hebrew. The rhymes are usually improvised for the occasion and built around the names, qualities, and lineages of the bride and the groom. From Yiddish *batkhn,* derived from Hebrew *badchan,* 'jester, merrymaker.'

badeken. A brief ritual performed among Ashkenazim just before the wedding ceremony, in which a veil is placed or lowered over the bride's face while reciting the blessing made on Rebecca (*Genesis 24:60*), "Our sister, may you come to be thousands of myriads." From Yiddish *badekns,* short for the phrase *badekn di kale,* 'to cover the bride.'

bashert. See the main entry.

bavarfns. The Ashkenazi custom of showering the groom with sweets during the *aufruf.* Also, the sweets showered on him. From Yiddish, literally, 'peltings,' from *bavafn,* 'to throw at, pelt.'

chasan, plural *chasanim.* 1. A bridegroom-to-be; fiancé, as in *She introduced me to her chasan.* 2. A bridegroom at his wedding, as in *The chasan wore a kittel under the chuppah.* From Yiddish and Ashkenazi Hebrew.

chasene. A wedding ceremony, preceded by a reception and often followed by a dinner. Broadly, a wedding, as in *It was a simple chasene, with no frills.* From Yiddish and Ashkenazi Hebrew.

chuppah or *chuppa,* plural *chuppahs, chuppas,* or (*Sephardi*) *chuppot.* The canopy under which the wedding ceremony takes place. From Yiddish and Hebrew, literally, 'covering, canopy.' See also the main entry **chuppah.**

erusin. The traditional betrothal, or preliminary act of marriage, to be completed by *nissuin,* the marriage proper. Since the Middle Ages, the two parts of the process have been combined into one ceremony. From Aramaic, from the verb *aras,* 'to betroth.'

forshpil. See the main entry.

gramen. See under **music and dance terms.**

kabbalas panim. The reception held before the wedding ceremony, often in the form of a buffet meal or smorgasbord. The groom's kabbalas panim, held separately from the main reception, is informally called the *chasan's tish.* The *tenaim* and the *kesubah* are signed at the groom's kabbalas panim. From Hebrew, literally, 'reception of guests.'

kallah. 1. A bride-to-be; a fiancée. 2. A bride at her wedding. From Yiddish and Hebrew. The Yiddish-origin term *chasan-kallah,* literally, 'groom-bride,' is used to refer to an engaged couple, either before or during the wedding.

kesubah or *ketubah,* plural *kesubos* or *ketubot.* The traditional marriage certificate or contract, specifying the groom's obligations to his bride, signed by two qualified witnesses before the wedding ceremony. Written in Aramaic, it is read out loud under the chuppah and handed to the groom, who gives it to the bride to keep. From Hebrew, literally, 'writ,' from *kasav,* 'to write.'

kiddushin. 1. The legal act of betrothing a woman Compare **erusin.** 2. The part of the wedding ceremony in which the bride becomes consecrated in marriage, effected by the groom's presenting a ring to her before two qualified witnesses and reciting the formula "Behold, you are consecrated unto me with this ring according to the law of Moses and Israel" as he places the ring on her finger. From Aramaic, literally, 'consecrations.' Compare *nissuin.*

kittel. A white linen robe or frock symbolizing purity, often worn by a groom over his clothes under the chuppah during the wedding ceremony. It is an Orthodox Ashkenazi custom. From Yiddish *kitl.* See also the main entry **kittel.**

lechayim. An informal celebration of an engagement. See *lechayim* under **greetings and salutations.**

mechuten. See the main entry.

nissuin or *nesuin.* The part of the wedding ceremony in which marriage is effected. It takes place after *kiddushin* as the bride and groom stand together under the chuppah and the *sheva berachos* are recited. From Hebrew, literally, 'marriage.'

open chuppah. See under the main entry **chuppah.**

shadchen, plural *shadchonim* or (*Anglicized*) *shadchens.* A matchmaker or marriage broker, especially a professional one, whose usual fee is traditionally a percentage of the dowry. From Yiddish *shatkhn* and Hebrew *shadchan*, derived from *shidduch*, 'matrimonial match.' A female matchmaker is a *shadchente* (from Yiddish).

sheva berachos. The seven blessings recited under the chuppah during the wedding ceremony. These blessings are also recited after every meal attended by the married couple during the week following the wedding. From Hebrew, literally, 'seven blessings.'

shidduch, plural *shidduchim* or (*Anglicized*) *shidduchs.* The matching up of a man and a woman for purposes of marriage; a match. In popular usage, any match or alliance, as in *The shidduch between the two organizations was a success.* Compare *zivug.* From Yiddish *shidekh* and Hebrew *shidduch*, 'match, marriage arrangement,' derived from the verb *shidech*, 'to arrange a marriage.'

shoshvin, plural *shoshvinim.* A close friend who accompanies the groom to the chuppah; a best man. A bridesmaid is *shoshvinah.* From Hebrew. Compare *unterfirer.*

tenaim. A document of betrothal, consisting of an agreement written in Hebrew that contains all the conditions and settlements agreed upon by the parents of the bride and groom or their representatives. After the reading of the tenaim, the mothers or nearest female relatives of the bride and groom break a dish (originally an earthen vessel), a custom that parallels the breaking of the glass by the groom under the chuppah. The writing of the tenaim usually takes place at the *kabbalas panim* before the wedding. From Hebrew, plural of *tenai*, 'condition.'

tish. Also, *chasan's tish.* The groom's reception at a wedding. See *kabbalas panim.* From Yiddish, literally, 'table.' See also under **Hasidic terms.**

unterfirer. The Yiddish-origin term for the best man at a wedding; the *shoshvin.* The corresponding term for a bridesmaid is *unterfirerin.* From Yiddish, literally, 'accompanier,' from *unterfirn*, 'to accompany.'

vort. An informal social gathering among Orthodox Jews to celebrate a couple's engagement. From Yiddish, literally, 'word.' See also the main entry **vort.**

yichud. The sequestering of the bride and groom after the wedding ceremony in a private room, where they can spend time together in seclusion. The yichud is an essential part of the wedding, making the marriage valid and binding. From Hebrew, literally, 'oneness, unity, privacy.'

zivug, plural *zivugim.* 1. A matrimonial match; a marriage, as in *This was a zivug made in heaven.* 2. A mate or spouse, as in *He has yet to meet his zivug.* From Yiddish *ziveg,* derived from Hebrew *zivvug,* literally, 'coupling, mating,' from *zug,* 'a pair, couple.'

Weeks. An English name of Shavuos. See *Shavuos* under **holiday terms.**

Writings. See **Hagiographa.**

Written Law. Translation of Hebrew *torah she-be-kesav* (literally, 'Torah that is written'), meaning the **Tanach** or Hebrew Scriptures. Compare **Oral Law.** See also **Torah.**

–Y–

Yaavetz. See **Jabez.**

yachsn. See under **Yiddishisms.**

yahadus or **yahadut.** See **Judaism.**

yahrzeit, plural **yahrzeits.** The anniversary of the death of a parent or close relative (brother, sister, daughter, son, husband, wife), observed annually by lighting a 24-hour memorial candle (*yahrzeit candle*) and reciting the mourner's kaddish at the evening, morning, and afternoon services. Also, the observance of such an anniversary, as in *My brothers and I have yahrzeit next Monday.* Informally, the term is sometimes applied to a person observing a yahrzeit, as in *The aliyah for maftir belongs to the yahrzeit.* (A more appropriate term for such a person is the Yiddish *baal-yortsayt.*) The anniversary of the death of a noted rabbi, rebbe, teacher, or Jewish leader is also commonly called a yahrzeit, as in *Moshe Rabbenu's yahrzeit is on the seventh of Adar.* The word comes from Yiddish *yortsayt* (plural *yortsaytn*) derived from Middle High German *jārzīt,* 'anniversary,' literally, 'year's time.' The spelling *yahrzeit* is an Anglicized form of Ashkenazic German *Jahrzeit*, itself a Germanization of Yiddish *yortsayt.* Compare **annos.** See also **mourning terms.**

Yahudic. Any of various dialects of Arabic (Iraqi, Moroccan, Yemenite, etc.) containing many Hebrew words and expressions, spoken and written by Jews in Arab countries, in Israel, and in the Iberian Peninsula before 1492. From Arabic *yahudi*, 'Jew' (from Hebrew *yehudi*) + English *–ic*. Formerly called **Judeo-Arabic.**

yarche kallah. See **kallah.**

yarmulke or **yarmulka.** The skullcap worn by religious males (instead of a hat or other head covering), in accordance with the rabbinical injunction against going bareheaded (*giluy rosh*). In the United States, *yarmulke* has been the commonly accepted term since the early 1900s, while in Great Britain *kapl* prevailed. Since the mid-1900s, however, the Israeli Hebrew *kippah* has made inroads among American Ashkenazim and is now used among them interchangeably with *yarmulke.* The Yiddish word has been falsely etymologized in many sources. Among the folk etymologies assigned to the word, the one best known is the Hebrew-Aramaic *yarey malka*, 'fear of the king' (meaning 'God-fearing'). Others have conjectured the word's ultimate origin to be Turkish *yagmurluk*, 'raincoat.' Actually, Yiddish *yarmlke* came from Polish *jarmulka*, 'a kind of skullcap,' which was borrowed from Medieval Latin *almunicum*, *almucia*, or *armutia*, 'clergyman's cap or hood,' words apparently related to the source of English *almuce* and *amice*. The variant spelling *yarmulka* derives from the Polish form. Compare **kippah.** See also *kapl* under **clothing terms.**

yasher koach! See under **congratulatory terms.**

yechidus. See under **Hasidic terms.**

yeke. See under **Yiddishisms.**

yenta. A busybody or gossipy person. From Yiddish. See **Yentl:** the story of a name.

yeshiva or **yeshivah**, plural **yeshivas** or **yeshivot.** The primary sense of this word is that of an Orthodox school or institution devoted to Talmudic studies, especially a seminary that prepares students for the rabbinate. A more

Yentl: the story of a name

In the 1980s the Yiddish female name Yentl gained brief prominence as the title of a motion picture based on a story by Isaac Bashevis Singer entitled "Yentl, the Yeshiva Boy," about a girl named Yentl who disguises herself as a boy in order to attend a yeshiva. Yet Yentl has not been favored as a given name among American Ashkenazic Jews, whether religious or secular, and probably for the following reason.

Almost fifty years before the movie *Yentl*, a Yiddish humorist named B. Kovner (actually a pseudonym of Jacob Adler) wrote a popular comic series in the *Jewish Daily Forward* entitled "Yente Telebende," whose chief character was Yente, a henpecking, shrewish wife. The character's popularity was such in the 1920s and 1930s that the name Yente came to be applied to any woman (later, even a man) who was a henpecking busybody or gossip. The name was eventually Anglicized as Yenta and generically written in lower-case (see **yenta**). Since the Yiddish form Yente was merely a clipped form of Yentl and the two forms closely resembled each other, parents were understandably reluctant to bestow the name Yentl on a daughter.

The irony in this story is that historically the name Yentl connoted a maiden or lady of noble and genteel character. It was derived over a thousand years ago from Old Italian *Gentile*, meaning 'noble, genteel.' Old Italian, or rather a Jewish variety of Old Italian (see **Jewish Italian**), was one of two precursors of Yiddish, the other being a Jewish variety of Old French. A number of common Yiddish words have been traced to one or the other of these medieval Romance languages, words like *bentshn*, 'to recite the grace after meals,' and *tsholnt*, the hot dish of meat and vegetables that is a staple of the traditional Sabbath meal. The name *Yentl* has thus a distinguished lineage and deserves more respect than fate has accorded it.

But it would be unfair to put all the blame for the devaluation of the Yiddish name Yente on B. Kovner. Long before Kovner invented the character Yente Telebende, that name was applied in Yiddish to any old-fashioned or plain woman. Alexander Harkavy, in his Yiddish-English-Hebrew Dictionary (published in 1925 and reissued by Shocken Books in 1988), lists *yente* in that sense, and illustrates it with a couple of idiomatic phrases, one of which is *a yente vi ale yentes*, 'a woman like all other women.' Perhaps confusion with the word *yidene*, often used in Yiddish in the sense of an old-fashioned or plain Jewish woman, was the starting point of Yente's fall into disrepute.

recent sense is that of an Orthodox day school that provides both religious and secular education on an elementary-school level. This type of school is often called a *yeshiva ketana* ('minor yeshiva') and is contrasted with a *yeshiva gedola* ('major yeshiva'), which is a regular yeshiva attended by high school, college, or graduate students. Historically, the oldest yeshivas, mentioned in the Talmud, were places where Jewish scholars and sages sat together and studied the Torah. The first great yeshivas were those of the amoraim in Eretz Israel and Babylonia, especially the yeshivas of Sura and Pumbedita. (See **academy.**) From Talmudic Hebrew *yeshivah*, literally, 'a sitting, session,' from Hebrew *yashav*, 'to sit.' Compare **mesivta.** See also **rosh yeshiva.**

Yevanic. The variety of Greek spoken and written by the Jews of Greece during and after the Middle Ages in Egypt, Spain, and other countries. Like other Jewish languages, Yevanic contained many Hebrew elements and was often written in Hebrew characters. The name derives from Hebrew *Yavan*, 'Greece,' after one of the sons of Japhet mentioned in Genesis 10:2. Formerly called **Judeo-Greek.** See also **Jewish languages.**

YHVH. See **Tetragrammaton.**

yibbum or **yibum.** The marriage of a man to the widow of his deceased brother who died childless, "so that his name shall not be blotted out of Israel" (*Deuteronomy 25:5–6*). If he refuses to marry his sister-in-law, the ceremony of **chalitzah** ('removal, pulling off') takes place, in which she removes from his right foot a leather shoe to indicate the mourning he has caused, and spits before him, saying, "So is done to the man who will not build the house of his brother." **Levirate marriage**, as yibbum is called in formal English, is no longer practiced, and instead, the brother-in-law (the *yavam*) is obliged to free the widow (the *yevamah*) through chalitzah. The laws of yibbum are treated in the Talmudic tractate *Yevamos*. From Hebrew *yibbum*, 'levirate.'

yichud. See under **wedding terms.**

yichus. See under **Yiddishisms.**

yid. See **Jew.**

Yiddish. The Yiddish language has been used by European Ashkenazic Jews and their descendants for about a thousand years. The name *yidish* (literally, 'Jewish') is the most widely used name for the language. An affectionate Yiddish name for it is *mame-loshn*, literally, 'mother tongue.' The earliest known use of the name *yidish* to designate the language is in a dirge commemorating the Jews slaughtered in Ukraine during the Chmielnicki massacres of 1648 and 1649. Since the language arose in the German-speaking region of the Rhine Valley, it was called originally (1100s) *leshon ashkenaz*, 'language of Ashkenaz (Germany).' Not until the 16th century did the German word *Jüdisch*, meaning 'Jewish,' begin to be applied by non-Jews to the language of the Jews, often in the compound *jüdisch-teutsch*, 'Jewish German.' Gradually, Yiddish-speakers adopted the German phrase as a name for their language, shortening it to *jüdisch*, which eventually became *yidish*. Yet even as late as in the 18th century, Jewish intellectuals did not regard Yiddish as a bona-fide language, referring to it disparagingly as *zhargon*, 'jargon.' The English word *Yiddish* first showed up in the 1880s, but the language still lacked strong credentials as a legitimate language. To this day one hears Jews and non-Jews occasionally refer to the language as "Jewish" rather than Yiddish.

Yet most scholars today regard Yiddish as a genuine language in a class with other Germanic languages such as English, Dutch, and Swedish. Once the language of all of Ashkenazic Jewry, Yiddish began to decline in western Europe in the latter part of the eighteenth century. Western Yiddish, once spoken in Germany, Switzerland, Holland, and Alsace-Lorraine, is no longer in use, though vestiges of it remain in other languages, including English, like the words *kosher* and *nebbish*. Eastern Yiddish, by contrast, remained strong until the Holocaust, although beginning in the mid-1800s and increasingly in the early 1900s large numbers of urban, secular Jews shifted to other languages, such as Polish, Romanian, and Russian. Today, Yiddish is used mostly by strictly Orthodox Ashkenazim in parts of Israel (especially Jerusalem and Bene-Berak) and in the United States, in urban areas such as New York, Chicago, Boston, and Los Angeles. The growth of yeshivas, where until recently Yiddish was often a language of instruction, has been instrumental in preserving the language.

Reflecting its historical development, Yiddish has a vocabulary largely derived from Middle High German, but with a distinctive component of about 18 percent Hebrew-Aramaic and 16 percent Slavic (Czech, Polish, Russian, Ukrainian) as well as a substratum of Romance elements from the Jewish correlates of Old French and Old Italian. Yiddish is the only Germanic language written in the Hebrew alphabet, and words of Hebrew or Aramaic origin retain their original spellings (regardless of how they are pronounced), while those of Germanic or other origin are spelled as they are pronounced. Eastern Yiddish is usually divided into Northeastern Yiddish (Lithuania, Latvia, Belarus), Southeastern Yiddish (Ukrainia, Romania, eastern Galicia), and Central Yiddish (Poland, western Galicia).

Standard Yiddish, which is taught in secular and non-Jewish schools and colleges, is closest to Northeastern Yiddish in pronunciation and closest to Central Yiddish in grammar. By way of illustration, the Yiddish of Frankfurt am Main is Western Yiddish; that of Warsaw is Central Yiddish; that of Vilnius is Northeastern Yiddish; and that of Kiev is Southeastern Yiddish.

Like other Jewish languages, such as Judezmo, Yiddish has a special variety called **ivre-taytsh**, which was formerly used to translate sacred Jewish texts.

In the United States, Yiddish absorbed many American English words, some embodying distinctly American concepts (*sobvey,* 'subway,' *kemp,* 'summer camp,' *hayskul,* 'high school') but most others reflecting the dominance of everyday English.

In return, however, it gave to American English numerous Yiddish words and expressions, many of which became part of the colloquial language of non-Jewish Americans. See also **Jewish English; Yiddishisms.**

Yiddish continues to be promoted as a modern language by *Yiddishists* (students and devotees of the Yiddish language and culture) who write Yiddish books, textbooks, and periodicals, teach the language, compile dictionaries, and continuously do research in what has come to be known in the academic world as "the field of Yiddish." Devotion to the Yiddish language and culture is known as *Yiddishism*, a term more commonly used to mean a word or expression of Yiddish origin.

Yiddishisms. Hundreds of Yiddish-origin words and expressions are part of the everyday vocabulary of English-speaking Ashkenazi Jews. Over the past hundred years, a number of such words and phrases have passed into general English, especially American English slang. Some of these words, such as **bobkes, chutzpah, goy, maven,** and **mensch,** are listed separately as main entries. The list that follows is a selection of common Yiddish-origin words and phrases used mainly by English-speaking Ashkenazi Jews. Many of the terms are used only in speech and rarely found in print. Such terms are spelled according to the Standard Yiddish Romanization system. Pronunciations given in parenthesis are also rendered in this system.

> *abi gezunt.* As long as one has health; the main thing is (a person's) health.
>
> *aderabe.* See under **exclamations and interjections.**
>
> *agmes nefesh.* Anguish; distress.
>
> *akshen.* A stubborn person.
>
> *alef-beys.* The Jewish alphabet.
>
> *alevay!* Would that it be so! Also, *halevay!*

almone. A widow.

amorets, plural *ameratsim.* A Jew lacking Jewish learning; an ignorant or uneducated Jew. See also the main entry **am-haaretz.**

avade. Certainly, of course.

aveyre. A sin.

azes ponem. An impudent person.

beheyme. An animal. Also, a dull-witted person.

bobe or *bobbe.* Grandmother; grandma.

bobkes. See the main entry.

bocher (bo'kher). 1. A youth, as in *a yeshiva bocher.* 2. A bachelor, especially in the phrase *an alter bocher* (literally, 'an old bachelor').

boki, plural *bekiim.* One who is well versed or learned, as in *a boki in Shas.*

breyre. A choice or alternative; recourse (used usually in the negative, as in *to have no breyre* or *What breyre did I have?*).

bulvan. A boorish, brutish person.

chiddush (khi'desh), plural *chiddushim* (khidu'shim). Something new; a novelty, especially a new explanation of a Talmudic or halachic concept.

chochom. See the main entry **chacham.**

chosev (kho'shev). Respected; distinguished; important.

choyzek (khoy'zek). Ridicule, as in *to make choyzek of someone.*

chutzpah. See the main entry **chutzpah.**

davke. See under **exclamations and interjections.**

dayge. Worry; care; concern, as in *a family with many dayges.*

dreykop. A scatterbrain. Also, a pest or nuisance.

farbisn. Mean; dour.

farblondzhet. Lost; confused, as in *We got farblondzhet in the city.*

farbrente. Ardent; zealous, as in *a farbrente Zionist.*

farklemt. Moved deeply, as if about to cry.

farshlept. Drawn out; dragged out.

fonfe. To talk through the nose; hem and haw. Also, to doubletalk; bluff.

fres or *fress.* To gorge on food; eat like a pig.

galach (ga'lekh). A gentile clergyman, especially a priest.

ganev or *ganef,* plural *ganovim* (gano'vim). A thief. Also, a troublemaker; rascal.

gazlen, plural *gazlonim* (gazlo'nim). A robber or bandit.

gelt. Money, as in *to give Chanukah gelt.*

geshmak. Tasty; delicious; delightful.

gevalt or *gevald.* A cry for help; hue and cry; alarm.

gezunterheyt. In good health, as in *Go gezunterheyt!*

gotenyu! Oh, God! Dear God!

goy. See the main entry **goy.**

grober yung. A coarse, ignorant person; a boor.

halevay! See under **exclamations and interjections.**

hanoe. Enjoyment; satisfaction.

hashkofe. Viewpoint; outlook.

hashpoe. Influence; inspiration.

hatslokhe. Good fortune; success; prosperity.

hefker. Ownerless. Also, lawless; licentious.

heymish. Homelike; cozy, as in *a heymish atmosphere.*

ikar. Main point; essence.

iluy. A young genius; a prodigy, especially in Talmudic study, as in *the Rogachover iluy.*

inyen, plural *inyonim.* Matter; subject; case, as in *a difficult inyen.*

kabtsn. A poor man.

kanehore or *kan eyn-hore.* See under **exclamations and interjections.**

kapitl. A chapter, as in *a whole new kapitl.*

kashe. A question or problem; a difficulty.

kavyochl. See under **exclamations and interjections.**

kibitz. To make fun; banter; tease.

kinder. Children. The endearing form is *kinderlech* (-lekh).

klap or *klop*, plural *klep.* A blow; hit; knock; strike.

klutz. A clumsy person.

klutzy. Clumsy; awkward.

knaker (k'na'ker). A big shot, often in the phrase *a groyser knaker.*

kochlefl. A busybody (literally, 'cooking-spoon').

korev, plural *kroyvim.* A relative.

koved. Honor.

koyekh. Strength.

krekhts. To groan. *A krekhts* means a groan.

kunts, plural *kuntsn.* A stunt; feat.

kvell (k'vel). To overflow with pride; beam with joy; take great delight in.

kvetch (k'vetsh). To complain. A *kvetch* is a complainer. (Literally, squeeze, pinch).

kvitsh (k'vitsh). To scream. A *kvitsh* is a scream.

lebedik. Lively.

lehakhes. So as to spite; spitefully.

lehavdl. See under **exclamations and interjections.**

lets, plural *leytsim* or *leytsonim.* A joker, buffoon; wag.

leydikgeyer. A loafer or idler.

loshn-hore. Evil talk; slander.

luftmentsh. See the main entry **luftmentsh.**

malekhamoves. The angel of death.

mame-loshn. See the main entry **mame-loshn.**

maven. See the main entry **maven.**

mekhaye. Something refreshing or delicious; a pleasure; a delight.

mekhile. Forgiveness, as in *asking someone mekhile on Yom Kippur.*

mensch. See the main entry **mensch.**

meshuga or *meshuge.* Crazy.

meshugas. A craze or madness.

meshugener. A madman; lunatic.

meshugoim. Crazy people; madmen.

metsie. A bargain; a find.

mise meshune. An unnatural or freakish death.

mishpoche. Family, especially immediate family.

naches. See the main entry **naches.**

nebech! See under **exclamations and interjections.**

nebbish. A pathetically inept person; a sad sack. From Western Yiddish
  (Holland) *nebish,* corresponding to Eastern Yiddish *nebekh.*

nochshleper (nokh'shleper). A hanger-on; tagalong.

noodge. Variant of *nudzh.*

nosh. A snack. Also, to snack or nibble. From Yiddish *nash, nashn.*

nudnik. A bothersome person; a pest or bore.

nudzh or *noodge.* To bother or pester; to nag. Also, a pest or nudnik.
  From Yiddish *nudyen,* 'to pester, nag, bore.'

ongeshtopt. Stuffed, as in *ongeshtopt with money.*

oylem. An audience; a crowd or turnout. Also, the people or public at
  large.

parnose. A living or livelihood.

plotz. To burst or explode (with laughter, from chagrin, etc.). From Yiddish *platsn.*

probe. (pro'be). A tryout or audition, as in *a cantor's probe.*

pupik. Bellybutton; navel; also, gizzard.

pushke. A charity box.

roshe, plural *reshoim.* An evil person; malefactor; wrongdoer; villain.

schlemiel. Variant of *shlemiel.*

schlep or *shlep.* To drag, pull. Also, a clod, bore, drag. From Yiddish
  shlepn.

schlimazl. Variant of *shlimazl.*

schlock. An item or items of cheap or inferior quality. From Yiddish *shlak*, literally, 'stroke, mishap, nuisance.'

schlocky. Of cheap or inferior quality, as in *schlocky furniture.*

schlump. A shabby, sloppy person.

schmaltz. Excessive sentimentality; mawkishness. From Yiddish *shmalts*, literally, 'melted fat.'

schmaltzy. Overly sentimental; mawkish; gooey.

schmooze or *shmooze.* To converse informally; chat. Also, a chat. From Yiddish *shmuesn* (verb), *shmues* (noun). See also *shmues.*

schmutz. Dirt; smut.

schnorrer or *shnorrer.* A beggar or sponger.

schvitz. A Turkish bath. From Yiddish *shvitsbod.*

seykhl. Brains; intelligence.

sha! Silence! Quiet!

shammes. See the main entry **shammes.**

sheygetz. See the main entry **sheygetz.**

shiker. Drunk. Also, a drunkard.

shiksa. See the main entry **shiksa.**

shlemiel or *schlemiel.* A simpleton; bungler; fool. See sidebar **shlemiel: the story of a word** (page 156).

shlep. Variant of *schlep.*

shlimazl or *schlimazl.* An unlucky person.

shmate. A rag.

shmegege. A silly or stupid person; fool.

shmendrik. An inept or unimportant person; a nobody.

shmontses. Idle talk; nonsense.

shmooze. Variant of *schmooze.*

shmues. A talk, chat, or discussion; as in *a musar shmues.*

shnorrer. Variant of *schnorrer.*

shokel. See the main entry **shokel.**

shoyte. A stupid person; fool; imbecile.

shpilkes. Pins; needles, as in *sitting on shpilkes.*

shtetl. See the main entry **shtetl.**

shtick. An act or routine. From Yiddish *shtik*, 'tricks, pranks'; literally, 'piece.'

shtus. Foolishness; nonsense.

shul. See the main entry **shul.**

tachlis. Practical purpose or goal; end; aim.

tararam. Noise; commotion; fuss.

tshotshke. Variant of *tzatzke.*

tumler. A noisy, boisterous person. Also, a master of ceremonies.

tzatzke. A toy; bauble; trinket.

tzimmes. A big production or fuss; to-do. From Yiddish *tsimes*, literally, 'a sweet stew.'

tzores. Trouble; worries; care.

vitz. A funny or witty observation or story; a joke or witticism.

vort. See the main entry **vort.**

yachsn. One who has or claims noble descent. See *yichus.*

yeke, yekke. An informal name for a German Jew.

yenta. See the main entry **yenta.**

yichus. Noble descent; prestigious genealogy; pedigree.

yid, plural *yidn.* A Jew. See also the main entry **Jew.**

Yiddishkeit. See main entry below.

yold. A fool; dope.

yontev or *yontef.* A holiday, especially a Jewish holiday. The plural is *yon-toyvim.*

yosem, plural *yesoymim.* An orphan. A female orphan is a *yesoyme.*

zaftig or **zoftig.** Juicy; luscious. Also, plump, chubby.

zechus. Merit; privilege.

zeyde. Grandfather.

zhlub. A coarse, boorish person.

Yiddishkeit. A Yiddish-origin term meaning both 'Judaism' and 'Jewishness.' Because of this twofold meaning, the term has a divided usage that often results in confusion. For Orthodox Ashkenazi Jews, the term *Yiddishkeit* means Judaism, the Jewish religion, especially in the sense of traditional, rabbinic Judaism. For non-Orthodox Jews, the term has come to be widely used to mean Jewishness, that is, the condition of being Jewish, irrespective of religious affiliation (e.g., *secular Yiddishkeit, Socialist Yiddishkeit.*) The term *Yiddishism* used by secular Yiddishists, means devotion to the Yiddish language and culture, and should not be confused with *Yiddishkeit* in either of its senses. From the Yiddish *yidishkeyt.* See also **Judaism.**

yizkor. See under **mourning terms.**

yoetzet halachah, plural **yoatzot halachah.** A woman qualified to act as a counselor or advisor on halachic matters. From Hebrew, literally, 'halachah counselor.'

Yom Haatzmaut. See under **holiday terms.**

Yom Hashoah. A memorial day observed on the twenty-seventh Nisan for the victims and martyrs of the Holocaust, established by the Israeli parliament in 1963 and held annually in many parts of the world. The official Hebrew name is *yom hashoah vehagevurah* 'Day of Holocaust and Heroism.' Also called **Holocaust (Memorial) Day.**

yomim neroim. See under **holiday terms.**

Yom Iyun or **Yom Iyyun.** A day of Torah study, especially one set aside for group learning. From Hebrew, literally, 'study day.'

Yom Kippur. See under **holiday terms.**

yom tov, plural **yomim tovim.** A Jewish holiday. The Yiddish form is *yontev* or *yontef* (plural *yon-toyvim*). From Hebrew, literally, 'good day.' Compare **chag.**

Yom Yerushalayim. A celebration on the 28th of Iyar to commemorate the reunification of Jerusalem on June 7, 1967, the third day of the Six-Day War. From Hebrew, literally, 'Jerusalem Day.'

yordim. See under **Israeli terms.**

yortsayt. See **yahrzeit.**

yotzros, singular **yotzer.** Hymns or poems (*piyyutim*) inserted into the morning (*shacharis*) service on certain Sabbaths and holiday, between the blessing of *yotzer or* ("Who forms light") and the **shemone-esrei.** However, the term *yotzros* is often mistakenly applied to all *piyyutim*. See **piyyut.**

yovel. The fiftieth or jubilee year following seven Sabbatical (*shemitah*) years, when all land reverted to the original owners and all Jewish slaves were emancipated. See **Jubilee** (word history).

–Z–

Zarfatic. The variety of Old French spoken and written by Jews during the Middle Ages. It contained many Gallicized Hebrew-Aramaic and other Jewish words and was often written in Hebrew characters. Many of the Old French glosses on the Bible and the Talmud written by Rashi, who lived in Troyes, France, are in Zarfatic. For example, Rashi's gloss of Hebrew *bimah* (see **bimah**) in several Talmudic tractates (e.g., *Sotah 41a*) is *almenbre*, a Zarfatic word derived from Yahudic (see **almemar**). A number of Yiddish words and names are traceable to Zarfatic, e.g., *tsholnt* (see **cholent** under **food terms**) and the name *Bunim* (from Old French *Bonhomme*). The name *Zarfatic* derives from Hebrew *Tzarfat*, 'France.' Also called **Jewish French**. Formerly called **Judeo-French**.

zav, plural **zavim**. A man who is afflicted with an abnormal (nonseminal) emission or discharge. This form of ritual impurity is described in Leviticus 15:1–15 and dealt with in detail in the Mishnaic tractate *Zavim*. Similarly, a **zavah** is a woman who experiences an abnormal (nonmenstrual) discharge of blood, an impurity described in Leviticus 15:25–33. Various English commentators and translators have identified or labeled the abnormal flux as gonorrhea, which is a sexually transmitted bacterial (gonococcal) disease. As in the case of a **metzora** being described as a leper, the identification of the ritual impurity of a zav or a zavah with a treatable medical condition is unfounded and inappropriate. The Biblical terms can be explained without resorting to modern medical diagnostics. From Hebrew, literally, 'one having a flow,' derived from *zov*, 'flow, discharge, secretion.'

zebed habat. See under **ritual terms**.

zimmun. See **mezumen**.

zivug. See under **wedding terms**.

Zohar. The most important work of the kabbalah, consisting primarily of a mystical commentary in Aramaic on parts of the Pentateuch and Hagiographa (e.g., Ruth, the Song of Songs). Its authorship has been ascribed by kabbalists to the second-century tanna R. Simeon bar Yochai and his circle, but in the opinion of modern scholars it is an anthology of numerous works by unknown kabbalists. It became widely known in the 1300s, after its introduction into Spain by the kabbalist R. Moses de Leon (1250–1305). The work's name is the Hebrew word for 'radiance, splendor,' and derives from the verse in Daniel 12:3: "The wise will shine like the radiance of the firmament (*kezohar horokiya*). The work is especially revered by Hasidim and is often called *Zohar hakadosh*, 'the holy Zohar.' Students of the Zohar are called **Zoharists**, and studies of the Zohar are termed **Zoharic.**

zugos or **Zugos.** Any of the five pairs of outstanding religious scholars in the time of the Second Temple who preceded the tannaim or Mishnaic teach-

---

Zion: The story of a name

The name *Zion* derives from Hebrew *Tziyon* (צִיּוֹן), yet it is spelled and pronounced with a z . This peculiarity is due to the influence of German, in which the letter z is pronounced as *tz*, as in *Zionismus*, 'Zionism,' pronounced "tzi-o-nis'-mus." Most other languages, including English, have no sound in the alphabet that approximates the "tz" sound of Hebrew *tzadi* or *tzadik*. Hence historically this sound was represented by the letter *s*, and the name appears as *Sion* in the King James Version of the Bible (1611), as it does in Old English, which took it from Latin, which borrowed the name from Greek *Seon*. The Hebrew letter *tzadi* or *tzadik* is also often rendered in English as *sadhe* or *sade*.

The Hebrew word *Tziyon* is first found in the Scriptures as the name of a stronghold (*metzudas tziyon*) situated on a hill in the southeastern corner of Jerusalem that was captured by King David (*II Samuel 5:7*). The name was later extended to Jerusalem (*Isaiah 4:3*), to the Temple Mount (*Joel 4:17*), and to the Land of Israel (*Psalms 137:1*). Various theories have been proposed for the origin of the name, among them Hebrew *tziyun*, 'signpost, landmark,' related to *tziyan*, 'to mark, indicate' and *tzayon*, 'wilderness, desert.'

The term *Zionism* was coined as *Zionismus* in 1890 by the philosopher Nathan Birnbaum (1864–1937) in the German-Jewish political journal *Selbstemanzipation* (Self-emancipation), which he had founded in 1885. The term first appeared in English in 1896, along with the derivative *Zionist*.

---

ers. One of each pair was the **Nasi,** or president of the Sanhedrin, and the other the **av bet din,** the deputy of the Nasi. The five pairs (listed in the Mishnah, *Avos 1: 4–12*) were Yose ben Yoezer and Yose ben Yochanan; Yehoshua ben Perachyah and Nittai Hoarbeli; Yehudah ben Tabbai and Shimon ben Shotach; Shemayah and Avtalyon; and Hillel and Shammai. The term *zugos* (Hebrew, literally, 'pairs'), as applied to the five sets of scholars, is found in the Mishnah (*Peah 2:6*). The fact that the first of each pair was the Nasi and the second the av bet din is stated in the Mishnah (*Chagigah 2:2*).

Appendix I

Methods and Sources

To construct a dictionary of any kind, one must begin with a list of the terms that need to be defined or explained to the reader. Compiling such a list may be an easy or daunting task, depending on the size and complexity of the corpus. Since this Dictionary was not intended to cover the entire range of Jewish vocabulary, the list of terms was necessarily restricted. It was restricted, first, to those lexical terms that are either of Jewish origin (i.e., derived from some Jewish language, such as Hebrew, Aramaic, Yiddish, or Judezmo) or that are of Jewish interest. And secondly, it was restricted particularly to those terms of Jewish origin or interest whose usage is uncertain, questionable, or in dispute.

Such a list of terms does not spring from the head. It must come from research. In dictionary-making, research consists of thumbing and reading through countless books and periodicals in search of words, phrases, and idioms that are new, or that show a new meaning or spelling, or that suggest a new pronunciation or etymology. When any such item is spotted, it is underlined or highlighted, and the sentence or brief passage in which it appears is clipped or copied on a slip. The clipping or slip constitutes a citation, since it cites the source and date of the excerpt. All dictionaries are, to a large extent, based on citations. These citations are collected over many years and filed by hand or electronically. Dictionary editors pore over them, extracting the information they need to frame accurate entries and definitions.

The citations that formed the basis for this Dictionary were collected over a period of three decades from a variety of sources, primarily Jewish, but also including many non-Jewish ones, such as standard English dictionaries and encyclopedias as well as popular newspapers and magazines. The Jewish sources consisted of Jewish reference books written in English; English books of fiction and nonfiction dealing with Jews or Jewish subjects; and Anglo-Jewish daily, weekly, monthly, and quarterly periodicals published in the United States and Great Britain. A partial list of sources appears below.

From the file of thousands of citations thus accumulated, the ones selected were those that featured new or unusual terms of Jewish interest or origin, or Jewish terms that showed new meanings or shifts in usage. Those terms came to form the main entries in this Dictionary. The spellings of these entries were determined by the frequency of their appearance in citations: the two or three most frequent spellings were chosen, the first being the most frequent of the two or three recorded.

Collecting the citations and extracting the data from them was assiduous and time-consuming work, a fact noted long ago by Samuel Johnson, who defined a lexicographer as "a harmless drudge, that busies himself in tracing the original, and detailing the signification, of words."

The Anglo-Jewish periodicals from which citations were excerpted for this book are mostly the familiar ones still found in Jewish communities throughout the English-speaking world, and are too many and varied to be listed here. So are the numerous Web sites of Jewish interest consulted on the Internet. What follows is a selection of the books that were used for citations and for research purposes in developing the Dictionary.

General

Alter, Robert. *After the Tradition: Essays in Modern Jewish Writing.* New York: E.P. Dutton & Co., 1971.

Ansky, S. *The Dybbuk and Other Writings.* Translated by Golda Werman. New York: Schocken Books, 1992.

Bunim, Amos. *A Fire In His Soul.* Jerusalem, New York: Feldheim Publishers, 1989.

Der Nister (Pinhas Kahanovitch). *The Family Mashber.* Translated by Leonard Wolf. New York: Summit Books, 1987.

Donat, A. (1963). *The Holocaust Kingdom.* New York: Holt, Rinehart and Winston, 1963.

Eliot, G. *Daniel Deronda.* New York: Modern Library.

Feldstein, Stanley. *The Land that I Show You: Three Centuries of Jewish Life in America.* New York: Anchor Books, 1979.

Fendel, Zechariah. *Anvil of Sinai.* New York: Hashkafah Publications, 1977.

Frank, Gerold. *The Deed.* New York: Simon and Schuster, 1963.

Friedlander, Albert H. *Out of the Whirlwind: A Reader of Holocaust Literature.* New York: Schocken Books, 1976.

Gaster, Theodor H. *The Holy and the Profane.* New York: William Sloane Associates Publishers, 1955.

Gillman, Neil. *The Way Into Encountering God in Judaism.* Woodstock, Vt.: Jewish Lights Publishing, 2000.
Goldhagen, Daniel Jonah. *Hitler's Willing Executioners: Ordinary Germans and the Holocaust.* New York: Alfred A. Knopf, 1996.
Goldin, Hyman E. *The Jewish Woman and Her Home.* New York: Hebrew Publishing Co., 1941.
Grade, Chaim. *Rabbis and Wives.* Translated by Harold Rabinowitz and Inna Hecker Grade. New York: Vintage Books, 1983.
Gross, David C. *The Jewish People's Almanac.* New York: Doubleday & Company, 1981.
Hartman, David. *Conflicting Visions: Spiritual Possibilities of Modern Israel.* New York: Schocken Books, 1990.
Heilman, Samuel C. *Synagogue Life: A Study of Symbolic Interaction.* Chicago: The University of Chicago Press, 1973.
———. *When a Jew Dies: The Ethnography of a Bereaved Son.* Berkeley: University of California Press, 2001.
Herberg, Will. *Judaism and Modern Man: An Interpretation of Jewish Religion.* New York: Farrar, Straus and Young, 1951.
Herzl, T. *The Diaries of Theodor Herzl.* Edited and translated by Marvin Lowenthal. New York: Dial Press, 1956.
Heschel, Abraham Joshua. *God In Search of Man.* Northvale, N.J.: Jason Aronson Inc., 1955, 1987.
Hoobler, Dorothy and Thomas. *The Jewish American Family Album.* New York: Oxford University Press, 1995.
Howe, Irving. *World of Our Fathers: the Journey of East European Jews to America and the Life They Found and Made.* New York: Harcourt Brace Jovanovich, 1976.
Lamm, M. *The Jewish Way of Death and Mourning.* Middle Village, NY: Jonathan David, 1969.
Lamm, Norman. *Torah Lishmah: Torah for Torah's Sake.* Hoboken, N.J.: Ktav Publishing House, 1989.
———. *The Religious Thought of Hasidism: Text and Commentary.* Hoboken, N.J.: Ktav Publishing House, 1999.
Malamud, Bernard. *The Magic Barrel.* New York: Farrar, Straus, 1958.
Nathan, Joan. *Jewish Cooking In America.* New York: Alfred A. Knopf, 1994.
Patai, Raphael. *Tents of Jacob: The Diaspora – Yesterday and Today.* Englewood Cliffs, N.J.: Prentice-Hall, 1971.
Peretz, I.L. *The I.L. Peretz Reader.* Edited by Ruth R. Wisse. New York: Schocken Books, 1990.
Picard, Jacob. *The Marked One And Twelve Other Stories.* Translated by Ludwig Lewisohn. Philadelphia: The Jewish Publication Society of America, 1956.
Poll, Solomon. *The Hasidic Community of Williamsburg: A Study in the Sociology of Religion.* New York: Schocken Books, 1962.
Potok, Chaim. *The Promise.* New York: Fawcett Crest, 1969.
Reich, Tova. *The Jewish War.* New York: Pantheon Books, 1995.
Richler, Mordecai. *Solomon Gursky Was Here.* New York: Alfred A. Knopf, 1990.
Roden, Claudia. *The Book of Jewish Food: An Oddyssey From Samarkand To New York.* New York: Alfred A. Knopf, 1996.

Roth, Philip. *Portnoy's Complaint*. New York: Random House, 1969.

———. *Operation Shylock: A Confession*. New York: Simon & Schuster, 1993.

Schafer, P. *Judeophobia*. Cambridge, Mass.: Harvard University Press, 1997

Schwartz, Leo W., ed. *Great Ages and Ideas of the Jewish People*. New York: Random House, 1956.

Sholom Aleichem. *From the Fair: The Autobiography of Sholom Aleichem*. Translated by Curt Leviant. New York: Viking, 1985.

———. *Tevye the Dairyman and the Railroad Stories*. Translated by Hillel Halkin. New York: Schocken Books, 1987.

Singer, Isaac Bashevis. *In My Father's Court*. Translated by Curt Leviant. New York: Fawcett, 1980.

———. *More Stories From My Father's Court*. Translated by Curt Leviant. New York: Farrar, Straus and Giroux, 1956, 2000.

Singer, Israel Joshua. *The Brothers Ashkenazi*. Translated by Joseph Singer. New York: Carroll & Graf, 1985.

Smith, Harold P. *A Treasure Hunt In Judaism*. New York: Hebrew Publishing Company, 1942, 1950.

Stein, S. *Finding Your Bashert*. Brooklyn, NY: Judaica Press, 1999.

Steinsaltz, Adin. *The Long Shorter Way: Discourses on Chasidic Thought*. Northvale, N.J.: Jason Aronson Inc., 1988.

Tarr, Herbert. *The Conversion of Chaplain Cohen*. New York: Avon Books, 1963.

Urofsky, Melvin I. *We are One! American Jewry and Israel*. New York: Anchor Press/ Doubleday, 1978.

Wilkinson, Bruce H. *The Prayer of Jabez: Breaking Through the Blessed Life*. Portland, Oreg.: Multnomah Publishers, 2000.

Wouk, Herman. *This is My God*. New York: Doubleday & Company, 1959.

Zangwill, I. *Children of the Ghetto*. Detroit: Wayne University Press, 1892, 1998.

History and Folklore

Ausubel, Nathan. *A Treasury of Jewish Folklore*. New York: Crown Publishers, 1948, 1975.

———. *Pictorial History of the Jewish People*. New York: Crown Publishers, 1968.

Bialik, Hayim Nahman and Yehoshua H. Ravnitzky. *The Book of Legends*. [Sefer Ha-Aggadah]. Translated by William G. Braude. New York: Schocken Books, 1992.

Elbogen, Ismar. *A Century of Jewish Life*. Translated by Moses Hadas. Philadelphia: The Jewish Publication Society of America, 1945.

Potok, Chaim. *Wanderings: Chaim Potok's History of the Jews*. New York: Alfred A. Knopf, 1978.

Sachar, Abram Leon. *A History of the Jews*. New York: Alfred A. Knopf, 1953.

Sachar, Howard M. *A History of Israel From the Rise of Zionism To Our Time*. New York: Alfred A. Knopf, 1976, 1996.

Schappes, Morris U. *A Documentary History of the Jews of the United States 1654–1875*. New York: The Citadel Press, 1950.

Weinreich, Beatrice Silverman. *Yiddish Folktales.* Translated by Leonard Wolf. New York: Pantheon Books and YIVO Institute for Jewish Research, 1988.

Language

Birnbaum, Solomon A. "Jewish Languages." *Encyclopaedia Judaica,* vol. 10 (1972), 66–70.

Feinsilver, Lillian Mermin. *The Taste of Yiddish.* New York and London: Thomas Yoseloff, 1970.

Fishman, Joshua A. "The Sociology of Jewish Languages from the Perspective of the General Sociology of Language: A Preliminary Formulation." *International Journal of the Sociology of Language* 30 (1981): 5–16.

Gold, David L. "Jewish Intralinguistics as a Field of Study." *International Journal of the Sociology of Language* 30 (1981): 31–46.

———. "Recent American Studies in Jewish Languages." *Jewish Language Review* 1 (1981): 11–88.

———. "Jewish English." In *Readings in the Sociology of Jewish Languages*, edited by Joshua A. Fishman, 280–298. Leiden: E.J. Brill, 1985.

———. "Etymological Studies of Jewish Interest." *Comments on Etymology* 12, 5–6, 9–10 (1982, 1983).

Safire, W. *Language Maven Strikes Again.* New York: Doubleday, 1990.

———. *Quoth the Maven.* New York: Random House, 1993.

Steinmetz, S. *Yiddish and English: The Story of Yiddish in America*, 2d ed. Tuscaloosa: University of Alabama Press, 2001.

Steinmetz, S., C. M. Levine, and P. Stevens. *Meshuggenary: Celebrating the World of Yiddish.* New York: Simon and Schuster, 2002.

Weinberg, Bella Hass. *Ambiguities in the Romanization of Yiddish.* New York: YIVO Institute for Jewish Research, 1997.

Weinreich, Max. "Prehistory and Early History of Yiddish: Facts and Conceptual Framework." *The Field of Yiddish*, edited by Uriel Weinreich, 73–101. New York: Linguistic Circle of New York, 1954.

———. *History of the Yiddish Language.* Translated from the Yiddish by Shlomo Noble and Joshua A. Fishman. Chicago: The University of Chicago Press, 1980.

Weinreich, Uriel. *Languages in Contact.* New York: Linguistic Circle of New York, 1953.

———. *College Yiddish.* 5th revised ed. New York: YIVO Institute for Jewish Research, 1971.

Reference Books, Anthologies, and Sacred Texts

Alcalay, Reuben. *Milon Ivri-Angli Shalem* [The Complete Hebrew-English Dictionary]. Yedioth Ahronoth, Massada: Chemed Books, 1990.

American Jewish Desk Reference. New York: Random House, Inc., 1999.

Beider, Alexander. *A Dictionary of Jewish Surnames from the Russian Empire.* Teaneck, N.J.: Avotaynu, Inc. 1993.

Browning, W.R.F. *Oxford Dictionary of the Bible.* Oxford University Press, 1996.

The Chumash, Stone Edition. Brooklyn, NY: Mesorah Publications, 1993.

The Complete Artscroll Siddur. Brooklyn, NY: Mesorah Publications, 1984.

The Complete Artscroll Machzor. Brooklyn, NY: Mesorah Publications, 1986.

Dobrinsky, H. C. *A Treasury of Sephardic Laws and Customs,* Third Revised Edition. Hoboken, NJ: Ktov Publishing and Yeshiva University Press, 2001.

Encyclopaedia Judaica. Jerusalem, 1972.

Even-Shoshan, Abraham. *Konkordatziya Chadashah LeTorah, Neviim, Uchtuvim* [A New Concordance of the Bible]. Jerusalem: Kiryat Sefer Publishing House, 1989.

Fishman, Joshua A., ed. *Never Say Die: A Thousand Years of Yiddish in Jewish Life and Letters* The Hague: Mouton, 1981.

Friedman, Theodore and Robert Gordis, eds. *Jewish Life in America.* New York: Horizon Press, 1955.

Harkavy, Alexander. *Yidish-english-hebreisher verterbukh* [Yiddish-English-Hebrew Dictionary.] New York: Schocken Books and the YIVO Institute for Jewish Research, 1988.

Jacobs, Louis. *The Jewish Religion: A Companion.* Oxford University Press, 1995.

Jastrow, Marcus. *Dictionary of Talmud Babli, Yerushalmi, Midrashic Literature, and Targumim.* New York: Pardes Publishing House, Inc., 1950.

Joffe, Judah A. and Mark Yudel. *Groyser verterbukh fun der yidisher shprakh* [Great Dictionary of the Yiddish Language], 2 vols. New York: Yiddish Dictionary Committee, Inc. 1961–1966.

Mark, Yudel. *Groyser verterbukh fun der yidisher shprakh,* vol. 3. New York: Yiddish Dictionary Committee, Inc. 1971.

Petruszka, Symcha. *Yidishe folks-entsiklopedie* [Jewish Popular Encyclopedia]. Montreal: The Eagle Publishing Co., Ltd., 1943.

Rosenbaum, Samuel. *A Yiddish Word Book for English-Speaking People.* New York: Van Nostrand Reinhold Co., 1978.

Rosten, Leo. *The Joys of Yiddish.* New York: McGraw-Hill, 1968.

———. *Hooray for Yiddish!* New York: Simon and Schuster, 1982.

Runes, Dagobert D. *Concise Dictionary of Judaism.* New York: Philosophical Library, 1959.

Schonfield, Hugh. *A Popular Dictionary of Judaism.* New York: The Citadel Press, 1966.

Steinsaltz, Adin. *The Talmud: The Steinsaltz Edition, A Reference Guide.* New York: Random House, 1989.

Stutchkoff, Nahum. *Der oytser fun der yidisher shprakh* [The Thesaurus of the Yiddish Language]. New York: YIVO Institute for Jewish Research, 1950.

The Tanach, Stone Edition. Brooklyn, NY: Mesorah Publication, 1996.

Weinreich, U. *Modern English-Yiddish Yiddish-English Dictionary.* New York: McGraw Hill, 1968.

Weiser, Chaim M. *Frumspeak: The First Dictionary of Yeshivish.* Northvale, N.J.: Jason Aronson Inc., 1995.

Werblowsky, R. J. Z. and Geoffrey Wigoder. *The Encyclopedia of the Jewish Religion.* New York: Holt, Rinehart and Winston, Inc., 1965.

Wigoder, Geoffrey. *Encyclopedic Dictionary of Judaica.* Jerusalem: Keter Publishing House Ltd., 1974

Appendix II

Systems of Romanization

When Hebrew or Yiddish words, which are written in the Jewish alphabet, are introduced into English or another non-Jewish language, it usually becomes necessary to transliterate or transcribe them into Roman letters so that those unfamiliar with Hebrew or Yiddish may be able to read the words. Transliteration denotes the representation of the Hebrew or Yiddish letters; transcription denotes the representation of Hebrew or Yiddish speech sounds. *Romanization* is a cover term for both of these methods. As mentioned in the Introduction, a system of Romanization for Yiddish and one for Hebrew were developed in the last century: the Standardized Yiddish Romanization (also known as the YIVO system, after the YIVO Institute for Jewish Research), and the American National Standard Romanization of Hebrew. Varieties of these systems are used widely by scholars, librarians, teachers, and writers. One variety, the General-Purpose Romanization of Hebrew, is designed specifically for popular rather than scholarly use.

A simplified form of each system is given below as a guide to readers who wish to transliterate or transcribe Hebrew or Yiddish words into English.

General-Purpose Romanization of Hebrew

Consonants		*Vowels*	
א	Disregard	◌ַ = a	
ב	b	◌ֶ = e	
		◌ֵ = ei	

בּ	v		.	= i
ג	g			
ד	d		וֹ	= o
			וּ	= u
ה	h			
ו	v			
ז	z			
ח	ch [as in English *loch*]			
ט	t			
י	y			
כּ, ך	k			
כ, ך	ch [as in English *loch*]			
ל	l			
מ, ם	m			
נ, ן	n			
ס	s			
ע	disregard			
פּ	p			
פ, ף	f			
צ, ץ	ts			
ק	k			
ר	r			
שׁ	sh			
שׂ	s			
ת, תּ	t			

Standardized Yiddish Romanization

א	a
אָ	o
ב	b
בֿ	v
ג	g
ד	d
ה	h
ו	u
וו	v
וי	oy
ז	z
זש	zh

ח	kh [as in English *loch*]
ט	t
טש	tsh
׳	i
׳	y
״	ey
ײַ	ay
ך, כ	kh [as in English *loch*]
כ	k
ל	l
ם, מ	m
ן, נ	n
ס	s
ע	e
פ	p
ף, פֿ	f
ץ, צ	ts
ק	k
ר	r
ש	sh
שׂ	s
ת	t
ת	s

Index

This is an index of terms that are found in the book but not listed in the **Dictionary**. To look up a term, first consult the **Dictionary**. If it is not found there, use the Index. Included in the Index are the terms in the special sections (holiday terms, ritual terms, etc.) as well as various references occurring in other parts of the book.

shurah, shura, 118
shvitzer, 78
sichah, sicha, 78
siddur, 162
(be)siman tov!, 31
Simchas Torah, 69
sitra achra, 90
Sonderbehandlung, 74
Sonderkommando, 74
spellings, variant, xiv
Stammlager, 72
Standardized Yiddish Romanization,
   xiii, 195
strudel, 44
sufganiyot, 44, 66
Sukkos, 69

taanis, taanit, 146
taanis ester, 41
Tabernacles, 69
tachlis, 183
tachrichim, 118
tafsik!, 78
taharah, tahara, 118
tararam, 183
tate, 1
tayglech, 44
tefillas haderech, 147
tenai, 58
teudah, teuda, 78
tevilah, 147
tischadesh!, 39
tish, 62, 173
tiyul, 78
tizke leshanim rabot!, 55
tochnit, 78
Todah!, 78
Todah rabbah!, 78
tshotshke, 183
Tu Bishvat, 69
tumler, 183
Tzahal, 78
tzatzke, 183
tzidduk hadin, 36, 118
tzimes, tzimmes, 44, 184

tzimtzum, 90
tzores, 184
tzu gezunt!, 55

ulpan, 78
Umschlagplatz, 74
Umsiedlung, 74

varenikes, 44
vitz, 183

Yaale Veyavo, 66, 68
yachsn, 184
yad, 162–3
yafe, 78
yeke, yekke, 184
yeshiva ketanah, 28
yichus, 184
yid, 184
Yigdal, 8
yimach shemo!, 39
Yinglish, 82
yishuv, 78
yizkor, 118
yofi, 78
yold, 184
Yom Haatzmaut, 70
yom hadin, 36
yomim neroim, 70
Yom Kippur, 70
yom tov, 70
yontev, yontef, 184
yordim, 78
yosem, 184

zaftig, zoftig, 184
zay gezunt!, 55
zebed habat, 147
zechus, 184
zemiros, zemirot, 147
zeyde, 184
zhlub, 184
zichrono livrocho(h), 2, 39
zivug, 174
Zyklon B, 74

About the Author

Sol Steinmetz is a linguist, lexicographer, and ordained rabbi, who was educated at Yeshiva University and Columbia University. He has edited over thirty dictionaries and many reference books including *The World Book Dictionary*, the *Barnhart Dictionary of New English* series, *Safire's New Political Dictionary* (Random House, 1993), *Random House Webster's College Dictionary* (1997), and the *American Jewish Desk Reference* (Random House, 1999). He is also the author of *Yiddish and English: The Story of Yiddish in America* (University of Alabama Press, 2001), of a novel, *Youthopia USA* (Writer's Showcase, 2000), and coauthor of *Meshuggenary: Celebrating the World of Yiddish* (Simon and Schuster, 2002). He has contributed articles to *Encyclopedia Americana*, *The Oxford Companion to the English Language*, *American Speech*, *Jewish Language Review*, *The New York Times Magazine*, *Verbatim*, and other journals. He has served on the advisory board of the *Encarta World English Dictionary* (1999) and is currently a consultant on Jewish terms to the *Oxford English Dictionary*.

He and his wife reside in New Rochelle, New York.